GREAT
ADVENTURES

EXPERIENCE THE WORLD AT ITS BREATHTAKING BEST

lonely planet

HIKE

TASMAN SEA

Milford Sound
Homer Tunnel
Queenstown
Te Anua
Fiordland National Park

NEW ZEALAND
SOUTH ISLAND

PACIFIC OCEAN

TRAMP THE MILFORD IN NEW ZEALAND

ONCE DESCRIBED AS THE FINEST WALK IN THE WORLD, THE SOUTH ISLAND'S MILFORD TRACK IS A MULTIDAY FOOT JOURNEY BESIDE GIN-CLEAR STREAMS, BETWEEN MENACING CANYON WALLS, OVER AN ALPINE PASS, AND PAST ONE OF THE WORLD'S HIGHEST WATERFALLS. WHAT'S NOT TO LIKE?

Every day, busloads, carloads and planeloads of people squirm through the mountains of Fiordland National Park to visit New Zealand's postcard-perfect Milford Sound, but once it was only walkers who could make it to these shores.

A path to the long-inaccessible sound was made possible with the discovery of 1069m Mackinnon Pass in 1888 by Quintin Mackinnon and Ernest Mitchell. This alpine saddle immediately became – and remains – the midpoint and centrepiece of the Milford Track, opening up access to Milford Sound decades before the road was carved through the mountains. Mackinnon would become its first guide (though, tragically, he drowned in Lake Te Anau in 1892), and the track would spend decades as the private domain of guided trampers. It wasn't until 1966 that independent walkers were allowed onto the Milford Track.

Dubbed the 'finest walk in the world' by the *London Spectator* in 1908, the 53.5km track has since gained such popularity that access is now heavily regulated. During the tramping season, which runs from late October to late April, only 40 walkers can begin the track each day. You can walk in only one direction – Lake Te Anau to Milford Sound – and you must follow a set itinerary, staying in designated huts each night.

If the experience is regimented, the landscape you'll experience is far from it. From Lake Te Anau, the track funnels through Clinton Valley, with its glacier-scratched walls closing to little more than a crack at its head. From here it climbs to the crest of wind-whipped Mackinnon Pass. The descent follows the headwaters of the Arthur River, passing by 580m-high Sutherland Falls, the highest waterfall in New Zealand, and a string of other waterfalls cocooned inside rainforest. The four-day tramp ends at Sandfly Point on the shores of Milford Sound.

ESSENTIAL EXPERIENCES

* **Stepping through lush beech forest along the banks of the Clinton River.**

* Wondering at the winter carnage as you pass avalanche clearings near Hidden Lake.

* **Bracing against the weather atop Mackinnon Pass – there's a reason the shelter was built here.**

* Standing in the showery mist of 580m-high Sutherland Falls.

* **Crossing high swing bridges as you descend through the Arthur Valley.**

DISTANCE 53.5KM | **LOCATION** FIORDLAND NATIONAL PARK, SOUTH ISLAND, NEW ZEALAND | **IDEAL TIME COMMITMENT** FOUR DAYS | **BEST TIME OF YEAR** OCTOBER TO APRIL | **ESSENTIAL TIP** BOOK WELL AHEAD; THIS IS NEW ZEALAND'S MOST FAMOUS AND POPULAR TRACK

FIORDLAND NATIONAL PARK

With its coast frayed by fiords – or sounds – Fiordland National Park, at 12,523 sq km, is the largest national park in New Zealand and one of the largest in the world; in comparison, Yellowstone National Park covers 8987 sq km. It contains New Zealand's finest assortment of waterfalls, sharp granite peaks and 14 fiords, most famously Milford Sound. The park was established in 1952 and now forms the largest slice of the Te Wahipounamu World Heritage Site. It was inscribed onto the list in 1990, which noted it as the least disturbed area of New Zealand, and containing the best modern representation of Gondwanaland's ancient flora and fauna.

TREK CHILE'S TORRES DEL PAINE

TREK AROUND OR INTO THE HEART OF ONE OF THE WORLD'S MOST FANTASTICALLY SHAPED MOUNTAIN RANGES, PUSHING THROUGH PATAGONIA'S NOTORIOUS WINDS TO VIEWS THAT WILL WOW EVEN THE MOST SEASONED MOUNTAIN TRAVELLERS.

22

Near the southern tip of South America, the Torres del Paine rises like a fistful of broken fingers, its multitude of peaks and spires tortured into otherworldly shapes by time and wild weather. Trekkers who journey south to the national park invariably come to hike one of two routes: the Paine Circuit or the W Trek.

The W Trek is named for its shape as it angles into a trio of valleys cut deep into the range. The most striking of these are the Ascencio and Frances valleys, which provide the finest trekking views on offer in the Torres del Paine. The Ascencio valley rises to meet an enormous terminal moraine, atop which is found a lake set beneath the trio of towers that give the mountains and the national park their name. The trail through the Frances valley skirts the crevassed base of the Frances Glacier, climbing onto a lookout set inside a ring of impressive peaks.

The Paine Circuit does exactly as the name suggests, looping around the Torres del Paine. It's more committing than the W Trek, but is also less busy – in summer there can be more than 2000 people in Torres del Paine National Park every day. For the extra effort, trekkers add a string of lakes and glaciers, as well as a wild pass crossing above Grey Glacier. Stepping onto Paso John Garner on a fine day can be a sublime experience, staring directly down onto Grey Glacier. On a foul day, with gale-force winds spearing ice into your face, it can feel as perilous as the poles.

In early 2012, a huge fire tore through the national park, burning most of the land between the Frances valley and Refugio Grey, about a 16km stretch of both treks. The devastated area will take decades to recover, though fortunately the bulk of the Torres del Paine's natural attractions lie outside of the fire zone.

ESSENTIAL EXPERIENCES

* **Viewing the eponymous towers from the lakeside lookout above the Ascencio valley.**
* Battling winds at the aptly named Paso de los Ventos (Pass of the Winds) or atop the Frances Glacier lookout.
* **Bracing for the brawn and beauty of nature on the exposed crossing of Paso John Garner.**
* Celebrating day's end with a pisco sour in one of the refuges.
* **Listening for ice falls as you walk high above Grey Glacier.**

DISTANCE 100KM (PAINE CIRCUIT), 69KM (W TREK) | **LOCATION** TORRES DEL PAINE NATIONAL PARK, CHILE | **IDEAL TIME COMMITMENT** EIGHT DAYS (PAINE CIRCUIT), FOUR DAYS (W TREK) | **BEST TIME OF YEAR** DECEMBER TO MARCH | **ESSENTIAL TIP** THE NATIONAL-PARK AUTHORITY, CONAF, DOESN'T ALLOW SOLO HIKERS TO CROSS PASO JOHN GARNER, SO JOIN UP WITH OTHER TREKKERS AT CAMPAMENTO LOS PERROS IF WALKING ALONE

SENDERO DE CHILE

Conceived as a multidistance adventure on the scale of the USA's Appalachian or Pacific Crest trails, Chile's Sendero de Chile aims to become one of the longest pathways in the world. Stretching for around 8000km from Arica, in the country's north, to its southern tip at Cape Horn, and designated for hiking, mountain biking and horse riding, it will pass through around 40 watersheds. Note that some stretches will follow gravel roads instead of beautiful trails, so it's worth researching the parts you wish to undertake before setting out – there are updates and maps on the trail's website (www.senderodechile.cl).

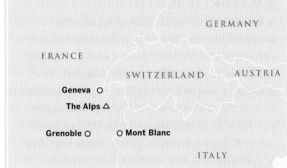

TAKE ON THE TOUR DU MONT BLANC

DO A COMPLETE CIRCUIT AROUND THE EUROPEAN ALPS' HIGHEST MOUNTAIN, WANDERING THROUGH THREE COUNTRIES AS YOU GO, AND CROSSING A SUCCESSION OF PASSES IN SIGHT OF SOME OF THE FINEST ROCK SPIRES AND PEAKS ON THE CONTINENT.

30

The Chamonix valley is arguably the European Alps' most appealing and fashionable destination. It also serves as the springboard for one of the world's finest long-distance hikes: the Tour du Mont Blanc (TMB). This international route has sections in France, Italy and Switzerland, and the views encapsulate the entire Alpine landscape, taking in the valleys, passes and mountains that crowd its rim.

Alpine history walks large beside you on the TMB. The trails take you right to the foot of the towering rock faces and glaciers where alpinism was born, and it's fitting that the first tour of Mont Blanc is credited to Horace-Benedict de Saussure, the man who put up the reward that inspired the first ascent of the mountain. From a starting point in Chamonix, he crossed the Col du Bonhomme and Col de la Seigne to reach Courmayeur, before entering Switzerland via the Col du Grand St-Bernard.

The route became popular in the Victorian era as the English flocked to the Alps. Those who could climb enjoyed the fruits of the 'Golden Age' of mountaineering, while those with lesser ambition crossed passes, using donkeys to carry food, clothing and equipment. In the 20th century, with the construction and development of paths used purely for recreation, the TMB evolved into a more compact circuit with variant routings tackling the higher passes and allowing walkers to get even closer to the world of permanent snow.

Today, the TMB remains a challenging route. Even the easiest variations mean you'll be ascending and descending more than 8000m. If you take the most strenuous route, it becomes as much as 11,000m of climbing. That means you'll be ascending and descending at least the equivalent of Mt Everest from sea level as you circuit this European mountain icon.

ESSENTIAL EXPERIENCES

* **Spending a night at Rifugio Elisabetta, almost in touch of the icefalls of the Glacier de la Lée Blanche.**

* Border hopping as you cross Col de la Seigne and Grand Col Ferret.

* **Peering down onto the heavily crevassed Glacier du Tirent from the 2665m Fenêtre d'Arpette pass.**

* Marvelling at the ever-changing view of Mont Blanc along the trail's final stretch, the aptly named Grand Balcon Sud on the slopes of the Aiguilles Rouges.

* **Reflecting on the mountains – literally – as you gaze across the surface of Lac Blanc.**

DISTANCE 167KM | **LOCATION** FRANCE, SWITZERLAND AND ITALY | **IDEAL TIME COMMITMENT** 10 TO 14 DAYS | **BEST TIME OF YEAR** MID-JUNE TO MID-SEPTEMBER | **ESSENTIAL TIP** FROM THE START AT LES HOUCHES, HIKE ANTICLOCKWISE SO THE VIEWS GET STEADILY MORE IMPRESSIVE AS YOU WALK

Once you've walked around Mont Blanc, the temptation is often to then stand atop the 'White Mountain'. Climbing this peak is a tradition that dates back to 1786 when Jacques Balmat and Dr Michel Paccard became the first to summit the 4810m peak. Today, a fine summer day might see 100 or more people summiting. Mont Blanc is not a technically demanding mountain if climbed by the popular Goûter route, and is within the reach of fit walkers with a good head for heights who are prepared to hire a guide. Walkers with mountaineering experience could easily go it alone, as long as they are extremely careful in choosing the weather conditions.

WALTER BONATTI

One climber's name is more intrinsically linked to Mont Blanc than any other, and that is Walter Bonatti, as reflected in the name of the Rifugio Bonatti below the Col Sapin. Born in Bergamo in 1930, Bonatti was arguably the finest alpinist of his generation and pioneered several of the Alps' classic mountaineering routes, like the Bonatti Pillar on the Dru, which he climbed solo over a six-day period in 1955. Bonatti also made difficult first ascents on the Grand Capucin, the Red Pillar of Mont Blanc, the Piz Badile and the Pilier d'Angle – all in the Mont Blanc area – as well as audacious winter solo ascents of the north face of the Grandes Jorasses.

THE ADVENTURE UNFOLDS

The climb to Col de la Seigne has been long and steady – more than 600m of ascent since lunch. Wind whips up from the valley but you've not only reached a pass, you've reached another country. Another step forward and you're in Italy – it may be just one small step, but the change in the view is one giant leap. For the first time, the eastern side of the Mont Blanc massif opens up before you. In the distance the Miage and Brenva Glaciers resemble roads of loose mountain rock, seemingly intent on devouring the Courmayeur valley.

If the view seems good now, it's just a foretaste of things to come. Two days from now, at the head of yet another 600m climb, you step out from the front door of Rifugio Bertone into a broth of dawn cloud. It feels as though the world has been snatched from you, but as you rise up the slopes of Mont de la Saxe, running parallel to the massif, you step out of the cloud. It's like the parting of a curtain, and you're suddenly standing in air so crisp and clear it's as though you've stepped into a painting.

Below, the mist remains balled in the valley of the Doire Torrent, and the fins of the Grandes Jorasses – pin-ups of the mountaineering world – poke through, seemingly scratching at the perfect sky. The broad shoulder of Mont de la Saxe continues to rise, until you top out at the summit of 2584m Tête de la Tranche. The cloud is beginning to break up below, piping out of the valley like steam. If this isn't the finest view in the world this morning, you'd be surprised. You could stand here all day, though it's time to move on – Switzerland awaits you.

MAKING IT HAPPEN

The TMB is well served by refuges at strategic points, though this is a busy summer trail and they can be noisy and crowded in July and August. Several refuges permit camping close by. A list of accommodation for the route, including prices and phone numbers, is available free from the Office de Haute Montagne in Chamonix. Many adventure-travel companies offer guided Tour du Mont Blanc trips.

AN ALTERNATIVE CHALLENGE

For most people, walking the TMB is challenge enough, but for others there's the Ultra-Trail du Tour du Mont Blanc. The task for this annual ultramarathon, first held in 2003, is simple (in theory): run the 167km of the TMB. Competitors must complete the trail within 46 hours (the winners run it in about 20 hours), having crossed passes with ascents totalling almost 10,000m. Entry is limited to 2300 runners, who must qualify through a series of other ultramarathons.

OPENING SPREAD On top of L'Aiguille du Midi (the Needle of the South) in the Mont Blanc massif. **ABOVE (L) AND (R)** Chamonix is the adventure sports capital of France with climbers, hikers and mountain bikers exploring its network of trails in summer. **LEFT** The six peaks of the Grandes Jorasses.

ARMCHAIR

* *Tour of Mont Blanc* (Kev Reynolds) Dedicated TMB guidebook, describing the route in both directions, including variants.

* *Walking in the Alps* (Lonely Planet) Features a special chapter on the Tour du Mont Blanc.

* *Savage Snows: The Story of Mont Blanc* (Walt Unsworth) Enjoyable history of climbing on Mont Blanc.

* *The Great Days* (Walter Bonatti) The great climber recounts some of his mountain moments, including climbs on the Grandes Jorasses.

* *Mont Blanc: Discovery and Conquest of the Giant of the Alps* (Stefano Ardito) Ode to the mountain, mixing great photography with the history of its climbs.

◼ THE ADVENTURE UNFOLDS

Sunrise is two hours away but you're already on the trail. Ahead of you, a line of head torches snakes up the slopes, looking like a procession of fireflies. It's another group of trekkers heading for the summit of Ras Dashen. The air is thin at 4000m – about 60% of the oxygen rate at sea level – but after five days at altitude your lungs feel as big as hot-air balloons.

As dawn begins to light the sky, you rise to a crest to catch the first view of your goal: the rocky summit of Ras Dashen. You ascend along a dirt road for a while, villagers passing you with sacks of grain or rolls of corrugated iron on their shoulders. The trail then heads up to the top of an escarpment through a line of piled stones, placed here as a gun post during the country's civil war more than a decade ago.

You round a bend and step into an enormous scree field – even the hardy giant lobelias don't grow here – stopping every few minutes to suck in precious air. Ahead, the walls of the summit escarpment look impenetrable –

is there really a line through that rock face? – but then you see movement off to the left as the group ahead makes its final push to the summit. Sure enough, it's a simple scramble to the top, where a shepherd boy wrapped in animal skins stands waiting for you.

The view is quite simply too massive to comprehend. It's said to cover 10,000 sq km of African expanse, an area about the size of Jamaica. Ridge lines curl away from the summit like wishbones, and two gelada baboons sit grooming each other on a nearby peak. Their mountain looks somehow higher than yours, but it's not, for you are standing on the apex of the 'roof of Africa'.

ARMCHAIR

* **Kebra Negast** Written during the 14th century, this is Ethiopia's great national epic, creating the legend of Queen Sheba.

* **The Ethiopian Revolution: War in the Horn of Africa** (Gebru Tareke) You'll see reminders of the recent wars across the Simiens, so browse up on them in this 2009 book.

* **The Emperor** (Ryszard Kapuscinski) Fascinating campside reading about the Ethiopian leader Haile Selassie, the man worshipped by Rastafarians.

* **Planet Earth** (BBC) Watch this beautiful series for a segment on the Simien Mountains and gelada baboons.

■ MAKING IT HAPPEN

Treks can be organised in the gateway town of Debark, which is accessed by bus from the former Ethiopian capital city of Gonder. Guides, cooks, mules and armed national park scouts can be arranged at the park headquarters here, though only the scout is compulsory (guides are highly recommended, and the decision on whether you want to cook your own food and carry all your own gear is entirely down to you).

A number of well regarded international trekking companies, including Peregrine Adventures, operate hikes in the Simiens with options to ascend Ras Dashen.

■ AN ALTERNATIVE CHALLENGE

If you haven't got the time – or perhaps don't have the head for the altitude – to climb Ras Dashen, a good shorter option is to hike to the village of Geech and ascend 3926m Imet Gogo, the classic Simiens viewpoint.

From Imet Gogo, return to Geech via Saha, a small peak with a heady view deep into a narrow canyon topped with an array of spires – keep an eye out for walia ibex around the foot of the cliffs. This shorter trek will take around five days.

OPENING SPREAD Simian appeal: gelada baboons groom each other to reinforce family relationships. **ABOVE** Chenek Camp in Simien National Park is a good spot for wildlife watching. **BELOW** After millions of years of erosion, precipices in the park drop 1500m.

HIKE CALIFORNIA'S JOHN MUIR TRAIL

STEP OUT INTO A WILDERNESS THAT INSPIRED OVER A CENTURY OF CONSERVATION, FOLLOWING A HISTORIC TRAIL THROUGH THE LOFTY RANGES, PEACEFUL MEADOWS, BEAR-GRAZED FORESTS AND FRESH-AIR SPLENDOUR OF CALIFORNIA'S SIERRA NEVADA.

John Muir: inventor, conservationist, writer, tramp – and one of the most important men of the past millennium. Yet most people outside the US have never heard of him, and might wonder what his claim is on one of that country's best-known hikes. The answer's simple: without Muir there'd likely be no trail, and no wilderness here worth walking through. This eccentric Scot, who immigrated to the States at the age of 11, was at the forefront of the national parks movement. He spent years walking across backwoods America, living off the land, living for the land, getting 'as near to the heart of the world' as he could. His passions stoked, he focused them on persuading presidents to safe-keep the country's wildest places. We owe him much.

Fitting, then, that this 344km hike across Muir's beloved Sierra Nevadas, from the great granite valley of Yosemite to 4421m Mt Whitney, bears his name. The trail was advocated by the Sierra Club, the environmental organisation Muir founded; construction began in 1914, the year he died. It was 1938 before the route was finished, having forded rivers, negotiated forests and surmounted high-altitude passes. It is the ultimate access to the land that Muir so loved.

There's lots of up and down (walk the entire route, north to south, and the total ascent is 12,800m; walk south–north and it's 14,234m). But, despite this, the trail seldom feels tough – gradients are mostly gentle, the way largely sheltered. The toughest part is being self-sufficient. There are no real towns or shops en route, and hikers must carry much of what they need, meaning weeks of dried food and watery porridge.

But the trail compensates for this culinary fatigue with sheer wow. This is magnificent countryside, where every step seems to reward with yet another deer-nibbled valley or lake-reflected mountain range; where every night's camp, even if busy with other hikers, makes you feel a bit like a pioneer.

ESSENTIAL EXPERIENCES

* **Watching the sun set and rise over Thousand Island Lake.**

* Marvelling at the basalt columns of the Devil's Postpile – and nipping to nearby Red Meadows Resort for a hot-spring-powered shower.

* **Looking out for lupines, Indian paintbrush and other wildflowers, as well as mule deer, marmots and black bears.**

* Camping beside mountain-hugged Evolution Lake, one of the JMT's remoter reaches.

* **Casting a line (if you have a fishing permit) into the five serene pools of Rae Lakes.**

* Standing atop Mt Whitney, gazing over the rugged wilderness you've just traversed.

DISTANCE 344KM | **LOCATION** SIERRA NEVADA, CALIFORNIA, USA | **IDEAL TIME COMMITMENT** THREE WEEKS | **BEST TIME OF YEAR** MID-JULY TO EARLY SEPTEMBER | **ESSENTIAL TIP** NEVER APPROACH OR RUN FROM A BEAR – BACK OFF SLOWLY

THE GRAND TRAVERSE

John Muir Trail too tiny? The Pacific Crest Trail follows the JMT through southern Yosemite – though this is merely one small step on its 4240km journey from the Mexican border (near the small town of Campo) to the Canadian border at Manning Park. This epic hike across California, Oregon and Washington traverses old-growth rainforests, high deserts, low deserts and all the major western mountain ranges. Every year it's reckoned around 300 'thru-hikers' attempt it in one go; tramping an average of 32km a day, and allowing for plenty of rest days, it generally takes five or six months.

THE WILD WEST

There's a wealth of wildlife in the Sierra Nevadas. More than 1500 types of flower fleck the region: blooms such as mountain violet, azaleas and red columbine colour lower elevations, while orchids, mariposa lilies and alpine monkey flowers grow higher. Easily spotted birds include red-tailed hawks, turkey vultures and bold Steller's jays; listen for owls after dark. Ground squirrels, racoons and marmots are the mammals most commonly seen; mule deer thrive, as hunting is not permitted in protected areas. Black bears might be seen, and often raid camping grounds at night – keep your food stored in a bear barrel.

■ THE ADVENTURE UNFOLDS

Your legs ache. Your armpits smell. And your shoulders burn from the weight of your backpack. But you've never felt more alive. It's that blissful hour, when the day's walk is done and memories are flashbacking in your brain as you rest by the glow of your stove. The sun has dipped, rendering the cold grey mountains a warmer hue; the lake by your tent glitters as a breeze riffles its surface.

Dinner is uninspiring – mush with dried something – but you're famished so it tastes fantastic, especially when gulped down with those views. There are others camped here too – some in groups, some hiking solo. One starts to play a harmonica. You lie back and feel the last of the earth's warmth seep into your tired but contented bones. Later, stars sprinkle the sky like fairy dust. Inside your tent you lay awake, listening for snuffles – is that a black bear?

The days adopt a basic rhythm: rise with the sun, brew a cuppa, pack the tent, away you go. There's little to consider other than your physical motion and the beauty of the world around. That, and when you'll meet your next food drop – is it three days? Five? It's easy to lose time in this world of lakes and mountains – though you're looking forward to that chocolate ration.

Food is a bit of an obsession on the trail; it's the main topic when you meet fellow trekkers – which you do, frequently. The JMT is too popular to be a total step out of civilisation, but it's good to know there are others around in case you have an accident – or accidentally come face to face with a bear...

You have spotted one, foraging in a far-off meadow. It paid you no mind and you carried on carefully, feeling privileged to have entered, briefly, its domain.

■ MAKING IT HAPPEN

Most hikers tackle the JMT north–south (Yosemite–Mt Whitney); buses run from San Francisco to Yosemite, via Merced. You need a Wilderness Permit from the reservation station nearest your starting point; apply online or by post, up to 24 weeks in advance. You must be self-sufficient, carrying camp kit and filtering water. Pack plenty of food and prearrange resupplies at points en route; keep food in bear barrels. Local companies run organised full and shorter JMT hikes.

■ DETOUR

The great granite baldy of Half Dome, Yosemite's most iconic outcrop, is not officially on the John Muir Trail. However, it's only a short diversion on day one (if walking north–south). The JMT–Half Dome trail junction is just after Little Yosemite Valley Campground; allow three hours for the round trip from here. The climb is well marked but strenuous, the final section entailing a haul up bare rock with the aid of a fixed cableway. Take gloves, and don't attempt it if you suffer from vertigo.

41

OPENING SPREAD Dawn reflected in First Lake on the Big Pine Creek trail. **ABOVE (L)** Owens Valley, on the east side of the Sierra Nevada, doesn't get much rain. **ABOVE (R)** Wild sage flowers on Mt Williamson. **LEFT** Mule deer are a common sight. This buck is ready for the rutting season.

ARMCHAIR

* ***The John Muir Trail*** (Cicerone) Dedicated trekking guide that breaks the route into 21 stages and includes planning and preparation info.

* ***On the Trail of John Muir*** (Cherry Good) An investigation of the man behind the hike; looks at Muir's life and work, as well as his legacy.

* ***Sierra Nevada: The John Muir Trail*** (Ansel Adams) Iconic black-and-white images by the famed American photographer.

* ***John Muir Trail: The Essential Guide*** (Elizabeth Wenk & Kathy Morey) The latest edition of this US hiking guide contains GPS coordinates for landmarks and updated topographical maps.

* ***The Eight Wilderness Discovery Books*** (John Muir) A compendium of Muir's nature and conservation writing, including 'My First Summer in the Sierra' and 'The Yosemite'.

FOOD ON THE GO

Walkers work up a healthy appetite. Luckily, Corsica's cuisine makes use of the island's bounty to create distinctively Corsican flavours. Hearty *soupe corse*, a vegetable soup with a meat-bone stock, fortifies trekkers in many refuges. Delicious charcuterie (cured meats) owe their taste to the chestnuts foraged by pigs and wild boar that snuffle among forest roots. Chestnut flour is also the basis of *beignets* (savoury doughnuts) and *fiadone*, a honey-sweetened flan. Traditional ewes-milk cheeses are often pungent – most renowned is the soft *brocciu*, best bought from source at *bergeries* (shepherds' huts) in the mountains.

THE ADVENTURE UNFOLDS

Your hiking partner has already wolfed down his *beignet* (chestnut-flour doughnut) and espresso. It's not yet 7am, but a trickle of hikers are already passing the cafe. Like you, they're en route to the small chapel above Calenzana where the trail begins. You wonder if, also like you, they're both exhilarated and nervous about their first day on the infamous GR20.

Hoisting your rucksack onto your back, you're almost unbalanced by its weight, heavily loaded with a tent, wet-weather gear and a mountain of *saucisson* (dried sausage), pasta and bread. But your resolve stiffens and you stride along the mule track that winds up into the hills, turning your back on the olive groves and delving into the maquis. A few hours of gentle uphill strolling past pines and chestnut trees confirms your belief in your trekking prowess – a fragile confidence that evaporates as the path takes a sudden turn for the steep, the start of a sweat-soaked 400m haul up to the pass of Bocca a u Saltu. But as the gradient finally softens and lean on your walking poles, the sweeping views back across the maquis to the Balagne coast soothe the pain.

Knowing you've climbed nearly 1000m this morning, breaking the back of the day's ascent, also gives you a boost, and you put on your best mountain-sheep impression to scramble through the granite outcrops, through pine forest and across a mountain stream to the Refuge d'Ortu di u Piobbu, your home for the night. Thanks to your dawn start, it's still early – time enough for a leg-stretching extra climb to the peak of Monte Corona before settling in with a cold beer to toast the setting sun as it sizzles into the Mediterranean. Salut, indeed!

MAKING IT HAPPEN

International flights serve Bastia, Figari, Ajaccio (the island's capital) and Calvi, the nearest airport to the trailhead. Ferries sail to several Corsican ports from French and Italian cities. Accommodation along the trail is mostly at simple refuges, with dormitories and camping areas; beds are limited, so book well ahead in summer. Several operators offer guided or self-guided tours, accommodation bookings and baggage transfers; try World Expeditions, KE Adventure or Exodus.

AN ALTERNATIVE CHALLENGE

Several other long-distance trails tempt trekkers in Corsica, notably the Tra Mare e Monti ('Between Sea and Mountains') route skirting the rugged coastline of the northwest, and three Mare a Mare ('Sea to Sea') itineraries slicing the island east–west. The five-day Mare a Mare Sud (south) takes in traditional villages, prehistoric remains and chestnut woods – and with less-demanding terrain and more opportunities for stays in *gîtes d'étapes* (walking lodges), it's far easier than the GR20.

OPENING SPREAD The mountain town of Soveria in the heart of Corsica. Once bandit country, the hills are the domain of hikers today. **ABOVE (L)** The sure-footed Corsican mouflon is at home on the rocky trails. **ABOVE (R)** Descending Monte Cinto. **LEFT** Carry all your kit for two weeks on the trail.

ARMCHAIR

* **Corsica Trekking GR20** (David Abram) Comprehensive guide to the trail, with detailed hand-drawn maps.

* **GR20: Corsica – The High Level Route** (Paddy Dillon) Expert route guide with ample information and maps.

* **An Account of Corsica** (James Boswell) An intriguing 18th-century travelogue by the noted biographer of Samuel Johnson.

* **Granite Island** (Dorothy Carrington) The classic overview of Corsica, published over 40 years ago, still provides insights into the island's history and psyche.

* **Les Randonneurs** (1997) The French comedy film about a pair of brothers accompanying two girls and their hiking guide along the GR20 brought attention – and ample visitors – to the trail.

WALK AUSTRALIA'S LARAPINTA TRAIL

SEE ONE OF THE WORLD'S OLDEST MOUNTAIN RANGES USING THE OLDEST FORM OF TRANSPORT: YOUR FEET. AS IT TRAVERSES THE MACDONNELLS, THE LARAPINTA TRAIL DIPS IN AND OUT OF WATERHOLES AND GORGES, OFFERING VIEWS OF THE RED CENTRE DESERT FROM ON TOP OF THE RANGE.

Not all desert adventures need be about hardship and Herculean endurance. First mooted as a walking trail in 1987, and completed 15 years later, the Larapinta Trail delves into many of central Australia's finest natural features – waterholes, gorges, razorback ridges – squeezing the beauty out of Australia's harshest desert environment. Such is its beauty, accessibility and infrastructure, the Larapinta has quickly become one of the most popular long-distance trails in the country.

The trail begins (or ends, depending on which direction you choose to walk it in) at the actual springs that the township of Alice Springs is named after. Prior to that, it follows the length of the West MacDonnell Ranges to the summit of its most striking peak, Mt Sonder. The trail's 223km of twists, turns, spinifex, mountains and gorges are divided into 12 sections, each one somewhere between 13km and 31km in length. Every section represents a day or two of walking, and each is determinedly intent on showing off hidden mountain wonders.

Camp sites are spaced at manageable distances and, though the land is as dry as bones, there are water tanks acting as virtual oases. These are found no more than 33km apart, making this a delightful desert experience that's far from barren.

Along the way the trail passes through tourist set pieces such as Simpsons Gap, Standley Chasm, Ellery Creek Big Hole, Serpentine Gorge, the Ochre Pits, Ormiston Gorge and Glen Helen Resort, but also seeks out walker-only delights like Hugh Gorge, Inhalanga Pass and the signature Larapinta view at Counts Point, considered one of the West MacDonnells' best lookouts.

ESSENTIAL EXPERIENCES

* **Watching for euros bounding across the eponymous Euro Ridge, with Alice Springs still in sight.**

* Swimming off the day's sweat at waterholes such as Ellery Creek Big Hole and Redbank Gorge.

* **Hiking through predawn chill to Counts Point for a sunrise view over the Red Centre.**

* Balancing along the knife-sharp Razorback Ridge near Hugh Gorge.

* **Looking east over much of the trail's journey as you stand atop Mt Sonder at the trail's end.**

46

DISTANCE 223KM | **LOCATION** WEST MACDONNELL RANGES, NORTHERN TERRITORY, AUSTRALIA | **IDEAL TIME COMMITMENT** 12 TO 16 DAYS | **BEST TIME OF YEAR** APRIL TO SEPTEMBER | **ESSENTIAL TIP** MAKE FOOD DROPS ALONG THE TRAIL TO REDUCE YOUR WALKING BURDEN

A PRICKLY COMPANION

If there's one plant you're going to get to know well on the Larapinta Trail, it's spinifex. This grass forms in tussocky clumps on the sandy soils of central Australia and lines the trail, often overreaching it. The characteristic of spinifex that walkers will most come to recognise is its prickliness, with the points of its leaves being almost needle-sharp – those walking without gaiters will probably spend plenty of time picking out spinifex tips from their legs. Spinifex's bristliness, in turn, makes it a great safehouse for small creatures, who live protected from predators deep within the tussocks. There are around 30 different species of spinifex – Larapinta walkers will become best acquainted with weeping spinifex.

FEELING OLD?

Look carefully and you'll notice a curious design
feature to the West MacDonnell Ranges. Here, the
rivers don't flow between the ranges but through them,
indicating that the waterways were here long before
the mountains. The Finke River, which slices through
the mountains at Glen Helen Gorge, at the western end
of the Larapinta Trail, is often claimed to be the oldest
river in the world, said to have formed over 300 million
years ago. The river's headwaters are just north of Glen
Helen — you'll walk past them on section 11 — and it
eventually flows out into the Simpson Desert in South
Australia, though it's usually dry except for waterholes.

THE ADVENTURE UNFOLDS

It's been a long haul across the desert plain, switching from one line of mountains to the other, but you've finally arrived at Hugh Gorge. Inside the gorge, the rock walls are as smooth as plates, towering above you as you step around waterholes. At Hugh Gorge Junction, the trail turns east into Linear Valley but you continue up the gorge for a few hundred metres, until its walls almost clamp shut above a waterhole as frigid as the polar ice caps.

You turn back to camp at the base of Razorback Ridge, saving this gymnastic mountain ascent for the morning. The cry of a dingo cuts through the evening, and temperatures slip below freezing as you lie beneath a sky flecked with more stars than you knew existed.

When the sun hits in the morning, the mercury rises almost instantly by 20°C. It's a long hot day across the ridge, the exposed rock feeling like the very bones of the land, but soon you're weaving through dry Spencer Gorge to Birthday Waterhole. The gift here is rest. It's been a tough few days and tomorrow brings another ascent to Brinkley Bluff, its summit like a red bubble atop the range.

Approached from the west like this it's a grunt of a climb, ascending 500m to its summit, where you make camp and are rewarded with a golden sunset. You half expect to be able to look west and see Mt Sonder yet again. This mountain, shaped like a sleeping woman, has been part of your view for so many days, mocking the slowness of walking. But the mountain is gone; you've finally left it behind. Instead, to the east, there's a faint glow of light on the horizon that can only be Alice Springs. The end is nigh.

MAKING IT HAPPEN

Independent walkers can ease the walking burden by making food drops at Standley Chasm, Ormiston Gorge, Glen Helen Resort and the walkers' camp at Serpentine Gorge, meaning they need carry no more than four or five days of food at a time. A number of companies lead guided walks on the trail, from sample sections to through hikes. Locally operated Trek Larapinta is one of the most experienced. There are also walker shuttle services to Mt Sonder from Alice Springs.

AN ALTERNATIVE CHALLENGE

If you want to walk in the Northern Territory but haven't the time to commit to the Larapinta Trail, head north to Nitmiluk National Park to hike the Jatbula Trail. This 66km walk links Katherine Gorge with Leliyn (Edith Falls) along the edge of the Arnhem Land escarpment, passing waterfalls, secluded swimming holes and the Aboriginal art site at the Amphitheatre, with its wonderful curving rock set above a remnant of monsoon rainforest. Allow four days to truly appreciate the trail.

49

OPENING SPREAD A sunburnt country of ragged mountain ranges: West MacDonnell National Park in the Northern Territory. **ABOVE (L)** Walking Razorback Ridge on the Larapinta Trail. **ABOVE (R)** Glen Helen Gorge. **LEFT** The course of Finke River through the Western MacDonnell Ranges.

ARMCHAIR

* ***Take a Walk on the Larapinta Trail*** (John & Lyn Daly) Track notes for the entire trail, plus planning information.

* ***A Field Guide to Central Australia*** (Penny van Oosterzee) Detailed natural history guide to the Red Centre that will help identify flora and fauna along the trail.

* ***Lasseter's Last Ride*** (Ion L Idriess) One of Australia's epic bush legends, about one man's ill-fated search for a gold reef in central Australia.

* ***Larapinta Trail*** (John & Monica Chapman) Trail guide featuring full track notes (in both directions) and colour topo maps.

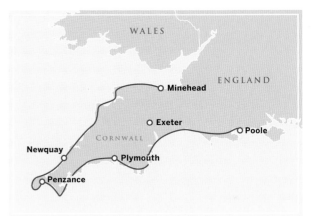

AMBLE ENGLAND'S SOUTHWEST COAST

BASKING SHARKS, SMUGGLERS, WORLD-FAMOUS CHEFS, SURF BEACHES AND AN ENDLESS AZURE SEA – THIS 1000KM OUTLINE OF ENGLAND'S SOUTHWEST CORNER IS COASTAL WALKING AT ITS MOST DIVERSE, MOST SPECTACULAR AND MOST DELICIOUS.

50

The Smugglers' Way – that'd be a good name for it. Because the more prosaically titled South West Coast Path – which traces the outlines of Somerset, Devon, Cornwall and Dorset for over 1000km – only exists due to the ne'er-do-wells that once bothered these shores. In the early 19th century, when import duties were high, bootleggers were rampant. So the coastguard service was set up to stop them. These law-upholding men created continuous patrol paths along the cliff tops so they could peer into every cove, cave and cranny (of which there are legion). Today, walkers do the same.

The SWCP has been an official National Trail since 1978, and it's a cracker. The sea is a constant companion; the cliffs are immense and varied, ranging from outcrops steeped in Arthurian legend to Jurassic remnants thick with fossils. The highest point is just 318m (Great Hangman, near Combe Martin), but walk the whole path, from Minehead to Poole Harbour, and you'll climb a total of 35,000m. Indeed, the path is unbelievably undulating. No sooner have you hiked down to, and up out of, one wave-lashed bay or fishing harbour, you're tackling the next. All (with a few tourist-tack exceptions) are worth the effort.

This trail has everything. There are lighthouses and manor houses. There are rolling hills, towering cliffs, frenzied foam, sand dunes, nudist beaches, surf beaches and quiet creeks where smugglers must have hidden. There's witchcraft, naval history and the possible location of Camelot – plus cream teas, pasties, pilchards and pubs. And, of course, the views are unremittingly spectacular.

But the best thing about walking the South West Coast Path is leaving the world behind. Though millions of holidaymakers flock to these shores, most stay in the main honey pots and barely leave. Walk 15 minutes beyond a candyfloss-and-kiss-me-quick seaside town, and the crowds melt away. Leaving just you, the strength of your legs, the chat of the birds and the inescapable *boof!* of the sea.

ESSENTIAL EXPERIENCES

* **Finding your favourite fishing village: maybe hillside-tumbling Clovelly, pretty Port Isaac, smuggler-infested Polperro or tiny Penberth Cove?**

* Meeting wild goats on the walk from Lynton to the Valley of the Rocks, followed by super scones at the Lee Abbey teashop.

* **Gorging on gourmet seafood at one of Padstow's fine fish eateries.**

* Spying seals and basking sharks as you picnic on remote cliff tops.

* **Walking (low tide) or ferrying (high tide) to St Michael's Mount from Marazion, to wander the ancient island abbey.**

* Watching wild waves crash around the striking rock arch of Durdle Door.

DISTANCE 1008KM | **LOCATION** SOUTHWEST ENGLAND | **IDEAL TIME COMMITMENT** SEVEN TO EIGHT WEEKS | **BEST TIME OF YEAR** MAY TO JUNE, SEPTEMBER | **ESSENTIAL TIP** BOOK ACCOMMODATION EARLY IN SUMMER

FOOTPATH OF THE FAMOUS

Many big names appear along the coast path. Poet John Betjeman is buried at St Enodoc Church at Trebetherick. Nearby, Padstow is virtually owned by Rick Stein – the celebrity chef has several restaurants there. Godrevy Lighthouse inspired Virginia Woolf's *To the Lighthouse* (the author holidayed in nearby St Ives). Rudyard Kipling went to school in Westward Ho!, which itself is named after the Charles Kingsley novel. Writer Daphne du Maurier lived at Menabilly (near Fowey), Agatha Christie resided in Torquay and John Fowles died in Lyme Regis, the setting for his acclaimed novel *The French Lieutenant's Woman*.

■ THE ADVENTURE UNFOLDS

A limp sandwich has never tasted so good. You're eating it while resting on a day-warmed boulder, gentle gusts wafting around your shoulders, which are enjoying the break from your backpack. The view ahead is eye watering. A knobbly headland reaches out into an emerald sea, which fizzes brilliant-white where it wallops the unyielding rock. Inland, fields of wildflowers nod in the breezy sunshine; offshore, a dark shape is cutting calmly through the swell – the dorsal fin of a basking shark, looking for its own lunch.

This 'holiday' has been hard. You've never been more physically depleted. You wake early, when daylight begins to invade your canvas castle. Then it's a speedy teeth-toilet-tent-pack-up to hit the path while most tourists are still sleeping, and while the sands and cliff tops are still bathed in a golden glow. You never seem to make it up and out before the surfers, though.

You're carrying your world on your back – house, bed, kitchen, wardrobe – which triples the effort of every footstep. And you've been taken aback by the unrelenting abundance of ups and downs; thank goodness for your walking poles, which ease the pressure on your tested knees.

But you've never, ever been happier. The freedom and simplicity of life on the trail is the perfect antidote to the modern world (though a few nights swapping camp sites for B&Bs is a welcome treat). And the beauty! You chastise your own cheesiness, but this land and seascape is epic – promontories that look artistically sculpted, trails that snake through seaside pines, whitewashed cottages squeezed round tiny fishing harbours.

There are 'proper' sites: St Ives' Tate Gallery, Porthcurno's cliff-perched Minack Theatre, Plymouth's historic harbour. But, really, it's all

ARMCHAIR

* **Cornwall Coast Path** (Trailblazer) Excellent guide to the Bude–Falmouth stretch, with detailed hand-drawn maps.

* **South West Coast Path** (National Trail Guides) Four NT volumes cover the path: Minehead–Padstow, Padstow–Falmouth, Falmouth–Exmouth, Exmouth–Poole.

* **Seashore Life of Britain and Europe** (Bob Gibbons) Pocket-size guide to the seaweeds, molluscs and crustaceans found along the coast.

* **Rebecca** (Daphne du Maurier) Du Maurier set several novels in Cornwall; this tale of a young woman living with the ghost of her husband's first wife is a gothic classic.

* **And Then There Were None** (Agatha Christie) The queen of crime lived in Devon, and used it as a stage for many of her murders. Devon's Burgh Island – written here as Soldier Island – features in this thriller.

about the bits in between, where you can pause on a rock, with a Cornish pasty and some tasty views.

▓ MAKING IT HAPPEN

Minehead is 75 minutes by bus from Taunton train station; Poole Harbour is one hour (on two buses) from Bournemouth. Places en route with rail access include Newquay, St Ives, Penzance, Falmouth, Plymouth, Exmouth and Weymouth; buses connect some areas (eg Exeter–Bude). There are camp sites, B&Bs and some hostels along the path, though not always evenly spaced. Luggage Transfers can transport bags between nightly stops.

▓ AN ALTERNATIVE CHALLENGE

The All Wales Coast Path opened in spring 2012. It runs for 1400km from Queensferry in Flintshire, northeast Wales, via the island of Anglesey, the Llyn Peninsula, Cardigan Bay, Pembrokeshire and Cardiff to the Bristol Channel at Chepstow. On its way it traces every inch of seaboard, to create a continuous route around the nation's shore – a world first. The fully committed could then pick up Offa's Dyke National Trail, which heads north from Chepstow and roughly follows the Welsh–English border for 285km to Prestatyn – to complete an entire perambulation of Wales.

VISITBRITAIN | BRITAIN ON VIEW | GETTY

OPENING SPREAD The footpaths above Dorset's chalk cliffs are at their best in summer.
ABOVE The Cobb at Lyme Regis starred in the film of *The French Lieutenant's Woman*.
BELOW The limestone of Durdle Door in Lulworth Cove, Dorset, is 140 million years old.

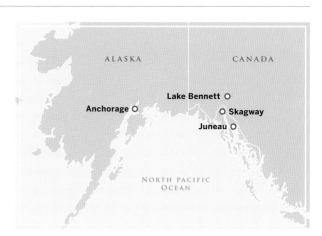

HIKE ALASKA'S CHILKOOT TRAIL

THE KLONDIKE GOLD RUSH WAS 'THE LAST GRAND ADVENTURE', WHEN THOUSANDS FOLLOWED THE CHILKOOT TRAIL TO SEEK THEIR FORTUNE IN THE YUKON. THESE DAYS IT'S HIKERS IN SEARCH OF ADVENTURE WHO ARE RETRACING THE STAMPEDERS' STEPS ACROSS ALASKA'S FAMOUS TRAIL.

54

In 1896, Skookum Jim Mason, Dawson Charlie and George Washington Carmack found 'colour' in a tributary of the Klondike River in Canada's Yukon territory. A year later, when a steamship landed in Seattle with a couple of tonnes of gold, the Klondike Gold Rush was on. Thousands of people quit their jobs and sold their homes to finance a trip to the newly created boomtown of Skagway in Southeast Alaska. In 1897–98 alone, almost 30,000 prospectors tackled the steep Chilkoot Trail to Lake Bennett, where they built crude rafts to float up the Yukon River to the goldfields. In all, it was a journey of around 1000km, with gold-seekers often arriving in Dawson City only to discover most of the streams were already staked.

At the height of this madness, Irish contractor Michael J Heney convinced a group of English investors that he could build a railroad from Skagway to Whitehorse over the White Pass. Construction began in 1898, with little more than picks, shovels and blasting powder, and the narrow-gauge railroad reached Whitehorse, today the Yukon's capital, in 1900. The construction of the White Pass & Yukon Railroad was nothing short of a superhuman feat and it sealed the fate of the Chilkoot Trail.

The actual Klondike Gold Rush lasted only to the early 1900s but its legacy has endured, even blossomed, and is now the basis for Skagway's economy. Today, most of downtown Skagway and the famous trail immortalised by stampeders are part of the Klondike Gold Rush National Historical Park, and a ride on the White Pass & Yukon Railroad is one of the most popular tours in Southeast Alaska. Not only have Skagway's historic buildings been restored to their boomtown appearance, but locals, dressed in turn-of-the-century garb, still welcome the modern-day stampeders stepping off ferries and cruise ships.

ESSENTIAL EXPERIENCES

* **Riding the historic White Pass & Yukon Railroad as it climbs from Skagway to White Pass.**

* Bellying up to the bar at Skagway's Mascot Saloon, a museum dedicated to gambling, drinking, prostitution and other vices during the Klondike Gold Rush.

* **Cruising to Skagway on the Alaska Marine Highway through glacier-studded Lynn Canal, North America's longest and deepest fjord.**

* Checking out the ton of supplies every miner had to carry over the Chilkoot Pass at Klondike Gold Rush National Historical Park Visitor Center.

* **Strolling Skagway's wooden sidewalks as if it's 1898.**

DISTANCE 53KM | **ELEVATION** 1057M | **LOCATION** SKAGWAY, ALASKA, USA, TO LAKE BENNETT, BC, CANADA | **IDEAL TIME COMMITMENT** FOUR TO FIVE DAYS | **BEST TIME OF YEAR** MID-JUNE TO MID-SEPTEMBER | **ESSENTIAL TIP** PACK YOUR PASSPORT – THE CHILKOOT TRAIL CROSSES AN INTERNATIONAL BORDER

CLIMBING THE CHILKOOT PASS

Before the arrival of the railway, leg power was the only way to cross the Klondike. One amazing photo – one that's displayed even along the trail – is of a line of men carrying their loads up the Golden Stairs in the winter of 1897–98. Unless they could afford porters, stampeders carried roughly 22kg on each trip up the pass, which included 1500 steps carved out of the snow and ice. Most could endure only one climb a day, which meant they made as many as 40 trips in 40 days before they could get the required 'year's worth of supplies' to the top.

THE ADVENTURE UNFOLDS

The Chilkoot Trail is as much a history lesson as it is a wilderness adventure. The well-developed trail is littered from one end to the other with artefacts from the era – everything from collapsed tramways and huge steam boilers to a rotting wagon wheel or a rusty coffee pot. The Chilkoot stretches 53km from Dyea, a ghost town that was once Skagway's rival, to Lake Bennett, just over the Canadian border. You can hike the trail in either direction but it's easier to begin in Dyea, following in the footsteps of the Klondike miners, which is what makes this adventure so appealing.

Located along the Chilkoot are nine camping grounds with wooden tent platforms and warming shelters. The 12km hike to the first two camping grounds is relatively easy, as the trail follows the Taiya River. The climbing begins after the second camp site, Canyon City, but the most important camping ground by far is Sheep Camp, reached at Mile 11.8. Just as in 1898, Sheep Camp still serves as the staging area for the climb to the summit. For most hikers, that's a 14.5km, 10-hour trek to the next camping ground, in which they gain more than 750m in the first half. The final ascent to the 1057m Chilkoot Pass is via the famed Golden Stairs, a 45-degree rocky chute that is usually climbed by scrambling from one large boulder to the next on all fours.

At the top are snowfields, the USA–Canada border and an emergency shelter. From there, the Chilkoot Trail is a gradual descent to Lake Bennett, where backpackers gather at the classic White Pass & Yukon Railroad depot for a scenic train ride back over the border to Skagway.

MAKING IT HAPPEN

Only 50 hikers per day are allowed on the trail. If you're intending to walk in the peak period from mid-July to mid-August, you will need to reserve your permits in advance through Parks Canada. For travel to Skagway, there's the Alaska Marine Highway. For other details about the hike, have a chat to the staff at the Chilkoot Trail Center. Contact the White Pass & Yukon Route for passage from Lake Bennett back to Skagway.

AN ALTERNATIVE CHALLENGE

Glacier Station, at Mile 14 of the White Pass & Yukon Railroad, is little more than a sweeping curve in the tracks, a sign and a trail. But the trail leads 2.5km to a US Forest Service cabin and then to Laughton Glacier, a dramatic hanging glacier that spills over the 900m walls of the Sawtooth Range. Combining the train ride and a hike to a remote cabin makes this an easy alternative to the Chilkoot, while flagging down a train to return to Skagway is still uniquely Alaska.

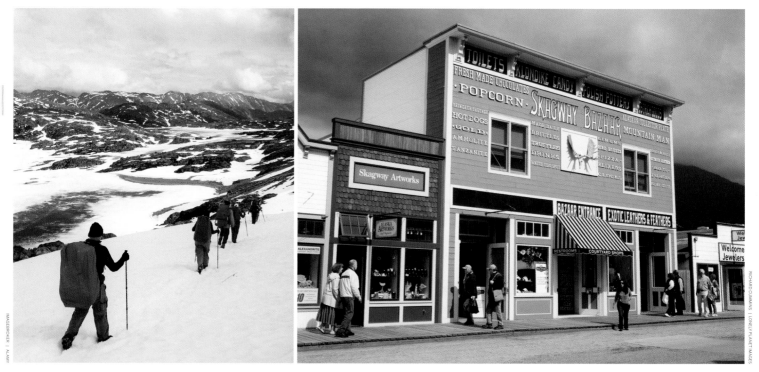

OPENING SPREAD Don't miss the end-of-the-trail meal for hikers of beef stew and apple pie on the White Pass and Yukon Railroad. **ABOVE (L)** The Chilkoot Trail dusted in snow. **ABOVE (R)** Today, customers at the general store in Skagway, Alaska, are souvenir hunters rather than gold prospectors.

ARMCHAIR

* ***The Floor of Heaven*** (Howard Blum) This novel of the Klondike Gold Rush has been made into a movie.

* ***Call of the Wild*** (Jack London) An adventure classic with a dog as chief protagonist and the Klondike as a backdrop.

* ***Good Time Girls of the Alaska–Yukon Gold Rush*** (Lael Morgan) Follow the women who followed the stampeders, including a prostitute who married the mayor of Fairbanks.

* ***Klondike Trail: The Complete Hiking and Paddling Guide*** (Jennifer Voss) From the Chilkoot Trail to paddling the Yukon River,

* ***Songs of a Sourdough*** (Robert Service) The 'Bard of the Yukon' knew well that 'There are strange things done 'neath the midnight sun,' as recounted in the poem 'The Cremation of Sam McGee'.

* ***Klondike Fever*** (1980) Based on London's Yukon adventures, this Canadian film starred Rod Steiger, Angie Dickenson and Lorne Green.

DIVE

DIVE BIKINI ATOLL

REGARDED AS THE ULTIMATE THEME PARK FOR WRECK DIVERS, THIS FORMER BOMB-TESTING SITE IN THE PACIFIC OCEAN IS LITTERED WITH THE WARPED WRECKAGE OF DESTROYERS, SUBMARINES AND RIPPED-OPEN BATTLE CRUISERS THAT HAVE BEEN REINVIGORATED BY A STUNNING ARRAY OF MARINE LIFE.

It's been just over 15 years since the islanders of Bikini opened their prized atoll to divers. Since then, Bikini Atoll has consistently ranked among the best dive sites in the world, renowned for its unique wreckage of decommissioned navy vessels. The jewel is USS *Saratoga*, the only aircraft carrier accessible to divers.

One of the 29 atolls and five islands that compose Micronesia's Marshall Islands, Bikini Atoll boasts an extraordinary collection of broken ships plus two submarines – but with an ominous heritage. After WWII, the United States declared Bikini Atoll a 'ship's graveyard' and in 1946 the Marshall Islands were chosen as the testing ground for nuclear tests.

Bikini Atoll proved a top spot to detonate bombs because of its remoteness from standard shipping routes. These days, the atoll's remoteness has ensured its exclusivity as a diving destination, despite it being jammed with mesmerising wreckage and an incredible abundance of aquatic life.

To get the most out of Bikini, it's recommended that you've done at least 50 dives, as getting to the sea floor requires a staged compression descent. Dives here are long and the approaches are spectacularly surreal, even for veterans. The sheer scale of the structures make it hard to absorb and make sense of the scene that emerges. It's not just that you're swimming with torpedo tubes and depth chargers or inspecting immense 16-inch guns – it's the historical significance of the sites that adds an extra punch of significance.

After nuclear tests were halted, the major concern for divers was radiation contamination. After 20 years' research, experts at the US-based Lawrence Livermore National Laboratory concluded there is no danger of radiation poisoning from swimming in the atoll. That said, if you set off any Geiger counters when you get home, you'll know why.

ESSENTIAL EXPERIENCES

* **Nervously heading out into the lagoon for the first time, imagining the spectacle of a mushroom cloud overhead.**

* Your first glimpse of the colossal *Saratoga* looming towards you like a mythical creature.

* **Observing aircraft instrument panels frozen at the moment the bomb was detonated more than half a century ago.**

* Marvelling at the warped, twisted havoc caused by one tiny atom split in two.

* **Standing on the seabed beside a rusting, barnacle-encrusted submarine.**

LOCATION BIKINI ATOLL, MARSHALL ISLANDS, MICRONESIA | **IDEAL TIME COMMITMENT** SEVEN DAYS | **BEST TIME OF YEAR** APRIL TO NOVEMBER | **ESSENTIAL TIP** GET FIT BEFORE YOU ARRIVE AS YOU CAN EXPECT TO DO 14 OR MORE DIVES IN A WEEK-LONG TRIP

BIRTH OF THE BIKINI

It is not a coincidence that Bikini Atoll is also a name for a swimsuit. While the atoll's name is derived from the indigenous names for surface (pik) and coconut (ni), it was a stroke of marketing genius that saw the bikini swimsuit named after the island just as the first nuclear tests were being conducted here and the atoll was headlining the news. In a scene that could have come straight out of *Mad Men*, the bikini was unveiled weeks after the 'Atome' one-piece was promoted as the 'smallest bathing suit in the world'. The bikini's slogan was that it had 'split the atom'.

TROUBLE IN PARADISE

After two thousand years living in their remote paradise, the people of the Marshall Islands suddenly found themselves subjugated when Germans set up an outpost in 1885. Thirty years on, Japanese soldiers took over at the start of WWI, until the islands and its people were 'liberated' following brutal fighting by the Americans at the end of WWII. Then, for 12 years after the war, the Marshall Islands were the venue for 67 nuclear tests, including 23 detonations on Bikini Atoll. Today, 2000 Bikinians hope that soil scraping will rid their atoll of radiation so they can return home. In the meantime, they await a settlement from the US Government for the destruction of their universe.

THE ADVENTURE UNFOLDS

Ironically, it is radioactivity that has made the lagoon such a place of wonder. The mesmerising abundance of aquatic life has been protected from overfishing, as any haul was for many decades considered inedible. The result is a plethora of inquisitive sharks and every type of fish you can imagine, heightening your senses as you move through the eerie wreckage.

What you're witnessing is a makeshift navy fleet arranged in battle formation and then blown to smithereens by an atomic bomb. Warped and mangled, the ghostly shells have come to rest in spectacular formations. USS *Saratoga* sticks out perpendicular to the seafloor while HIJMS *Nagato*, once the flagship of the Japanese Imperial navy, from which Admiral Yamamoto launched the attack on Pearl Harbor, lies eternally upside down.

The goats placed on deck to simulate how the explosions would impact humans are long gone but the hardware remains. You'll need to keep one hand on your regulator to stop it falling out of your mouth when your jaw drops while propelling yourself along the *Saratoga*'s flight deck, with planes strewn all about her awesome hulk. Photo opportunities are myriad. Pose beside rust-coloured barnacles enveloping a propeller five people tall, or flap your fins alongside anti-aircraft guns, their barrels seemingly searching for a target through the murky blue while reef sharks cruise nearby shrouded in the shadows.

Back on the surface, it's hard to describe what you've just seen. Around you the other 28 atolls of the Marshalls are out of sight. You are alone in the middle of the Pacific, where once mushroom clouds darkened the skies.

MAKING IT HAPPEN

The atoll is a 400km flight northwest of Majuro Atoll, which is usually reached via Honolulu or Cairns. Flying aboard a twin-engine aircraft adds to the sense that you're stepping back in time. On Bikini itself you'll find a somewhat rustic but air-conditioned resort equipped with a shuttle bus transporting you to the boats. Briefings are held before each morning dive, with an emphasis on safety. Two dives a day is the norm.

AN ALTERNATIVE CHALLENGE

Aside from soaking up the inestimable beauty of Bikini's lagoon, sport fishing is the 'other' activity you can do out here. It has been just over a decade since the atoll's fish have been declared safe for consumption. In the meantime they have been left to breed without the threat of overfishing that has destroyed ecosystems worldwide. On the reefs around Bikini you'll find giant trevally, mammoth-sized marlin and so many sharks you'd think they were sardines. And don't even start about the barracuda that got away.

OPENING SPREAD Ship and submarine wrecks around Bikini Atoll are now marine habitats. **ABOVE (L)** A 1954 thermonuclear test code-named Bravo created a 15-megaton explosion and a vast crater. **ABOVE (R)** Shining a light on the past. **LEFT** Bombers from the USS *Saratoga* scattered on the seabed.

ARMCHAIR

* ***Diving Micronesia*** (Eric Hanauer) A must-read for any diver travelling to the region.

* ***The Cruiser's Handbook of Fishing*** (Scott and Wendy Bannerot) Top tips about how to fish in the styles specific to people of the Pacific, including the Marshall Islands.

* **'Live from a Shark Cage from Bikini Atoll'** (Discovery Channel) Now over a decade old, this classic episode is still a beauty.

* ***USS Saratoga Cv-3: An Illustrated History of the Legendary Aircraft Carrier 1927–1946*** (John Fry) John Fry's impeccably crafted guide to USS *Saratoga* is a wonderful way to whet your appetite before you arrive at Bikini.

* ***Operation Crossroads: The Atomic Tests at Bikini Atoll*** (Jonathan Weisgall) Well-researched account of the US Government's program that changed Bikini forever.

ATLANTIC
OCEAN

SOUTH
AFRICA

Cape Town O

O Gansbaai

DIVE WITH SHARKS IN SOUTH AFRICA

IMAGINE IT: THE SEA'S SCARIEST, TOOTHIEST, MOST NOTORIOUS MANEATER, JUST INCHES AWAY FROM YOUR FACE… YOU DON'T NEED EXPERIENCE TO CAGE-DIVE WITH GREAT WHITES, BUT A TOUCH OF CRAZY MIGHT HELP. THIS IS AN ADVENTURE FOR THE MAD OR THE BRAVE. AND ONE NEITHER WILL FORGET.

Fitness needed: basic. Dive experience: none. Nerves of steel: 100% essential.

There's nothing difficult about cage-diving with great white sharks. You don't even travel far offshore, and then you dangle just under the surface, so scuba skills aren't required; most trips don't even use snorkels – instead, you simply hold your breath and dip your head. But – and it's a big but – you need to have the guts to be inches from 1000-plus kilos of thrashing, cold-eyed predator.

Great whites have a bad reputation, no small thanks to the movie *Jaws*. Peter Benchley, who wrote the novel on which it was based, actually spent the last years of his life campaigning for shark conservation, but the damage was done: it's impossible to think of these creatures without hearing John Williams' terror-inducing score, those two simple notes that, he said, mimic the shark: 'instinctual, relentless, unstoppable'.

Great whites *(Carcharodon carcharias)* are found in most seas and oceans, but the waters off South Africa are home to perhaps the largest concentration; some research suggests 2000, of a total global population of 5000, hunt here. They have a few favoured feeding spots, one of which is off the small Western Cape fishing village of Gansbaai. A strip of ocean between tiny Dyer Island and tinier Geyser Rock has been dubbed Shark Alley. The 60,000-strong resident colony of Cape fur seals provides a constant buffet for the great whites, particularly from May to August, when the new-born seal pups make perfect snacks. Local tour operators claim sharks are seen on 99% of trips.

It takes just 20 minutes to motor from the harbour to the big-fish feeding ground, aboard a boat carrying up to around 40 passengers. Viewing from deck is excellent – you might see a shark make an acrobatic leap out of the waves to catch a seal. But the biggest thrill is descending into a galvanised-steel cage (attached to the boat so it can't sink or float away) to enter the shark's realm.

ESSENTIAL EXPERIENCES

* **Keeping your eyes open for the Cape gannets, African penguins, whales, dolphins and 60,000-plus Cape fur seals that fly and frolic around Geyser Rock.**

* Scouring the swell for that spine-chilling telltale sign: a sleek grey dorsal cutting through the water.

* **Dropping into a (hopefully) sturdy cage to come face-to-gaping-maw with the most fearsome predator in the sea.**

* Dispelling the myths about these magnificent creatures: a good guide will fill you in on shark behaviour and the environmental issues as you sail.

* **Spending time on land at Gansbaai, hiking the many trails that spider across the surrounding hillsides.**

62

LOCATION GANSBAAI, WESTERN CAPE, SOUTH AFRICA | **IDEAL TIME COMMITMENT** FOUR TO FIVE HOURS | **BEST TIME OF YEAR** JUNE TO SEPTEMBER | **ESSENTIAL TIP** TAKE SEA-SICKNESS PILLS (JUST IN CASE)

BE SHARK AWARE

Though great white sharks look tough, they're classed 'Vulnerable' by the International Union for the Conservation of Nature. However, there is currently no ban on international trade in great white products: a single tooth might sell for up to US$8000. Don't be tempted by such macabre trinkets. There's also controversy about the use of bait; it's believed this causes sharks to link humans with food, leading to more attacks. Even the use of chum – a mix of fish oil and innards that attracts but is not food – has its detractors. Question your operator on these issues before booking.

ICELAND

O Þingvellir National Park
Reykjavík O

DIVE ICELAND'S TECTONIC PLATES

CRYSTAL CLARITY, CHECK. VOLCANIC ACTIVITY, CHECK. FLOATING BETWEEN TWO TECTONIC PLATES SLOWLY SHIFTING APART, CHECK. CRUISING BACK TO REYKJAVÍK FOR THE MOTHER OF ALL PARTIES, DOUBLE CHECK, 'CAUSE THAT'S HOW YOU ROLL.

Iceland's Silfra Rift is more than just a crack in the Earth's crust. It is the only place in the world where you can go for a swim, stretch out your arms and be touching Eurasia with one hand and America with the other. That's because it is one of the few, and certainly the most exhilarating, places on the planet where it's possible to dive between two tectonic plates, which is literally the stuff that makes up the Earth's crust.

Cutting a swathe from the shore into a glacial lake, the rift lies within the majestic Þingvellir National Park – declared a Unesco World Heritage Site for its natural and geological uniqueness. All you have to do is slip on a dry suit, plunge into the 50-year-old water and have your mind blown.

There are so many elements that make this the most surreal, jaw-dropping experience you will have in your lifetime. For a start, every moment you are submerged, you're shielded from death by just a few centimetres of dry suit. Exposure to the 4°C water – and that would be on a warm day – can result in death within just a few tortuous minutes. As if that isn't edgy enough, the water also happens to be so pure that you can remove your ventilator and drink it. Talk about a dichotomy: what can kill you is also great for quenching your thirst.

Frequently cited by veteran divers as the clearest dive-able water in the world, Þingvellir Lake is fed by glaciers around 50km away, as the melting ice water resurfaces via underground wells. Visibility at the Silfra Rift literally extends to end-of-sight.

What that means in practice can't be truly comprehended unless you're actually down there fathoming it, gasping at every gaping lava rock formation leaping out in spectacular vibrant detail like some mind-bending etching by Escher that wills itself into your mind.

ESSENTIAL EXPERIENCES

* **Surfacing after a midnight dive into the blazing summer sun.**
* Recalling long-lost colours and hues as you try to put a name to what you're seeing.
* **Feeling a strange sense like vertigo, the water so clear it's like you're hanging in space.**
* Taking a sip of water 10m under the lake.
* **Slowly descending between the walls of Silfra Cathedral.**
* Being eternally grateful you did this dive while you still have 20/20 vision.

DEPTH 63M | **LOCATION** ÞINGVELLIR NATIONAL PARK, ICELAND | **IDEAL TIME COMMITMENT** TWO NIGHTS | **BEST TIME OF YEAR** MAY TO AUGUST | **ESSENTIAL TIP** BRING A DECENT SCHNAPPS TO TOAST YOUR DIVE IN TRUE VIKING TRADITION

ALTHING ASSEMBLY

In the year 930, a tribal assembly known as the Althing was established on land that is now part of the Þingvellir National Park. Each year over a fortnight, the assembly would meet to set the laws and settle disputes, so that relative peace and prosperity could be enjoyed by the people of Iceland. The stone remnants of where the Althing took place are still regarded as something akin to sacred relics by locals, and more remnants are believed to be buried below ground. The national park has changed little in a thousand years and remains shaped by the toil of the old Nordic farmers who once called it home.

THE ADVENTURE UNFOLDS

Standing on your first launch platform, your heart pounds and your body is heating up in your thick dry suit. Without ceremony you must dive head first into a 16m vertical descent through a corridor of rock known affectionately as the Toilet that takes you into the Silfra Crack, where you'll get flushed along with glacial water pouring up from the underground wells, funnelled through the narrow crack and into the lake. Exiting the tunnel, you join up with the less-experienced divers and snorkellers who elected to take an easier entry.

A peaceful swim leads you into the Silfra Hall cave system that reaches a depth of 45m. Huge boulders are scattered like broken marbles, discarded playthings of the mighty Thor. The strewn rocks serve as both gallery and obstacle course as you swim the 200m to Silfra Cathedral, the most celebrated, and many would say divine, aspect of the dive.

The crystal clarity means you can see every detail from end to end of the cathedral. Its beauty is so powerful you have to remind yourself to breathe. Walls of petrified lava punch straight down at the opening of a fissure that extends for over 100m and to the depth of 10 divers. You don't want to leave, but the current has other ideas. It will deposit you in the lake unless you follow your guide into the final chapter of the experience, the Silfra Lagoon.

The water here is even clearer than in the Cathedral. Waiting for your fellow divers, you're granted an otherworldly sense of scale and perspective, allowing you to pick out every detail across the lagoon's 120m diameter. Sadly, you can also spot where you need to exit and leave the splendour of Silfra behind.

MAKING IT HAPPEN

The Sport Diving School of Iceland is a good place to begin. As the oldest dive centre in Iceland, the school has pioneered diving the Silfra Rift since 1997. The rift lies within the Þingvellir National Park, an easy drive by jeep from Reykjavík, which means you can typically do your dive in a day and be back at your hotel before night. Your guide will supply your dry suit, tanks and everything else you need, so all you have to do is turn up and be blown away.

AN ALTERNATIVE CHALLENGE

If you don't have your diving certification, you can still chill in the rift. Daily snorkelling tours are an absolutely ripper alternative that can be done by anyone capable of donning a dry suit. The tours are usually run in conjunction with the dive tours, giving you an awesome sense of perspective as you watch the scuba crew descend into the rift. Snorkelling is also the perfect way to experience the pristine Silfra Cathedral, a shallow formation that feels like you're staring into a looking glass.

OPENING SPREAD Growing apart: the tectonic plates of the east and west separate by 7mm per year. **ABOVE (L)** Gullfoss (Golden Falls) named for the effect sunshine has on the water as it hurtles into Hvítá River. **ABOVE (R) AND LEFT** Suspended in the magically clear water of Silfra lagoon.

ARMCHAIR

✳ **Icelandic Folktales and Legends** (Jon Arnason) The author gives ink to 85 tales full of fairies and trolls sprung from the rich veins of Iceland's spectacular natural beauty.

✳ **Dreamland** (Andri Snær Magnason) The latest offering from one of the country's leading cultural critics is a compelling introduction to the issues confronting modern Iceland.

✳ **101 Reykjavik** (2000) Multi award-winning film based on the book by Hallgrimur Helgason, presenting a darkly comic take of the capital set to a soundtrack by ex-Blur frontman Damon Albarn.

✳ **Embla** (1991) Also known as *The White Viking*, a striking cinematic portrayal of Iceland and Norway during the 10th-century reign of King Olaf I of Norway.

SNORKEL SOUTH AFRICA'S SARDINE RUN

FEEL THE CRACK OF CAPE GANNETS PIERCING THE WATER METRES FROM YOUR HEAD, WATCH SHARKS CIRCLING BRAZENLY WHILE DOLPHINS ZOOM PAST, CLICKING INSTRUCTIONS TO EACH OTHER AS THE ENDLESSLY HARASSED SARDINES SWIM FOR THEIR LIVES, ALL TO A SOUNDTRACK OF WHALE SONG.

70

Every year, millions of sardines migrate along the eastern shores of South Africa en route to their breeding grounds off the Southern Cape. Exactly how many and for how long this has been happening, we can't say, but word has certainly got around the animal kingdom. The migration, which local fishermen dubbed the sardine run, attracts unprecedented numbers of predators, from sharks, dolphins and orcas, to Cape gannets and other birds all eager to partake in this epic feast.

Securing a front-row seat at this all-you-can-eat buffet is easy. You just slip on a pair of goggles, fasten your snorkel and jump into the treacherous waters off the Wild Coast, so named because this has long been a rocky wrecking yard for the vessels of unfortunate sailors. With its vast unspoilt beaches and rolling grasslands framed beneath the Drakensberg Mountains to the west, and an endless stretch of Indian Ocean to the east, the Wild Coast is as picturesque a place as you could imagine, but it's what's happening under the sea that will rip your breath away.

With the sardine shoals reaching a staggering 30km in length, the predators' feeding displays are on a colossal scale. It is believed more than 20,000 dolphins alone follow the sardines' migration. Working together, dolphin pods strategically herd the sardines, rounding them up into gigantic 'bait balls', which are then ruthlessly gobbled up by an array of marine predators.

The beauty of snorkelling the sardine run is that anyone who doesn't mind sharing their bath with a great white, or seven, can do it. Your guide tracks the sardines using a combination of underwater sonar and by simply watching the skies – when you spot a huge cloud of birds circling overhead, it's a safe bet they've found a shoal. Once your boat arrives at the spot, it's simply a matter of taking that leap of faith into the unknown.

ESSENTIAL EXPERIENCES

* **Hearing the explosion of gannets bursting into the water and shooting past you like Formula 1 racers.**

* Eyeballing sharks, knowing that any minute they could launch into a feeding frenzy.

* **Trying not to surface while scuba diving, as migrating ragged tooths loom inquisitively all around you.**

* Believing your eyes when you spot a penguin among the predators.

* **Shedding a tear for the sardines that won't be making it to the Agulhas Bank.**

LOCATION WILD COAST, EASTERN CAPE, SOUTH AFRICA | **IDEAL TIME COMMITMENT** FIVE DAYS | **BEST TIME OF YEAR** END OF MAY TO JULY | **ESSENTIAL TIP** BRING AN UNDERWATER CAMERA WITH A STRAP – YOU WON'T WANT TO SWIM AFTER IT IF YOU DROP IT

AGULHAS BANK OR BUST

Sardines are seriously time-poor fish. With only a three-year lifespan at best, it is essential that as many as possible make it to their breeding grounds at Agulhas Bank, off South Africa's Southern Cape, in time for the summer love fest. It is here that their eggs have the best chance of survival in the nutrient-rich waters. Even so, each female still needs to release tens of thousands of eggs, which are then fertilised by the males. If they survive long enough to become juveniles, the sardines will form thick shoals and head south, only to return the following year from the north.

DIVE THE YUCATÁN'S CENOTES

THE MAYA REVERED THESE OTHERWORLDLY POOLS, WITH SHAFTS OF SUNLIGHT TANGIBLE ENOUGH TO CLIMB, CLUSTERS OF THIGH-THICK VINES AND VISIBILITY MEASURED IN HUNDREDS OF FEET. DIVERS WILL DISCOVER MANY SECRETS BELOW THE SURFACE OF THESE UNIQUE MEXICAN WONDERS.

74

Cenotes played a key role in prehistoric Maya civilisation, and they remain a central part of the natural heritage of the Yucatán. Formed by the erosion of calcium-laden rock in the shallow shelf that makes up the peninsula, cenotes are sink holes. What makes them unique is that these columnar caves reach far down into the freshwater aquifer, providing water in an area that, while lush and humid, often experiences droughts. Only a handful of rivers cut through the area, leaving much of this plateau and its plants, animals and humans dependent on rainwater. Scientists are realising that many of what were once thought to be independent caves are actually connected; indeed, Yucatán's cenotes may be part of the largest underground system in the world.

Even more interesting, thanks to centuries of cenotes being used as anything from ceremonial burial grounds to waste baskets, the silt at the bottom of these unique freshwater caves is often rich with information about the plants, animals and populations of prehistoric times. Many of the artefacts on display in museums in Mexico and at famous sites like Chichén Itzá were dredged up from the depths. Travelling into these caverns is like diving into a museum.

Cenote diving is both interesting and dangerous: this is not an open-water dive. You may encounter all sorts of interesting challenges that separate this experience from the run of the mill. Layers of silt are easily stirred up and, without currents to wash it away, can turn crystal-clear visibility into zero visibility in seconds. Extreme pressures at certain depths trap toxic gases, which remain suspended or dissolved in the water but which are poisonous and can even eat away at diving equipment if precautions aren't taken. Some cenotes have forests of dead trees at the bottom, which can tangle or ensnare the careless. So it's vital to dive here with someone experienced not just in diving, but in all the various surprises each cenote may have in store.

ESSENTIAL EXPERIENCES

* **Gazing up in awestruck wonder at a cavern ceiling pierced by shafts of sunlight that seem tangible as steel.**

* Gliding past ethereal rock formations in inky darkness larger than a football stadium.

* **Observing close up the bottom of these time capsules: prehistoric artefacts, indigenous peoples' skulls, even the occasional mastodon.**

* Plunging into the crystalline water hundreds of miles inland, knowing that if you could follow it indefinitely you'd find it leads all the way to the sea.

* **Taking in the wonders of the Maya ruin Chichén Itzá, where the Well of Sacrifice was used for sacrificing humans to the gods.**

LOCATION YUCATÁN, QUINTANA ROO, MEXICO | **IDEAL TIME COMMITMENT** ONE DAY PER DIVE | **BEST TIME OF YEAR** NOVEMBER TO MARCH | **ESSENTIAL TIP** RESERVE TWO-THIRDS OF YOUR TANK FOR THE RETURN

THE CHICXULUB CRATER

A vast number of the Yucatán's cenotes, especially those near Mérida in the state of Yucatán, trace the outer border of the Chicxulub crater, a massive meteor impact that dates back to prehistoric times. The event occurred right at the K–T boundary, which was the time the dinosaurs vanished, and the crater's size (over 180km wide) proves it had to have been an earth-changing catastrophe. It may be that the Chicxulub impact not only paved the way for mammals to thrive, but created the area's most interesting natural attractions as well.

HENEQUIN

In the late 19th century, the Yucatán was Mexico's richest and most prosperous *estado,* thanks to the use of local henequin fibres in ropemaking. Like tequila, the fibres come from agave. The industry took off after the invention of the henequin fibre press (an intricate Rube Goldberg–looking machine), and soon henequin plantations stretched for thousands of square miles, ruled by barons who exploited the indigenous populations and made fortunes off cheap land and labour. Only when the era of the clipper ships ended did the need for rope subside, and today most plantations remain as atmospheric ruins, if they remain at all.

THE ADVENTURE UNFOLDS

Cenote diving often begins with a hazard: just getting the gear down to the water can be tricky, requiring careful placement of feet on slippery rocks, climbing down ladders or even leaping in from above. But the care at the start pays off in spades when you're underwater, gliding through vast chambers or narrow tunnels in water so clear you almost forget it's not air.

Take time to absorb the above-ground portion of the cave: the sunlight filtering through the canopy and the tangle of vegetation, vines and moss on the cavern sides. Some cenotes have stalactites that almost kiss the surface. Others have shallows where you can see rocks and blind fish swimming.

Descending, you'll find that visibility is limited only by your torch, or by the sunlight that filters in from above. Use your fins sparingly, to avoid churning up dust. You may need to hold onto a guide rope to avoid getting lost. Make sure emergency procedures have been discussed before you dive, and always reserve two-thirds of the tank for your return trip.

As you dive deeper, the chambers take on the aura of cathedrals and it seems like you're flying, weightless, through Earth's natural apses. If your location is close to the sea, you may notice the blurry halocline, where the heavier saltwater mixes with the fresh rainwater in the aquifer above.

Only those experienced in deepwater scuba-diving should go all the way to the bottom of some cenotes. Many have 'Peligro – No Pase!' signs that must be heeded carefully. Layers of dissolved acid or treacherous passageways are just a few of the possible dangers, but the rewards of a cenote dive are long-lasting.

MAKING IT HAPPEN

Cancún, Mérida and Playa del Carmen hotels have cenote tours and there are cenote-experienced dive shops nearby. Trips start at around US$100 per person, and may be much more depending on the type of dive and location. Keep safety at the top of the priority list – two-thirds of your tank must remain for the return half of the dive. Lesser-known cenotes may require private permission and/or off-road driving to reach.

AN ALTERNATIVE CHALLENGE

For those not yet PADI-certified or who are uncomfortable assuming the risks inherent in a non open-water dive, cenote snorkelling may be the perfect alternative. Most of the popular tours such as Dos Ojos and Río Secreto have snorkel-only options; often the group is a mix of snorkellers and divers. Snorkellers should not apply any kind of sunscreen before entering the water, however, as the oils rub off into the water and leave a sheen that – in these current-free holes – has nowhere to go.

OPENING SPREAD AND ABOVE (L) Diving in a cenote near Akumal. There are more than 5000 cenotes in the Yucatán. **ABOVE (R)** Swimming in Sacred Blue Cenote in Ik Kil Parque, close to Chichén Itzá. **LEFT** Cenote Samula in Dzitnup, near Valladolid, is one of the prettiest cenotes in the Yucatán.

ARMCHAIR

* ***Cancún, Cozumel & the Yucatán*** (Lonely Planet) A great guide to the area, with lots of insider tips and practical advice about lodging, food, dives and more.

* ***Exploring Maya Ritual Caves*** (Stanislav Chládek) A unique look isnto many cenotes and other caves around the peninsula, with excellent photography.

* ***Fifty Places to Dive Before You Die*** (Chris Santella) Includes cenotes in the list, along with many other extreme, fascinating dives.

* ***Mayan Folktales, Cuentos Foklóricos*** (Susan C Thompson, Keith S Thompson & L Lopez) Explains some of the cultural history behind the cenotes and what they meant to the Maya who revered them.

* ***'The Watery Graves of the Maya'*** (National Geographic Magazine) This online magazine article is filled with interesting facts and excellent photos of these curious caves.

SWIM WITH WHALE SHARKS

REEF SHARKS, MOVE OVER. DOLPHINS, STEP ASIDE. SWIMMING WITH THE WORLD'S BIGGEST FISH LEAVES OTHER MARINE ENCOUNTERS IN THE SHADE. DONSOL IN THE PHILIPPINES IS WHALE-SHARK CENTRAL, SO GRAB YOUR MASK AND SNORKEL AND SWIM WITH THE BIG FISH.

78

Suddenly an onlooker spots a dark shadow and the shout goes up: 'Shark! Everybody get in the water!' At Donsol, the whale-shark capital of the Philippines, the aim is getting close to sharks, not getting away.

Fishermen have known about the *butanding* that gather in the watery depths off the coast of Bicol for centuries, but the transformation of Donsol from sleeping fishing village to whale-shark spotting mecca is a more recent phenomenon. In 1998, a Filipino dive team spotted startling numbers of whale sharks on an exploration dive and alerted the WWF, who set the wheels in motion for one of the most successful community ecotourism projects in Asia.

Historically, *butanding* were viewed with fear by local fishermen, who noted their resemblance to more deadly denizens of the deep. However, the involvement of marine experts led to an official ban on fishing for whale sharks, and a new-found respect for the *butanding* amongst Donsol residents. With money coming in from managed shark dives, *butanding* suddenly had a greater value alive than dead, providing a powerful incentive for conservation.

From the outset, diving at Donsol was promoted with the welfare of the whale sharks in mind. Scuba diving was banned – sharks are spooked by the noise of bubbles from diving equipment – and swimmers were only allowed to enter the water with a mask and snorkel, in small, managed groups. Without tanks and regulators, the encounter with whale sharks is more intimate; you are a visitor in their world, rather than the other way round.

While Donsol is firmly on the international diving map, this is not your average diving hub. Donsol remains a sleepy fishing village – aside from the visitor centre, a scattering of Filipino-style resorts and the occasional jeepney, there is little to disturb the peace. In the evening, nightlife takes the form of beers on the balcony and firefly-spotting cruises on the local creek.

ESSENTIAL EXPERIENCES

* **Feeling the spray on your face as the pumpboat skims across the waves.**
* Glimpsing your first *butanding* gliding through the silent depths.
* **Getting up close and personal with mantas off Ticao Island.**
* Scouting for fireflies on the Ogod River.
* **Admiring the symmetry of Mt Mayon, the world's most perfect volcano, in nearby Legaspi.**

LOCATION DONSOL, SORSOGON, BICOL, THE PHILIPPINES | **IDEAL TIME COMMITMENT** THREE DAYS | **BEST TIME OF YEAR** FEBRUARY TO MAY | **TOP TIP** BRING YOUR OWN MASK AND SNORKEL FOR A WATERTIGHT FIT

FILTER FEEDERS

Don't be alarmed by that gaping mouth. It may look large enough to swallow a diver whole, but the whale shark is a gentle giant... unless of course you happen to be plankton. Whale sharks use their 3000 modified teeth as a giant sieve to strain tonnes of microscopic crustaceans and other plankton from the sea. The remarkable thing is how such tiny critters can support such enormous predators – the blue whale and manta ray, two more of the largest creatures in the ocean, are also filter feeders.

MOUNTAIN BIKE MOAB'S SLICKROCK TRAIL

DISCOVER THE ICONIC SLICKROCK THAT HAS MADE THE UTAH TOWN OF MOAB A WORLD-FAMOUS DESTINATION FOR FAT TYRE FANS. PEDAL THROUGH THE DESERT ON A BIKE, EXPLORING ROCKY OUTCROPS AND TESTING YOUR METTLE ON STICKY DROP-OFFS IN THIS WILD WILE E COYOTE COUNTY.

82

Most people associate Utah with deserts and Mormons, but to mountain bikers the western town of Moab could be an acronym for Mother of All Biking towns.

Originally a ford on the Colorado River, Moab was first settled (and swiftly abandoned) as a Mormon outpost in 1855. It boomed with the discovery of uranium in the region in the 1950s. Thirty years later, the Cold War ended, and so did Moab's largest industry. In its place came mountain bikes, refashioning Moab as one of the States' premier outdoors destinations. How many other towns have generic-brand hotels that advertise on-site bike workshops?

Pinched between Arches and Canyonlands national parks, Moab's surrounds are a mat of sand and red rock – the so-called 'slickrock' that makes mountain biking here so magnificent. Named because its surface was so slick for horses, the ancient Navajo sandstone is more like stickrock for mountain bikes, allowing riders to almost defy gravity as their wheels grip to steeply sloped rock.

The trail that attracts the vast bulk of mountain bikers is the Slickrock Trail, arguably the most famous mountain bike route in the world. Originally designed for trail bikes, the 20km loop rolls across Swiss Cheese Ridge and the Lion's Back, a rock ridge looming above Moab. Its orange rock is like a set of cycling moguls, with ledges that drop into pits of sand followed by stiff climbs back out.

But there's no need to get fixated on the Slickrock Trail: Moab has myriad bike experiences and great natural beauty to help dilute the adrenalin rushes. Novices can admire the swirling patterns in the rock as they curl around Bartlett Wash, or pass dinosaur footprints on the Klondike Bluffs Trail. Experienced riders will want to add Porcupine Rim and Poison Spider Mesa to their resume– these trails are almost as famous as Slickrock – while multiday desert rides beckon the most adventurous on the White Rim and Kokopelli trails.

ESSENTIAL EXPERIENCES

❋ **Earning your mountain bike stripes on the mighty Slickrock Trail.**

❋ Touring through canyon country as you ride a ledge above the Colorado and Green Rivers on the White Rim Trail.

❋ **Braving the exposure of the Portal on Poison Spider Mesa.**

❋ Dodging dinosaur footprints on the ride to Klondike Bluffs.

❋ **Soaking in the view along Porcupine Rim, while still remembering to keep an eye on the ledges.**

DISTANCE 20KM | **LOCATION** MOAB, UTAH, USA | **IDEAL TIME COMMITMENT** THREE TO FOUR HOURS | **BEST TIME OF YEAR** APRIL TO MAY, SEPTEMBER TO OCTOBER | **ESSENTIAL TIP** IF CYCLING IN SUMMER, RIDE ONLY IN THE COOL OF THE EARLY MORNING OR EVENING

CRYPTOBIOTIC CRUSTS

One of the most fascinating features of the desert
around Moab are cryptobiotic crusts. These living
crusts cover and protect desert soils, literally gluing
sand particles together so they don't blow away.
Cyanobacteria, which are among the world's oldest
living forms, start the process by extending mucous-
covered filaments that wind through the dry soil.
Over time, these filaments and the sand particles
that stick to them form a thin crust that's colonised
by microscopic algae, lichens, fungi and mosses.
Unfortunately, this thin crust is instantly fragmented
under the heavy impact of bicycle wheels. Once broken,
the crust takes 50 to 250 years to repair itself, so it's
imperative to stick to trails when you ride.

DESERT SOLITAIRE

The landscapes you ride through around Moab can have a haunting, almost apocalyptic beauty that's captivated many, including one of America's great writers, Edward Abbey (1927–89). Abbey worked as a seasonal ranger at Arches National Monument (now Arches National Park, about 5km from Moab) in the 1950s. He wrote of his time here in *Desert Solitaire: A Season in the Wilderness*, describing the simple beauty and subtle power of the vast landscape. Read it – and its polemic against cars and the paving of the wilderness – and you may see this desert and its mountain biking potential in a new light.

THE ADVENTURE UNFOLDS

They call it the Slickrock practice loop, but really it's the procrastination loop as you delay the moment you must confront the trail more famous than Moab itself: the Slickrock. Even this short loop has moments that have you closing your eyes in hope, including a jump into sand that throws you over the bars.

On the Slickrock Trail, your guiding lines are the painted white dashes that stretch like roller-coaster tracks across the rock. Few people can ride this trail without stopping to push, and you've covered less than 3km before you're taking your bike for a walk, pulling it up and out of Wooly Gully. One more walk and you've emerged at the top of Swiss Cheese Ridge, the highest point of the trail, where you can pretend you're soaking in the view over Moab to the Portal and not simply trying to suck in more oxygen.

Past Portal Viewpoint, the descent begins. The Colorado River is below, carving its way towards the Grand Canyon, but your attention is on your braking hands. As you turn from the river, you round Shrimp Rock, wondering how this table of rock – it looks nothing like a shrimp – received such a name. Later someone reveals it's because of the shrimps that live in the pool of water at its base.

You're tiring as the trail continues over rock and through sand – is this really just 20km? – until eventually you're back at Abyss Viewpoint, staring deep into the box canyon below. There's just 2km to ride, following your outward trail back to the practice loop, though practice sure didn't make perfect on Slickrock, and you have the blood and scabs – the bacon, as mountain bikers call them – to prove it. But so does everyone else here.

MAKING IT HAPPEN

Great Lakes Airlines flies to Moab from Denver and Las Vegas, while Greyhound has buses to Green River, around 80km away, with shuttle connections to Moab. In town, a number of companies offer bicycle shuttles to trailheads. Bike stores abound, but book ahead for mountain bike hire. The Slickrock Trail is in Sand Flats Recreation Area.

AN ALTERNATIVE CHALLENGE

Moab's reputation for adventure may be founded on mountain bikes, but dig deeper and there's a lot more here than knobblies and slickrock. Rafting the Colorado River has become Moab's adventure understudy, with a menu that goes from flat-water trips to the Confluence up to turbulent week-long journeys into the legendary class V rapids of Cataract Canyon. Other Moab adventures of note include four-wheel driving (Hells Revenge trail is right beside Slickrock, while the Moab Jeep Safari is held every Easter) and canyoneering – there's a reason the national park is called Canyonlands.

85

OPENING SPREAD Off-road trails in Utah follow the undulating contours of the slickrock but its name is misleading; it's very grippy. **ABOVE (L)** Taking a break. **ABOVE (R)** Crossing a sandstone bridge in Canyonlands National Park. **LEFT** Mountain bikers following the White Rim trail in Canyonlands.

ARMCHAIR

* ***Mountain Biking Moab Pocket Guide*** (David Crowell) Excellent guide to 42 of the best mountain bike trails around Moab.

* ***Rider Mel's Mountain Bike Guide to Moab*** (Rider Mel) Irreverent guide to 39 Moab rides, spiral-bound for ease of use.

* ***In the Land of Moab*** (Tom Till) Ogle the Moab landscapes in this photographic ode to red-rock country.

* ***Between a Rock and a Hard Place*** (Aron Ralston) Epic real-life survival tale in which the author amputates an arm after being trapped in a Canyonlands canyon; the story hit the big screen as *127 Hours*.

* ***Wagon Master*** (1950) A John Ford western filmed around Moab.

* ***The Collective*** (2004) Visually stunning 16mm film about mountain biking with several scenes shot in Utah.

CYCLE THROUGH VIETNAM

WITH TERRAIN TO SUIT EVERY CYCLIST, VIETNAM IS ONE OF THE WORLD'S MOST BIKE-FRIENDLY COUNTRIES. CYCLE THE COAST FROM HUE TO NHA TRANG, CRUISE ABOUT THE SPIRIT-LEVEL-FLAT MEKONG DELTA, OR TACKLE THIGH-TAXING CLIMBS INTO THE HIGHLANDS.

Vietnam seems custom-made to be seen by bike. Look at classic images of the country, and they feature bicycles. Little wonder it has become one of the world's burgeoning cycle-touring destinations.

It's a wishbone-thin country – around 1600km in length, but as narrow as 50km at times – so it's inevitable that most cycle journeys run north–south, or vice versa. For those who don't like hills, the popular alternative to a linear ride is to cycle through the Mekong Delta, southern Vietnam's rice bowl, where you'll see as much water as land – the delta seems to have more bridges than similar locations in the world.

Perhaps the most enticing cycling area is central Vietnam. Pedalling between the ancient royal capital of Hue and the contemporary beach resort of Nha Trang, riders can choose between various permutations of coast and mountains, detouring up into the highlands whenever they wish or simply following sand and sea.

Most riders will want to explore the coast around Danang, the ever-romantic Hoi An and My Son, heading up to the heights around Buon Ma Thuot and Dalat. Up here in the steaming highlands, thick forest breaks open into coffee plantations, for Vietnam is one of the world's largest coffee producers. If you're riding here sometime around November, you'll probably be sharing the road with drying coffee beans.

At first glance, Vietnam's traffic can seem confounding and confronting for a cyclist. It swirls in typically Asian confusion, but after a few hours of pedalling you'll discover that appearance doesn't always equal reality. There's order in the disorder, with bikes an accepted part of the road equation...as you'd expect of a nation so intrinsically linked to the bicycle.

ESSENTIAL EXPERIENCES

* **Spending a full-moon night in Hoi An, when the only street lighting is silk lanterns.**
* Roaring downhill on a descent from Dalat to Nha Trang.
* **Cycling past floating markets in the Mekong Delta.**
* Indulging in some R&R on the islands offshore from Nha Trang.
* **Marvelling at the bustle of Hanoi's lively Old Quarter.**

DISTANCE 660KM FROM HUE TO NHA TRANG | **LOCATION** VIETNAM | **IDEAL TIME COMMITMENT** TWO TO FOUR WEEKS | **BEST TIME OF YEAR** DECEMBER TO MARCH | **ESSENTIAL TIP** USE TRAINS TO AVOID CYCLING IN LARGE CITIES SUCH AS HO CHI MINH CITY AND HANOI

HO CHI MINH TRAIL

When you escape the urban jungle and enter the highlands of Vietnam you will at some time brush past the legendary Ho Chi Minh Trail. The major supply link for the North Vietnamese and VC during the Vietnam War, it connected the port of Vinh to Saigon, crossing in and out of Laos, and covering somewhere between 5500km and 13,000km. Each man started out from Vinh with a 36kg pack of supplies plus a few personal items (tent, snake antivenin etc). What lay ahead was a rugged and mountainous course, plagued by flooding, disease and the constant threat of American bombing – at their peak, more than 500 American air strikes hit the trail every day. Today, the Ho Chi Minh Highway is the easiest way to get a trail fix.

THE ADVENTURE UNFOLDS

At Hoi An the sun is falling into the Thu Bon River as you ride into town. The sky is dimming but streetlamps around the old town are beginning to glow. The streets will soon close to motor vehicles, as they do each night – in this country full of bikes, you sense this World Heritage–listed town may be the most bike-friendly of all.

Early the next morning you cross the Thu Bon on a ferry, a gaggle of bikes and motorbikes squeezed onto a boat the size of a cricket pitch. From here a road hugs the coast, the ocean tantalisingly close but always just out of sight. The dunes are covered in casuarinas, graves and, as ever, waving children. Fishermen mend nets or caulk their basket boats at the roadside.

At the little village of Thanh Binh, the road turns to dirt. At times it's sandy; at other times it's like slush, still muddied from the recent wet season. There are traffic jams caused by cows and ducks, and quick manoeuvres to swerve around children so keen to high-five you, they almost run under your wheels.

After riding for a couple of days in earshot but out of sight of the coast, you finally come to a beach at My Khe, a couple of kilometres from the wartime massacre site at My Lai. The fishing boats look as colourful as packets of sweets. A day from now you'll be grinding up into the humid highlands, the land stepping up with you in layered rice fields as you leave the coast behind. Villagers will be preparing the fields to be planted, their buffaloes lurching through the waters looking like buses for the cattle egret that crowd their backs.

For now, though, you stop, lie back on the sand, and enjoy a moment of seaside solitude.

MAKING IT HAPPEN

Vietnam's national air carrier, Vietnam Airlines, will carry boxed bikes; excess baggage is inexpensive. Bikes can be carried on trains, though they go as cargo, sometimes even on a separate train. A number of companies, including World Expeditions and Exodus, operate cycling tours through Vietnam.

AN ALTERNATIVE CHALLENGE

If you're spending your time in the north of Vietnam, it's worth building in some extra days for a couple of nonbike adventures. While most visitors take to supernatural Halong Bay in boats, the more adventurous are beginning to discover its stack-studded waters in kayaks. Inland, Vietnam's highest mountain, 3143m Fansipan, can be climbed from Sapa in three to four days. The terrain is rough, adverse weather is frequent and you'll need to be self-sufficient as there are no mountain huts or other facilities along the way.

89

OPENING SPREAD Rush hour Hanoi-style: cyclists are a common feature on the city's streets. **ABOVE (L)** Bringing in the rice harvest. **ABOVE (R)** Passing through O Quan Chuong gate in Hanoi. **LEFT** End your trip admiring the limestone islands of Halong Bay, a World Heritage Site in Vietnam's north.

ARMCHAIR

* **Catfish and Mandala** (Andrew X Pham) The author fled Vietnam as a child and returned as an adult – to travel by bicycle.

* **A Bright Shining Lie** (Neil Sheehan) Pulitzer Prize–winning book about the Vietnam War, seen through the experience of Lieutenant Colonel John Paul Vann.

* **The Sorrow of War** (Bao Ninh) One of the finest books about the Vietnam War by a Vietnamese writer.

* **A Dragon Apparent** (Norman Lewis) Classic and fascinating account of the author's journeys through Vietnam, Laos and Cambodia in 1950 – an eloquent insight into the last days of colonial rule.

* **Three Moons in Vietnam** (Maria Coffey) A writer travels the length of Vietnam's coast – the Mekong Delta to Halong Bay – by boat and bicycle.

MOUNTAIN BIKE COED Y BRENIN

FOR MOUNTAIN BIKERS, COED Y BRENIN IN WALES IS A PIONEERING SITE. THE FIRST FOREST IN THE UK TO BE DEVELOPED FOR SINGLE-TRACK MOUNTAIN BIKING, THIS THICKLY WOODED TERRAIN IS CRISS-CROSSED WITH EXPERTLY MAINTAINED TRAILS FOR RIDERS OF ALL ABILITIES.

90

With mountaintop views that make your heart skip, crashing waterfalls and a rugged topography carved out by glaciers, Coed y Brenin, 'the King's Forest', is a foliage-knitted landscape with a huge sense of space. Stalked by massive trees, the area is centred around the wide, epic valleys of the rivers Mawddach, Eden, Gain and Wen, which cut majestic channels through the woodlands and fall steeply over cubist-looking cliffs. The shy packs of fallow deer that you'll occasionally sight flitting through the forest are reminders of its time as a royal hunting ground. To the west lie the rugged Rhinog mountains; to the east, shadowy Rhobell Fawr; and to the south, the hulking profile of imposing Cader Idris ('Cadair's Seat' – Cadair being a legendary giant warrior-poet).

It was local rider Dafydd Davis who came up with the idea of building trails specifically for mountain bikers here in the early 1990s, along old paths and ancient drovers' roads. Dedicated one-way paths meant riders could test their abilities while not having to worry about disturbing walkers. Davis used local volunteers to create the trails out of materials they found in the forest, especially rock, which shaped the nature of the routes.

Today, this 3600-hectare, seemingly wild expanse is known to mountain bikers all over the world, cut through as it is with hundreds of kilometres of exhilarating single-track pathways. It's particularly good for experienced riders, but will appeal whether you're a novice or a professional. Its trails are rated for difficulty rather like ski runs, with green being the most gentle, red equalling intermediate, and black being the fiercest ride.

Prepare yourself to race along constantly surprising pathways, zigzag precipitously through the forest, and fight your way up over rocky slopes before thundering downhill in some thrilling descents.

ESSENTIAL EXPERIENCES

* **Glimpsing part of Cader Idris' 11km ridge through the trees.**

* Meandering along the beautiful valley of the River Mawddach.

* **Watching the world fall away as you drop into the Cavity, the largest technical challenge in the False Teeth section of the Beast of Brenin.**

* Having a postadventure drink at the George III Hotel, overlooking the Mawddach estuary at Penmaenpool, 12.5km away.

LOCATION COED Y BRENIN, SNOWDONIA, WALES | **IDEAL TIME COMMITMENT** TWO DAYS TO ONE WEEK | **BEST TIME OF YEAR** YEAR-ROUND | **ESSENTIAL TIP** WHEN MOUNTAIN BIKING, LOOK OUT FOR UPCOMING OBSTACLES, BUT DON'T FOCUS ON THEM – KEEP YOUR EYE ON THE EASIEST LINE

COED Y BRENIN HISTORY

Today the forest is part of the Snowdonia National Park, but it has ancient origins. It was first established as princely woodlands in 1100, and was acquired by the Forestry Commission in the early 20th century. Much of the forest's original timber was used during WWI, and the area was replanted with a mix of evergreen and deciduous trees: conifers, Douglas fir, larch, oak and birch trees. Today, some of the Douglas firs are almost 50m high. The woodlands gained their current name, the King's Forest, in 1935, in honour of King George V's silver jubilee.

■ THE ADVENTURE UNFOLDS

For experienced riders, the most notorious route is the most tempting: the menacingly named Beast of Brenin, an adrenalin-pumping, mentally taxing challenge that takes around 4 hours. It's the longest of the park's trails: 38.2km, with a 1015m climb.

Starting off on a broad track, you are dappled by sunlight filtering through leaves, before you head deeper into the forest. You whirr through the wood, full of anticipation, before passing the trail's first markers. The Beast immediately begins to test you, as you wind through the forest on a narrow, uneven path that bucks and dives between the trees.

Sections that test your technical skills include the stone-pitched Badger, taking you juddering over boulders and then speeding up over straightened tracks. Later comes Abel, a tight, narrow path where you're surrounded by trees, some so tall their tops are out of sight, and with a series of launch pads to keep you jumping. Beating your nerves, you feel your bike soar as you take off or swoop downhill.

Then you reach the most thrillingly difficult section: False Teeth, 800m of hardcore technical cycling. You whizz down a steep path that snakes through the woods. It hugs the slope, suddenly taking you over a series of moguls, then terrifyingly descends over boulders, directly downhill through the wood. But this is not the most difficult part.

Suddenly the trail drops unexpectedly into a deep hole. This is the Cavity. Approaching, too fast to think, you see an edge where the trail appears to stop, and there's then just a big hole, with seemingly no continuation of the path beyond it. You can't see where you might land, but before you know it, you are being spat out

ARMCHAIR

✳ **Mastering Mountain Bike Skills** (Brian Lopes) Great for brushing up on technique before launching off on a track.

✳ **Wales: Epic Views of a Small Country** (Jan Morris) A love letter to Wales and an insight into its history by the renowned Anglo-Welsh travel writer.

✳ **Mountain Biking Trail Centres: The Guide** (Tom Fenton) Good overview of the UK's best trail centres, including Coed y Brenin.

✳ **Zinn and the Art of Mountain Bike Maintenance** (Lennard Zinn) Teaches mountain bike know-how, so you can keep your ride running smoothly and do on-the-spot repairs.

✳ **The Best Mountain Bike Trails in Snowdonia** (Sue Savege, Dafydd Davis & Paul Barbier) Includes detailed descriptions of the Coed y Brenin trails.

THE MAWDDACH ESTUARY

Beyond Coed y Brenin, the River Mawddach is joined by the Afon Wnion downstream from Dolgellau, before opening out into the sea. The Mawddach estuary is mesmerisingly beautiful, wide open and edged by hills and sea. A long rail viaduct stalks across the water, its wrought-iron stilts calligraphic black. The surrounding area boomed during the 19th-century gold rush that took place here, but the industry had foundered by the 1920s. Traversing the area, the Mawddach Way is a 50km, three-day walking trail around the estuary, while the Mawddach Trail follows the old railway line and is suitable for cycling.

the other side of the hole, carried through by the breathtaking momentum of your speed, hopefully emerging with a modicum of style, and not minus your bike.

MAKING IT HAPPEN

You'll need a good-quality mountain bike, helmet and outdoor activity clothing, plus a pair of gloves will come in handy. Coed y Brenin's impressive, eco-friendly visitor centre has bikes and helmets for hire, as well as trail maps. Dolgellau Tourist Office will help you find places to stay nearby, including cottages, hostels, B&Bs and hotels. The centre is around 8km from Dolgellau.

AN ALTERNATIVE CHALLENGE

Coed y Brenin also contains Go Ape, a complex network of treetop crossings, designed to make you feel like a monkey swinging through the trees. There are impressive zip wires, wood-stepped ladders across seemingly vast expanses, and clever monkey-bar-style challenges. You're given safety guidance, and instructors are on hand, but otherwise you're free to zoom about the treetops as you please. It's a great high-level activity that offers a new perspective on Coed y Brenin, as well as some astounding views.

OPENING SPREAD Taming the Beast at Coed y Brenin. **ABOVE** Mountain bikers earn their descents by climbing through the Welsh woodland. Getting out of the saddle helps on steep sections. **BELOW** Barmouth and the Mawddach Estuary are to the southwest.

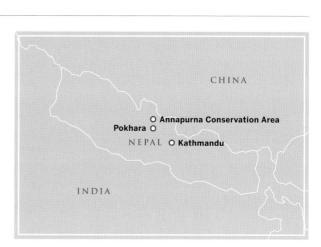

CYCLE THE ANNAPURNA CIRCUIT

THE FAMED ANNAPURNA CIRCUIT MIGHT BE DYING A DEATH AS ONE OF THE WORLD'S GREAT HIKING TRAILS, BUT IT'S EMERGING AS ONE OF THE GREAT ASPIRATIONAL MOUNTAIN BIKE TOURS. WOULD YOU DARE TO BRAVE A 5416M PASS ON TWO WHEELS?

94

The Annapurna Circuit is dead; long live the Annapurna Circuit...at least in the minds of mountain bikers. Opened to foreign trekkers in 1977, the Circuit was once the hiking pinnacle in Nepal – around two-thirds of the trekkers who visited the country in 2000 hiked in the Annapurna region. But the Circuit has lost much of its appeal in recent years, as roads have been forged through its valleys, bringing traffic and dust where once there was the sound of footsteps and prayer wheels.

The first half of the Circuit, on the Manang side to the east, is little affected by the construction of the road. On the western side, however, the Jomsom route through the Kali Gandaki valley (commonly said to be the deepest gorge in the world, with the river running around 6000m below the towering summit of Dhaulagiri) is now cut by a dirt road, busy with 4WD and motorbike traffic.

A series of new trails on the eastern side of the valley avoid the new road, but for many trekkers the Annapurna Circuit's shine has been well and truly dulled. In their place, rubbing together their gloved hands, have come mountain bikers, lured here by the chance to pedal one of the world's most famous trails, plus the rare opportunity to cycle to an altitude of 5416m across Thorung La.

The Circuit is a highly technical tour, far different from anything most people will have cycled. This is partly because some of the trail cannot be cycled at all; this is a tour on which you'll be pushing almost as much as pedalling – welcome to the sport of hike-a-bike. By some estimates, more than 20% of the Circuit is unrideable, including most of the ascent to Thorung La. Though for many, of course, the very term 'unrideable' is part of the challenge and besides, that 80% that you do try and ride, is absolutely epic.

ESSENTIAL EXPERIENCES

* **Challenging yourself to cycle across a high suspension bridge over the Marsyangdi River.**
* Sharing the thrill and the view of Thorung La with your bike.
* **Mingling with pilgrims and sadhus at Muktinath, with its temple holy to both Hindus and Buddhists.**
* Soaking away the cycling knots in your body in the concrete hot springs at Tatopani.
* **Paying homage to the mountains and mountaineers at Pokhara's International Mountain Museum.**

DISTANCE 300KM | **LOCATION** ANNAPURNA REGION, NEPAL | **IDEAL TIME COMMITMENT** TWO WEEKS | **BEST TIME OF YEAR** MARCH TO APRIL, OCTOBER TO NOVEMBER | **ESSENTIAL TIP** IT IS EASIEST AND SAFEST TO CROSS THORUNG LA FROM EAST TO WEST

ANNAPURNA I

In the annals of mountaineering, 8091m Annapurna I has a special place. The 10th-highest mountain in the world, it's also considered among the most difficult of the world's 8000m peaks, with one of the highest death rates – around four out of every 10 climbers on the mountain has been killed. And yet it was the first 8000m mountain to be climbed, three years before the conquest of Everest. On 3 June 1950, Frenchmen Maurice Herzog and Louis Lachenal summited Annapurna, though severe frostbite resulted in both men losing their toes. Herzog also lost most of his fingers. It would be another 20 years before Annapurna was successfully climbed again.

ACUTE MOUNTAIN SICKNESS

Acute mountain sickness (AMS) is a concern for anyone at high altitude. Due to their ability to go further and higher in a day than trekkers, mountain bikers should take particular care to avoid AMS. It is caused by the failure to acclimatise to the low levels of oxygen at high altitude, and symptoms include headache, nausea, sleeplessness, dizziness and loss of appetite. It's recommended that above 3000m, you don't increase your sleeping altitude by more than 300m per day. You should also have frequent rest days, spending two or three nights at each rise of 1000m. In Manang, the Himalayan Rescue Association gives a free daily lecture on AMS.

THE ADVENTURE UNFOLDS

It's still dark as you set out from Thorung Phedi, at the foot of the final climb to Thorung La. You're out early, hoping to beat the pass's notorious winds, which inevitably whip up as the day progresses.

You'd hoped to be riding part of the way but almost immediately the trail steepens, switchbacking up moraines and across rocky ridges. You resign yourself to pushing. It's going to be a tough morning, for you must ascend more than 1000m like this, reversing roles with your bike as you climb through the desertlike landscape, which is drained of both colour and oxygen.

Almost three hours have passed before you rise to a teashop, where you break, mustering energy for the final 200m of climbing. It's a tease of a pass – false summit after false summit – and briefly you wonder if you wouldn't rather be hauling a backpack than a bike. But you know that by the time you're freewheeling down the Kali Gandaki valley in a day or two, with the road in view, this bike is going to seem like old faithful itself.

When you do reach the pass, your front wheels making it seconds before you, the world opens up. From among the prayer flags, the scene takes in the Great Barrier ridge, the Annapurnas, rocky Thorungtse and the barren Kali Gandaki valley far below.

The oxygen is so thin you can hardly breathe, but you barely need to any more, for most of your work is done. You test your brakes a couple of times, vigilant about the steep 1600m descent from the pass – soon you will be coasting from these holy heights to the holy sights of Muktinath. Still, you descend cautiously. You wouldn't want to topple over the edge of one of these moraines.

MAKING IT HAPPEN

A growing number of tour companies are offering Annapurna Circuit mountain bike trips. If you're riding independently, you'll want to bring your own bike. The Circuit begins at Besi Sahar, which can be reached by bus from Kathmandu (about six hours) or Pokhara (five hours). From the Circuit's end at Naya Pul, it's a two-hour bus ride into Pokhara, or you can pedal back on minor roads.

DETOUR

By the time you reach the town of Manang, approaching the climb to Thorung La, you'll almost certainly be in need of some time off the bike to assist your altitude acclimatisation. From here, it makes a good walking side trip to head up to Tilicho Tal, a turquoise lake pooled at the base of the glacier system of the dramatic Great Barrier ridge. Most often, the lake is frozen but, if not, it can offer great reflections of the peaks around it.

OPENING SPREAD Spiritual sight: prayer flags flutter in the breeze on Annapurna's mountains. **ABOVE (L)** Be prepared to push on some sections of the Annapurna Circuit. **ABOVE (R)** Cyclists get a friendly welcome from locals. **LEFT** Off-road riding at Muktinath on the Annapurna Circuit.

ARMCHAIR

* *Biking Around Annapurna* (Nepa Maps) Contoured map that's a great resource for mountain bikers, showing gradients, likely spots you'll be pushing and 1:75,000 detail.

* *Annapurna* (Maurice Herzog) Since you're biking around it, read up on its first ascent in this classic book.

* *Annapurna: A Trekker's Guide* (Kev Reynolds) A walker's guide to the Circuit that will still be of use to bikers.

* *The Snow Leopard* (Peter Matthiessen) Get inspired about Nepal's landscape with this gorgeous account of walking through western Nepal in the 1970s.

* *Forget Kathmandu: An Elegy for Democracy* (Manjushree Thapa) Using the massacre of the royal family in 2001 as a foundation stone, a Nepali author journeys through a shambolic national political history.

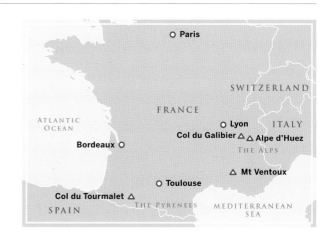

RIDE THE TOUR DE FRANCE HIGH PASSES

RIDE IN THE SLIPSTREAM OF TOUR DE FRANCE LEGENDS AS YOU TACKLE THE HIGH ALPINE AND PYRENEAN MOUNTAIN PASSES THAT HAVE TESTED, TORTURED AND DEFINED THE ABSOLUTE GREATS OF THE LYCRA-CLAD CYCLING WORLD FOR MORE THAN A CENTURY.

Few sporting events inspire emulation quite like the Tour de France. Each year, thousands of amateur cyclists pedal around France, retracing stages of the world's most famous cycling race. Some follow the entire course, all 3000km of it, but for most the ultimate challenge is to ride the classic high passes in the Alps and Pyrenees, taking on the climbs that bust open Tours.

When the Tour de France began in 1903 there were no mountain stages, just a couple of low cols on the stage between Paris and Lyon. Two years later the race was given its first official mountain climb, over 1171m Ballon d'Alsace in the Vosges, but it was the inclusion of the Col du Tourmalet in the Pyrenees in 1910 that truly saw the big race embrace the big mountains.

Tourmalet remains one of the classic Tour ascents, drawing hordes of cycling pilgrims, as does Col du Galibier, the first Alpine climb introduced into the race (in 1911). Prime among the other famed climbs are the Alpe d'Huez (first raced in 1952) and Mont Ventoux (1951), rising mighty above the Rhône valley. All four passes have been ranked *hors categorie*, meaning they're so steep as to be beyond classification – something like grade V rapids on wheels.

Alpe d'Huez (1860m) is a 13.8km climb, snaking around 21 numbered hairpin bends, with an average gradient of 8.1%. The most testing and famous approach to Mont Ventoux (1912m), named after the mountain's notorious winds, is from Bédoin, climbing more than 1600m over almost 22km at an average gradient of 7.4%. To Col du Tourmalet (2115m), the 17km, 1260m ascent from Ste-Marie de Campan has an average gradient of 8%; while the most impressive approach to Col du Galibier (2645m), which in 2011 became the site of the highest-ever stage finish in the Tour, is from Valloire to the north (18km climb, 7% gradient).

ESSENTIAL EXPERIENCES

* **Going big and picking off two passes – Col du Tourmalet and Col d'Aspin – in one day.**

* Counting off the 21 bends as you coil up the slopes of Alpe d'Huez.

* **Racing to clock your fastest speed on one of the pass descents.**

* Taking inspiration from the messages of encouragement and famous cycling names painted on the roads.

* **Paying homage at the 12th-century chapel of Notre Dame des Cyclistes, hung with jerseys belonging to famous cyclists and a bike used in the 1903 Tour, near the Pyrenees.**

ELEVATION 1860M TO 2645M | **LOCATION** FRENCH ALPS AND PYRENEES, FRANCE | **IDEAL TIME COMMITMENT** ONE DAY TO TWO WEEKS | **BEST TIME OF YEAR** JULY TO SEPTEMBER | **ESSENTIAL TIP** CARRY A WARM JACKET (OR, AS IN DAYS OF OLD, SOME NEWSPAPER) FOR THE DESCENTS – COLD WIND AND SWEAT AT SPEED CAN PRODUCE REAL CHILL

98

DRAMAS IN THE MOUNTAINS

It's on the high passes of the Alps and Pyrenees that Tour de France races are won or lost, that reputations are shattered or turned into legend. Here, swarms of people crowd the riders, shouting and gesticulating. These stages provide the race's greatest scenes, and its greatest dramas. In 1967, British rider Tommy Simpson died from heat exhaustion on the Mont Ventoux climb. In 1911, on the Col du Galibier, race leader André Leducq crashed at more than 90km/h. Remounting, he crashed again, snapping a pedal and bringing down another rider, Marcel Bidot. Bidot borrowed a spanner and pedal from a spectator and selflessly repaired Leducq's bike. Leducq went on to win the stage and the overall race.

FASTEST OF THE SLOW

It's a demoralising act but, inevitably, anyone who cycles up one of the high passes wants to know how their effort compares to that of the King of the Mountain types. If you wake up at the base of one of the passes with legs that itch to go fast, here are the times to beat:

Alpe d'Huez 37 minutes, 35 seconds (Marco Pantani)

Mont Ventoux 55 minutes, 51 seconds (Iban Mayo)

Col du Tourmalet 38 minutes, 43 seconds (Jan Ullrich)

Col du Galibier 48 minutes, 20 seconds (Marco Pantani)

■ THE ADVENTURE UNFOLDS

There are four road passes in the Pyrenees that are higher than Col du Tourmalet, but none of them have the cycling aura of the Tour de France's first big mountain climb. History has brought you to the base of the climb; now it's up to your legs and the bike to get you to the top.

Nerves are high as you clip into your pedals in Ste-Marie de Campan. This is the Col du Tourmalet – the so-called Terrible Mountain – after all: Merckx, Virenque and Andy Schleck have all led the race over this pass. It's time to saddle up and get moving.

The gradient starts gently, with the road rising as gradually as your confidence, though from the valley the peaks around you look frighteningly high. Road signs tick off your progress – 10km to go, this one tells you, though less encouragingly it also notes the gradient, which is now steepening to 8%.

Soon there are no trees. You've entered the Alpine zone. Bikes hurtle past you as other cyclists return from the summit, but on you climb, following the road as it coils through the green grassy slopes. The big names of cycling pass beneath your wheels, inscribed onto the road in flaking white paint.

It's been two hours since you left Ste-Marie de Campan, but suddenly there are buildings ahead. Bikes lean against stone walls, their riders indulging in liquid celebration or restocking on sugar. Above the road there's a larger-than-life statue of a mounted cyclist, his face contorted with effort. You know how he feels, though you're now smiling as you pass the sign that announces the top of the Col du Tourmalet. Allez!

■ MAKING IT HAPPEN

The big-name climbs are sprinkled through the French Alps and Pyrenees. A number of cycling tours focus on Tour de France high passes, and are often run in conjunction with the race. Some are run by past Tour cyclists, such as Australia's Phil Anderson. Grenoble or nearby Le Bourg d'Oisans make good bases for the Alpine climbs. Ryanair and easyJet fly to Grenoble from the UK.

■ AN ALTERNATIVE CHALLENGE

Inevitably, a single ride to the top of a pass, even one as difficult as Mont Ventoux, isn't enough for some cyclists. For those people, there's the Ventoux Masters, an event held each May in which cyclists ascend the mountain as many times as they can in 24 hours – the record stands at 11. In similar fashion, there's also Les Cinglés du Mont Ventoux (the Madmen of Mont Ventoux), an open challenge in which riders must pedal to the summit of Mont Ventoux from its three approaches (the towns of Malaucène, Bédoin and Sault) in a single day, gaining admission to the so-called Madmen Club.

OPENING SPREAD Climbing the Col du Galibier. **ABOVE (L)** The Tour's most diabolical fan, who is actually German. **ABOVE (R)** The bleak summit of Mont Ventoux, which means 'windy' in French, tests every rider. **LEFT** The countdown: Alpe d'Huez's 21 hairpin bends attract thousands of fans.

ARMCHAIR

* ***Ascent: The Mountains of the Tour de France*** (Richard Yates) Historical look at the mountain stages of the Tour.

* ***Tour Climbs: The Complete Guide to Every Mountain Stage on the Tour de France*** (Chris Sidwells) Detailed guide to every major climb featured in the Tour de France.

* ***Le Tour: A History of the Tour de France*** (Geoffrey Wheatcroft) More than a century of race history.

* ***Hell on Wheels*** (2005) Documentary video account of Team Telekom's 2003 Tour de France.

* ***The Yellow Jersey Companion to the Tour de France*** (ed. Les Woodland) Entertaining encyclopedia of the world's greatest race.

* ***The Tour is Won on the Alpe: Alpe d'Huez and the Classic Battles of the Tour de France*** (Jean-Paul Vespini) The Alpe d'Huez's role in the Tour de France, recounting every race climb since 1952.

MOUNTAIN BIKE THE GREAT DIVIDE

MOUNTAIN BIKE THE WORLD'S LONGEST OFF-ROAD CYCLING ROUTE, PEDALLING FROM BANFF IN CANADA TO ANTELOPE WELLS ON THE UNITED STATES-MEXICO BORDER, CROSSING THE CONTINENTAL DIVIDE 30 TIMES ON THE WAY. THIS IS A TRUE CYCLING EPIC TO DIGEST IN BITE-SIZE PIECES.

Hikers have long had options to walk the length of the United States, following the Pacific Crest, Continental Divide or Appalachian trails. Now mountain bikers have their own dedicated trail: the Great Divide Mountain Bike Route (GDMBR to its friends).

Conceived as an idea by the Adventure Cycling Association in the early 1990s, it became a reality in 1998, running from Antelope Wells to Roosville on the Canadian border; it was extended to Banff in 2003. Though the route is long and committing, it's not overly technical. Following mostly unsealed roads and trails, it's a touring-style trail rather than a single-track attack.

The trail statistics alone border on exhausting. Covering around 4400km, the GDMBR travels through two Canadian provinces and five US states. Crossing the Divide 30 times – the highest point is Indiana Pass in Colorado, at 3630m – its climbs total more than 60,000m, or the equivalent of cycling to the summit of Mt Everest from sea level almost seven times.

For most riders, the route begins in Canada at the Banff Springs Hotel, pedalling south towards the USA through a chain of national and provincial parks. By Great Divide standards, it's a low-elevation ride, rising only to 1960m at Elk Pass.

After the curiosity of a border crossing at Roosville, the route enters Montana and the most technically tricky sections of the ride. Through the mountains of Idaho, Wyoming and Colorado, the GDMBR ends across rough, corrugated tracks in New Mexico, hitting the Mexican border in the barren Chihuahuan Desert...an awfully long way, both in distance and terrain, from Banff.

If you want to do it the fast way, the entire route was once cycled in just under 23 days – an average of about 190km a day – though it's probably more realistic to aim for about 60km or 70km a day.

ESSENTIAL EXPERIENCES

* **Detouring to Fernie, for a day or two on some of Canada's finest mountain bike trails.**

* Handing over your passport at the border at Roosville.

* **Watching for bears as you ride through tough mountain country near Glacier National Park, with one of the highest concentrations of grizzlies in North America.**

* Rolling through autumnal aspen country in Colorado.

* **Coasting to a stop beside the lonely border-control building outside Antelope Wells at ride's end.**

DISTANCE 4400KM | **LOCATION** USA AND CANADA | **IDEAL TIME COMMITMENT** THREE MONTHS | **BEST TIME OF YEAR** JULY TO SEPTEMBER | **ESSENTIAL TIP** MOST RIDERS PEDAL NORTH-SOUTH TO BEST ALIGN WITH THE SEASONS

ROCKY MOUNTAINS

Even if you're riding alone, you'll have one fairly constant companion as you cycle the Great Divide Mountain Bike Route, and that's the Rocky Mountains. Stretching for around 5000km from the Cassiar Mountains near Canada's border with Alaska, to the Sangre de Cristo Mountains of northern New Mexico, the Rockies have rightly been called the 'backbone of North America'. The Continental Divide – the ridge line that sheds water either east to the Atlantic Ocean or west to the Pacific Ocean – meanders erratically through the Rockies, often far from the highest summits and ranges... to the inevitable relief of GDMBR mountain bikers.

DON'T JUST RIDE IT, RACE IT

The creation of the Great Divide Mountain Bike Route has, in turn, spawned a pair of mountain bike races along the route. In the Tour Divide, self-supported cyclists leave Banff in the second week of June and must follow the exact course of the GDMBR until they arrive in Antelope Wells, usually about four weeks after they began. The Great Divide Race also begins in June, but leaves from Roosville, cycling only the US section of the GDMBR. Rules in both are straightforward – follow the GDMBR to its end, with no prearranged outside assistance allowed.

THE ADVENTURE UNFOLDS

Packing your panniers at the Warm River Campground, you're excited at the thought of riding into another state today. The tough, forested climbs of Montana are behind you, and soon Idaho will be also. Two states down, three to go. Wyoming sits somewhere towards that mountain horizon ahead.

Crossing the border you enter natural royalty of sorts, with the road pinched beautifully between Yellowstone National Park to the north and Grand Teton National Park to the south, the latter's peaks rising with stunning abruptness. You're back in bear country, but it's the mosquitoes that force you to quicken your pace even as the ascent tries to slow you down.

The next few days will be ones of incredible contrast. Through the Wind River Range, you rise into a stunning alpine area, but there's desert not far ahead. Atlantic City has none of the bells and whistles its name suggests – this Atlantic City is a tumbleweed kind of place, making it an appropriate gateway into the Great Basin, North America's largest desert. Soon, the earth is just that: bare earth. You climb through heat, the land scuffed brown, with the Divide rising away in the distance. Wild horses roam far from the trail. Was it just a few days ago you were surrounded by water and mountains around Jackson Lake?

Still, the desert has its own beauty, and for a short time the trail even gives you the chance to ride along the Divide, rather than zigzagging across it, which has been the pattern much of the way. Into Rawlins, and another state is almost done. The Colorado Rockies, the highest points of your journey, loom to the south. But first you have one more tough climb out of Rawlins and this desert.

MAKING IT HAPPEN

Riders on the GDMBR must be totally self-supported and self-sufficient. You will need to camp much of the way, and distances between food and water sources can be lengthy and tough. Come well researched. Most towns along the route are small, so also come well provisioned with spare parts.

AN ALTERNATIVE CHALLENGE

Just as the GDMBR parallels the Continental Divide walking trail, so too does the newer Sierra Cascades Bicycle Route now follow the hikers' Pacific Crest Trail. Also created by the Adventure Cycling Association, this route begins in Sumas (Washington), on the Canadian border, and ends 3850km later in Tecate (California), on the Mexican border, following the Cascade Range and Sierra Nevada. Along the way, it passes through the likes of Mt Rainier, Crater Lake, Yosemite and Kings Canyon National Park, while crossing 20 mountain passes and bisecting the Pacific Crest Trail around 25 times.

OPENING SPREAD Some of the world's best biking is in Fernie, British Columbia. **ABOVE (L)** Explore the trails around Steamboat Springs, Colorado, a mecca for mountain bikers. **ABOVE (R)** Riders in Banff National Park, Alberta. **LEFT** Skip summer's heat: ride in the falling leaves of Colorado's aspens.

ARMCHAIR

* *Cycling the Great Divide: From Canada to Mexico on America's Premier Long Distance Mountain Bike Route* (Michael McCoy) Guidebook to cycling the trail from one of its creators.

* *National Audubon Society Field Guide to the Rocky Mountain States* (Peter Alden & John Grassy) All-in-one natural history guide to the Divide, covering geology, flora, fauna and even all-important weather patterns.

* *Journal of a Trapper* (Osborne Russell) For those days when it all seems too tough; a classic account of a young fur trapper's adventures in the Rockies and Grand Tetons in the mid-19th century.

* *Ride the Divide* (2010) Award-winning feature film by mountain biker Mike Dion following riders in the annual race along the length of the Great Divide Mountain Bike Route.

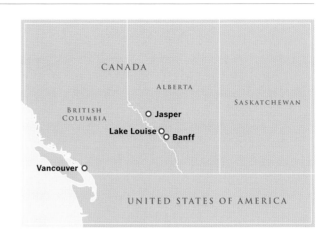

CYCLE CANADA'S ICEFIELDS PARKWAY

CYCLE PAST PIN-SHARP PEAKS AND THE LARGEST ICEFIELD IN NORTH AMERICA, FOLLOWING A ROAD WHERE WILDLIFE ROAMS WITH PEDESTRIAN-LIKE ABANDON, AND THE MOUNTAIN SCENERY BUILDS FROM EXCELLENT TO EXCEPTIONAL. IT'S WORTH ALL THE EFFORT OF THE TWO BIG ASCENTS.

When people describe the Icefields Parkway as the 'most beautiful road in the world', they mean it's the finest drive. What they don't say is that it's even better by bike. The Parkway stretches for 232km, from the watery jewel of the Rocky Mountains, Lake Louise, to Jasper, past some of the finest mountains in North America. On a bike, it's experienced with no degrees of separation: the scent of the meadows surrounds you, chill icefield winds keep you cool, deer graze oblivious to your presence and the chance of meeting bears is always there.

In summer, expect plenty of motor vehicles on the Parkway, though it has wide shoulders for much of its length, distancing you from the traffic. Some days you may even encounter almost as many bikes as cars, for the Parkway has become one of the most desirable cycle-touring destinations in the world. Even novice tourers can enjoy the ride, with camp sites and accommodation spread along its length, and two 500m climbs providing the only real tests of strength.

Most riders begin in Banff, 65km south of Lake Louise, along the Bow Valley Parkway. Following the banks of the Bow River, the road is said to be the best wildlife-viewing route in Canada, giving you the chance to spot elk, bighorn sheep, bald eagles and maybe that bear, before even getting on the Parkway.

Once on the Parkway, the first of the two 500m ascents begins immediately. This first climb, to Bow Summit, rises gradually, following a chain of lakes – Herbert, Hector and Bow Lakes – for 40km to the pass. The steepest moment will come if you decide to pedal up from the pass to the Peyto Lake Viewpoint.

By the head of the North Saskatchewan River, 60km on, the second climb to Sunwapta Pass is more challenging, making the same ascent in half the distance. From here it's reward time, descending (mostly) over almost 100km to Jasper, past the Athabasca Glacier – the only spot where the Columbia Icefield ventures near the road – and the white noise of Athabasca Falls.

ESSENTIAL EXPERIENCES

* **Sneaking a dawn view of Lake Louise before the daily crowds arrive.**

* Wandering to the Peyto Lake Viewpoint for an elevated look across one of the world's most beautiful mountain lakes.

* **Stepping quietly around the Waterfowl Lakes for the rare chance to spot moose.**

* Taking a special bus or a guided hike onto the ice of Athabasca Glacier.

* **Listening to the roar of thundering Athabasca Falls, pouring over a 23m drop.**

* Rising onto Sunwapta Pass with the knowledge that the way ahead to Jasper is now mostly downhill.

DISTANCE 232KM | **LOCATION** ALBERTA, CANADA | **IDEAL TIME COMMITMENT** FIVE DAYS | **BEST TIME OF YEAR** JULY TO SEPTEMBER | **ESSENTIAL TIP** CYCLE IN THE EARLY MORNING OR LATE AFTERNOON FOR THE BEST CHANCE OF SPOTTING WILDLIFE

THE COLUMBIA ICEFIELD

Tourism operators here will tell you that the Columbia Icefield – the main block of ice that gives the parkway its name – is the largest mass of ice south of the Arctic Circle. This tends to overlook a little place called Antarctica, but it's nonetheless an impressive chunk of frozen water. Icing the mountains to the west of the road, it's North America's largest icefield, covering an area of 325 sq km. Its meltwater drains away to three oceans – Pacific, Atlantic and Arctic – while 11 of the Canadian Rockies' 22 highest peaks rise around the icefield.

■ THE ADVENTURE UNFOLDS

The veritable souvenir city at The Crossing is finally behind you and you're back on the road, free again, legs turning, oblivious even to cars. There's been word of bears about, but the flowered meadows are clear and the berry bushes at the roadside have been stripped of their fruit, suggesting the animals have been and gone.

You are steadily pedalling upvalley but any climb is imperceptible as, slowly, the valley narrows, its bare rock walls closing in around you. A waterfall seeps over a cliff edge but is carried away on the wind long before it hits the valley floor.

You tell yourself that the scar ahead – the one climbing steeply across the hillside – isn't really the road, but deep down you know it is. And soon enough you're there, ascending through Big Bend, standing up on the pedals, the climb mounting towards Sunwapta Pass. Motorists stare at you in wonder and disbelief. You know exactly what they're thinking, but they're wrong. This is the proper way to see these mountains, really it is. Your brain is convinced, but your legs need to be coaxed through a bit more.

Sunwapta Pass greets you with a rude icy blast. The Columbia Icefield is straight ahead, muscling its way off the mountain tops briefly as the Athabasca Glacier, chilling the wind as it blows down from the north.

You experience that usual thought on top of the pass: 'it's surely all downhill from here...' But soon enough you discover that your front wheel is pointing at the sky once again as the road turns up onto Tangle Ridge. It's a short climb, this particular one, but who was that idiot who claimed short was sweet?

ARMCHAIR

* **On the Roof of the Rockies** (Lewis Freeman) Classic account of a 70-day trip in the 1920s exploring the region around the yet-to-be-built parkway.

* **50 Roadside Panoramas in the Canadian Rockies** (Dave Birrell) A panoramic vision of some classic views, with detailed notes and histories. Icefields Parkway scenes include Sunwapta Pass, Bow Lake and the Alexandra River Flats.

* **Bow Lake: Wellspring of Art** (Jane Lytton Gooch) A celebration of Bow Lake's artistic traditions, from the explorer Jimmy Simpson through to the modern artists in residence.

* **Jimmy Simpson** (EJ Hart) Biography of the Rockies legend, whose lodge became the modern-day Num-Ti-Jah Lodge on Bow Lake.

* **Flightless: Incredible Journeys Without Leaving the Ground** (Lonely Planet) Features an account of cycling the Icefields Parkway.

At the top of the ridge, a trio of bighorn sheep saunter across the road. Traffic backs up and cameras are pointed. It's as though a Hollywood star has arrived in town. You weave through the cars and the people, but at least they're not looking at you any more.

■ MAKING IT HAPPEN

Determined cyclists can cover the Parkway in as short a period as two or three days, but really this is scenery to linger over, so try to spread it across about five days. Bike hire is available at the Ski Stop in Banff, with the option to send the bike back by bus from Jasper.

■ AN ALTERNATIVE CHALLENGE

For a simple ride near Banff, cycle the 18km Goat Creek Trail from Canmore, cutting in behind Rundle Mountain and finishing at the Banff Springs Hotel. It's best ridden from Canmore to take advantage of the 300m descent. Banff National Park also has around 200km of mountain bike trails; for an edgier Canmore–Banff experience, ride the Rundle Riverside track, mixing single track and vehicle track over a rugged and rocky route.

OPENING SPREAD Would you like ice with that? The Columbia Icefield in Alberta. ABOVE Riding from Banff to Jasper on the Icefields Parkway takes you past magnificent Rocky Mountains scenery. BELOW Journey's end: Jasper National Park in Alberta.

COACH STOP

If you want someone else to do the steering for a couple of hours, park up at Athabasca Glacier and board one of the purpose-built Ice Explorer coaches that drive onto the glacier. Each day, graders smooth out a road across the ice, pasting over any potential crevasses. Coaches then follow this road up into the heart of the glacier, providing the sort of roadside scenery – the icy blue expanse of the glacier and the dark rock walls of the adjacent peaks – that even a bike can't supply. Now remind yourself that this glacier represents only 2% of the Columbia Icefield.

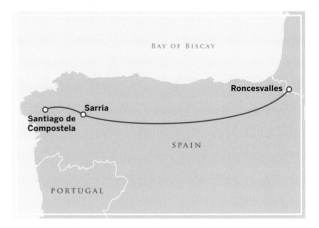

PEDAL THE CAMINO DE SANTIAGO

FOR CENTURIES, PILGRIMS HAVE BEEN FOOT-SLOGGING THEIR WAY ACROSS NORTHERN SPAIN TO SANTIAGO DE COMPOSTELA, TO PAY HOMAGE TO THE REMAINS OF THE APOSTLE JAMES. TODAY, A NEW BREED COMES ON WHEELS AND 27 GEARS.

One of Christ's disciples, James was executed by Herod in the year 44, possibly the first of the apostles to be martyred. Then, 800 years later, his tomb was discovered in Galicia, and the faithful started visiting. First a trickle, then a flood of pilgrims began to journey to Santiago de Compostela as it became the most important pilgrimage destination for Christians after Rome and Jerusalem.

The 11th and 12th centuries marked the Camino's heyday. The Reformation was devastating for Catholic pilgrimages, and by the 19th century the tradition had nearly died out. A startling late-20th-century reanimation saw the Camino reborn, and thousands of people now travel its trails every day. Most come on foot, but a growing number are riding bikes – Camino regulations permit pilgrims to walk, cycle or ride on horseback.

There are many Camino de Santiago routes that converge on Santiago de Compostela, from the Camino Primitivo out of Oviedo in northern Spain to the Camino Portugués from Porto in Portugal. Most popular by far is the Camino Francés from the Pyrenees, and it's this route that's been adopted by cyclists. For most of the ride, cyclists follow the walkers' trail, with a few on-road diversions through the steepest and most difficult ground.

Beginning in the border town of Roncesvalles, the ride descends the Pyrenees into the city of Pamplona before crossing the wine region of La Rioja, where fountains dispense wine for pilgrims. Crossing the high *meseta* (plateau) between Burgos and León is the Camino's version of penance – a long, bland haul that has many walkers jumping on buses. Here, you'll be very glad you came by bike.

Across the epic O Cebreiro climb, the Camino finally enters Galicia, a world apart from the dry meseta. Rainswept and green, this region provides a hilly final 150km into the mazelike old town of Santiago, where one final scallop shell – the symbol of St James – marks the pilgrimage's end outside the city's cathedral.

ESSENTIAL EXPERIENCES

✳ **Setting your wheels down, ready to ride, on the French border at Puerto de Ibañeta, the same Pyrenean pass Napoleon used to launch his 1802 occupation of Spain.**

✳ Drinking wine from a water fountain through La Rioja.

✳ **Carrying a stone to place at Cruz de Ferro, the cross atop the Montes de León.**

✳ Getting your Credencial del Peregrino stamped each day as you cycle west.

✳ **Threading through weary walkers as you arrive in Praza do Obradoiro, beside Santiago's cathedral.**

DISTANCE 783KM | **LOCATION** NORTHERN SPAIN | **IDEAL TIME COMMITMENT** TWO WEEKS | **BEST TIME OF YEAR** MAY TO JUNE, SEPTEMBER TO OCTOBER | **ESSENTIAL TIP** CARRY A BELL TO ENSURE GOOD RELATIONS WITH WALKING PILGRIMS

PILGRIM HOSTELS

Following the same spirit of charity as the medieval monasteries that gave hospitality to pilgrims, the *refugio* (refuge) system developed during the Camino's renaissance in the early 1990s. After making the pilgrimage herself, Catalan woman Lourdes Lluch decided that the Camino needed more facilities for pilgrims. During the summer of 1990, she rented a run-down house in Hornillos del Camino – one of the bleakest parts of the Camino – and set up a makeshift shelter and pulled pilgrims in off the street, offering them food, drink and a clean place to rest their weary bodies. The idea took off and there are now around 300 *refugios* along the Camino.

You're never far from the sea – and its harvest – on this adventure. As you ride through Galicia, nearing journey's end, it's worth joining the pilgrim crowds and indulging at a typical Galician *pulpería* – octopus restaurant. The octopus is boiled to perfection, then sprinkled with paprika. Chased down with fried pimientos (chillies) and a beer or two, it's a delight that may have you parking up at the next bit of shade for a siesta. The town of Melide, between Portomarin and Arzúa, is pulpería central. Modern Camino pilgrimages aren't all about deprivation.

THE ADVENTURE UNFOLDS

You've lingered in the village of Herrerias for a little too long, delaying the climb to O Cebreiro, fortifying yourself with coffee and carbs. Over the next 10km the road will ascend 800m, and pilgrims on the trail have been talking about this climb for days. It's time to just do it.

The slopes are covered in chestnut trees, their fruit bristling like sea mines, and though it seems to take forever, finally there's the rattle of cobblestones beneath your wheels – you've arrived at the thatched-roof village of O Cebreiro, its shops full of pilgrim gourds and scallop shells. You thought it was the top, but there are more climbs as the trail continues rolling across the crest of the ridge.

Just past O Cebreiro you pass a statue honouring pilgrims. The metal figure is holding onto his hat, a reminder that some days the wind atop this range can be much worse than today. Kindly, someone has placed a plaster across the statue's heel, as if nursing a blister. You've entered Galicia, and from here a countdown of kilometre markers begins. There's just 150km to ride to Santiago.

The 800m ascent was tough, but below Alto de Poio there's the final sting in this day's tail as the dirt track suddenly ramps up into impossibledom. You hop off and push your bike but, don't worry, you're not alone. Every cyclist behind you will be doing the same.

It's here that the descent begins, and it's glorious: a swooping, whooping run down dusty dirt tracks. Walking pilgrims are blurs as you rush by, brewing your own private dust storm. You arrive in the valley dust-coated, but you have entered the green embrace of Galicia – Santiago is just a couple of days away.

MAKING IT HAPPEN

To cover the traditional route, begin in Roncesvalles in the Pyrenees. León and Ponferrada make good alternative starting points if you're shorter on time. Roncesvalles can be accessed by bus from Pamplona. A mountain bike is almost essential, with much of the Camino route running along dirt tracks. A number of companies, including UTRACKS, offer tours or pack-carrying services along the route.

AN ALTERNATIVE CHALLENGE

They're a generous mob at the Camino de Santiago's pilgrim office. To be officially certified as pilgrims, cyclists need ride only 200km of the Camino Francés, making it possible to begin the journey in the Castilla y León town of Ponferrada, 60km from Astorga, riding into Santiago in just three or four days. By starting here, you skip the tough climb over the Montes de León but there's no escaping O Cebreiro, the pilgrimage's most notorious climb, an 800m ascent to one of Spain's prettiest hilltop villages.

OPENING SPREAD Resting place: the Catedral de Santiago de Compostela dates from 1075 and is reputed to be where St James is buried.
ABOVE (L) Ready for the ride. **ABOVE (R)** On the road: two-wheeled pilgrims crossing Leon. **LEFT** Preparing Galician octopus for the *pulperías*.

ARMCHAIR

* **The Cycling Pilgrim on the Camino Francés** (The Confraternity of Saint James) Snippety guide to cycling the Camino.

* **The Way of St James: A Cyclists' Guide** (John Higginson) Cycling guidebook covering an extended route from Le Puy in France.

* **The Pilgrimage** (Paulo Coelho) A mystical journey is described in this international bestseller, recounting Coelho's life-changing Camino walk in 1986, which led to a spiritual awakening.

* **Pilgrim Stories: On and Off to the Road to Santiago** (Nancy Frey) An anthropologist explores the pilgrimage's modern resurgence.

* **The Way** (2010) Martin Sheen plays a father who sets out to complete the pilgrimage for his son, who died on the Camino.

113

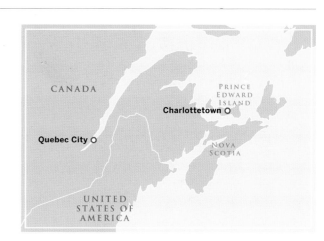

CYCLE PRINCE EDWARD ISLAND

PEDAL ACROSS CANADA'S SMALLEST PROVINCE, FOLLOWING ONE OF THE WORLD'S ORIGINAL RAIL TRAILS OR BRANCHING OFF TO EXPLORE THE GLEAMING COASTLINES AND THE SURPRISINGLY COSMOPOLITAN SMALL CAPITAL OF CHARLOTTETOWN.

114

Tiny Prince Edward Island, known almost universally as simply PEI, has the honour of being the only North American region to ban motor vehicles. It's therefore unsurprising that it's grown into one of the finest cycling destinations on the continent.

The backbone of PEI's cycling network is the Confederation Trail, a 279km route that bisects the island. The trail was conceived as an idea after the closure of PEI's railway in 1989, and was developed as a cycling rail trail throughout the 1990s. The hard-rolled dirt path was finally completed in 2000 and now stretches from Elmira to Tignish, the island's most eastern and western tips.

The trail cuts through PEI's rural heartland, only flirting with the coast between Morell and St Peters in the east. A web of side trails and quiet backroads branch out to the coast, however, making PEI's trail network a great spot on which to idly meander – to hurry is not a PEI thing. Recommended side trips include Souris and the beaches at Basin Head Provincial Park; the seaside play town of Cavendish; and the capital city of Charlottetown, home to just 40,000 people but with wine bars, architecture and restaurants to rival many major cities.

A second bike trail heads along the north coast through Prince Edward Island National Park, following the line of the dunes behind Brackley Beach and showcasing some of PEI's finest coastal scenery.

Adding to PEI's cycling appeal is the island topography. Its highest hill reaches just 142m above sea level, making for predominantly flat cycling (although if you ride against the grain of the land – south to north or vice versa – there are some steep short climbs).

ESSENTIAL EXPERIENCES

❋ **Cycling atop the sandstone cliffs and endless beaches of Prince Edward Island National Park near Cavendish.**

❋ Wandering the boardwalk to the coastal sand dunes at Greenwich.

❋ **Donning a bib for a traditional lobster supper at St Ann, New Glasgow or North Rustico.**

❋ Detouring into Charlottetown for a big-city fix in a small-town setting.

❋ **Celebrating PEI's lack of hills as you cut through the centre of the island on the Confederation Trail.**

DISTANCE 279KM | **LOCATION** PRINCE EDWARD ISLAND, CANADA | **IDEAL TIME COMMITMENT** ONE TO TWO WEEKS | **BEST TIME OF YEAR** JUNE TO SEPTEMBER | **ESSENTIAL TIP** THE PREVAILING WINDS ON PEI BLOW FROM THE WEST AND SOUTHWEST

SEAFOOD SUPPERS

Food is like a religion on Prince Edward Island, which becomes especially apparent when you see a 'fully licensed' sign hanging outside a village church. Across the island, in churches, dining halls and community centres, you'll encounter PEI's classic dining experience: no-frills lobster suppers. The lobster is served unadorned – no sauces or fanfare – with a slew of accompaniments, from chowder to mussels to PEI's famed potatoes. Lobster suppers are held daily from roughly mid-June to mid-October, and the most renowned are in New Glasgow, St Ann and North Rustico in central PEI.

▥ THE ADVENTURE UNFOLDS

At the entrance to the national park, cars are stopping to pay fees, but you just pedal on through to the bike lane that begins as soon as you enter the park.

Along the foot of the Brackley Beach dunes there's barely a tree in sight, just these coastal grasses and the sound of the ocean beyond the dunes. Soon enough you're turning back off the coast, wondering at the piety of this island where road signs warn of 'Church Traffic Ahead' as you rejoin the Confederation Trail at Tracadie.

At the town of Mt Stewart, built in the fork of the old railway, you pedal through the salt marshes above the Hillsborough River. Above the river, a bald eagle is perched to attention atop a spruce tree. The trail takes you back to the coast just beyond Morell, sometimes just metres in from the shores of St Peters Bay, a host of birdlife stirring its protected waters. Past St Peters, there are kilometres of ruler-straight track. Out here, alone in the woods, passing beaver ponds, it's hard to believe PEI is Canada's most densely populated province.

The names of the rural settlements are as entertaining as the chipmunks that bounce about the track: Bear River on this island with no animals larger than a beaver; New Zealand; and Harmony Junction, where you depart the main trail, following a branch line to the south coast in Souris.

You keep pedalling east, to Basin Head and the beach so many rate as the finest on the island. Red cliffs drop down to white sands and blue seas, and a crowd of bodies bake in the sun, looking like sausages on a barbecue. Elmira – ride's end – is just a few kilometres away, but for this it can wait.

▥ MAKING IT HAPPEN

Cycling independently is a simple task on Prince Edward Island. Bike rentals are available from Outside Expeditions in North Rustico and MacQueen's Bike Shop in Charlottetown – MacQueen's also offers transfers. Full planning details, including maps and trail descriptions, can be found via Tourism PEI.

▥ AN ALTERNATIVE CHALLENGE

Strapped in and ready for something really big? In creating the Confederation Trail, PEI became the first province to complete its section of the mammoth Trans Canada Trail, a proposed 22,500km coast-to-coast path across the entire country. Beginning at North America's most easterly point, Cape Spear, it will eventually extend right across to Victoria on Vancouver Island, crossing through every Canadian province on its way. When completed (the current forecast is that it will be open for action in 2017), it will be the world's longest network of trails, half as long as the Earth is round.

OPENING SPREAD Cape Tryon lighthouse was built in 1905 and stands above the red sandstone cliffs of Prince Edward Island's north coast.
ABOVE (L) Expect a windswept ride around Orby Head in Prince Edward Island National Park. **ABOVE (R)** A deserted farmhouse on the island.

ARMCHAIR

❋ **Anne of Green Gables** (Lucy Maud Montgomery) To know Prince Edward Island is to know the red-haired orphan who's more famous than the island.

❋ **Flavours of Prince Edward Island: A Culinary Journey** (Jeff McCourt, Allan Williams & Austin Clement) It's pretty clear, pretty fast that PEI is foodie heaven, and this book features recipes and tales from local chefs, farmers and fishers.

❋ **Prince Edward Island Book of Everything** (Martha Walls) If you wanted to know anything about PEI, it's probably in here, from the strange place names to the origins of all that red dirt.

❋ **Prince Edward Island: An (Un)Authorized History** (Boyde Beck) A PEI historian recounts some of the island's best historical yarns.

ABOVE & BELOW

———————— ❧ ————————

GREAT ADVENTURES

CANYONEER UTAH'S PARIA CANYON

A HIKE DOWN PARIA CANYON IS LIKE NOTHING YOU KNOW. WITH ITS NATURAL AMPHITHEATRES, ANCIENT PETROGLYPHS, MINIATURE RATTLESNAKES AND THE CONSTANT THREAT OF FLASH FLOODS, NEGOTIATING THE WORLD'S LONGEST SLOT CANYON IS AN EXERCISE IN AMAZEMENT.

118

Before Europeans 'discovered' it, Paria Canyon was part of a route used by the indigenous Paiute people to move between what is now southern Utah and northern Arizona. Archaeological evidence indicates that their ancestors inhabited the region for more than 10,000 years. Paria is actually Paiute for 'muddy water', which is something you'll get used to as the canyon narrows, forcing you to wade through the chocolate-coloured river.

As the last ice age came to an end, water runoff from ancient glaciers slowly cut deeper into the soft sandstone, bestowing Paria Canyon with a succession of bizarre and intriguing geological formations. This is Mother Nature at her most sublime and poetic, from the swirling patterns of the Wave at Coyote Buttes to the equally mesmerising red rock of the Paria amphitheatre.

As the water wore through the sandstone, the wind stripped the rock back to reveal changes in hue that have mesmerised visitors for millennia. The sun adds its final touch by glazing the shapes as if a potter on peyote had shaped the whole canyon. Thus, when you canyoneer through Paria, you are bearing witness to 85 million years of outrageous geology.

Typically, canyoneering is a hybrid of mountaineering that requires an acute route-finding sensibility plus the rope skills to descend and ascend any obstacles in your way. The awesomeness of Paria is that anyone with a good level of fitness is capable of negotiating any or all of the 60km route. That said, this is not a place you can take for granted: it's prone to flash floods, which means a happy hike can turn to disaster in an instant.

If you intend to tackle it yourself, make like a cub scout and 'be prepared'. Paria Canyon may be popular but it's still extremely remote, contains little drinking water and is largely inaccessible – getting rescued from here is not simply a matter of dialling emergency on your mobile phone.

ESSENTIAL EXPERIENCES

* **Marvelling at a brilliant ray of sun blasting through the Narrows onto the rock, illuminating it like pure gold.**

* Walking the Wave at Coyote Buttes.

* **Stargazing through the 'roof' of the canyon, and remembering the spirits of those who passed here long before.**

* Catching a glimpse of a bald eagle or peregrine falcon.

* **Giggling at the 'miniature' rattlesnakes common in the canyon, then remembering they can kill you with one bite.**

DISTANCE AROUND 60KM | **LOCATION** PARIA CANYON-VERMILION CLIFFS WILDERNESS, UTAH, USA | **IDEAL TIME COMMITMENT** FOUR TO SIX DAYS | **BEST TIME OF YEAR** SPRING AND AUTUMN | **ESSENTIAL TIP** BRING A WATERPROOF SACK FOR YOUR SLEEPING BAG

TSUNAMI IN A SLOT CANYON

In a region famous for its thunderstorms, a slot canyon is the last place you want to be when the rain comes down. Paria Canyon has an enormous catchment area, making a flash flood here more like a tsunami. With an average of eight flash floods a year that can reach speeds of up to 80km/h and 10m in height, bringing with them rolling rocks and all manner of debris, this is one mother of a wave nobody wants to catch. Fatalities in Utah slot canyons that occurred in 2005 and 2008 are a tragic reminder that the dangers of flash flooding cannot be overestimated.

KEEP CALM AND CARRY ON

If you're hiking the Paria River Canyon, the end of the line is technically where it meets the 'other' longest known slot canyon, Buckskin Gulch. Even more prone to flash floods than Paria, the gulch is ill advised for the inexperienced but a must-do for canyoneers who know their ropes. For 21km of its almost 60km length, Buckskin Gulch forms a corridor that is barely narrow enough to slip through and so steep you lose sight of the sky. A bewildering array of deep and shallow pools, fettered with perilous quicksand and rock jams, the gulch is the icing on Paria's cake.

■ THE ADVENTURE UNFOLDS

Paria Canyon's extraordinary length means it's packed with twists and turns that, while at times testing your physical dexterity, constantly leave you wide-eyed. When you first enter the canyon, it's little more than an unassuming desert streambed. Within a few hundred metres, you're moving through the Navajo sandstone. It's only after about 6km, when you enter the Narrows and are most at risk of getting caught in a flash flood, that suddenly you are moving between sheer walls of brightly coloured wind-streaked rock that stretch 150m straight up towards the deep blue sky. And so it begins.

A hike through Paria is all about the journey. Sure, you can't wait to arrive at star attractions such as the confluence with Buckskin Gulch or the wide arms of Wrather Arch, but it's the spaces, the moments in between, that carve themselves indelibly into your memory.

In parts you'll be scrambling up and along steep, smooth sections of limestone, so bring 'sticky' footwear, such as rubber-soled hiking shoes. Also carry your own drinking water. Hooking up with an experienced local or hiking with a guide is also strongly recommended, as this is the only way you'll discover many of the hidden gems that are all too easy to miss.

At all times only 20 people are allowed to start the hike each day, 10 by prior booking and 10 by lottery chosen 24 hours earlier. During peak season there are literally thousands of adventurers praying for one of the few hundred golden tickets available. If you really want to experience Paria in the sandstone flesh, you need to apply four months before you actually want to hike.

■ MAKING IT HAPPEN

There are several camp sites at the Whitehouse trailhead, just off Route 89, from where you can begin your adventure. Permits are required to hike Paria Canyon; get the latest information from the Bureau of Land Management. You must adhere to the 'leave no trace' policy, which means picking up any evidence you were there, including your poo, bagging it and carrying it out with you.

■ AN ALTERNATIVE CHALLENGE

You don't have to be in it to experience the beauty of Paria Canyon. Take a ride in a hot-air balloon and absorb the scenery as you float above this alien landscape. Or, make your way to one of the many strategically located lookouts, such as Paria View, where you might spot a majestic peregrine falcon. The surrounding meadows are home to mule deer and elk. If you're here just before the start of summer, you might get lucky and spy pronghorn antelopes heading to the forest, where they'll give birth to the next generation of mythical-looking creatures that inhabit this untamed region.

121

CHRISTIAN HEINRICH | GETTY

OPENING SPREAD Reaching Zebra Slot Canyon in Grand Staircase-Escalante National Monument, Utah, requires a 7km round-trip hike.
ABOVE The wind-sculpted rock formations of Coyote Buttes North in Paria Canyon-Vermilion Cliffs Wilderness. **LEFT** Buckskin Gulch, Utah.

ARMCHAIR

※ **Southern Paiute – A Portrait** (William Logan Hebner) Records the many trials and tribulations of the Paiute people since Europeans arrived, as told to Hebner by living members of the Paiute tribe. Accompanied by evocative photographs by Michael Pyler.

※ **Hiking and Exploring the Paria River** (Michael Kelsey) The guidebook covers the region's short and day walks, as well as the epic hike along the southern length of the Paria River gorge.

※ **Between a Rock and a Hard Place** (Aron Ralston) Ralston had to hack off his own arm after he got stuck in the Blue John Canyon. His autobiographical account offers a tantalising glimpse into what drives an outdoor adventurer.

※ **127 Hours** (2010) The six-time Oscar-nominated film tells Aron Ralston's story.

PARAGLIDE MONT BLANC

NOTHING SAYS ALPINE ADVENTURE LIKE MONT BLANC. WHETHER YOU ARE SCALING ITS ROCK-STUDDED SLOPES OR PARAGLIDING FROM ITS PEARLY WHITE SUMMIT, THIS 4810M GIANT WILL BLOW YOU AWAY. GIVE FLIGHT TO YOUR FANTASY AND LIVE THE MOUNTAIN DREAM.

Since time immemorial, Mont Blanc has been a source of wonder and fear, exhaustion and exhilaration. Straddling the French-Italian border, La Dame Blanche (the White Lady) is, as Lord Byron poetically put it, the 'monarch of mountains', the crowning glory of the Alps and Western Europe's highest peak. Its name alone suggests high-altitude escapades and has intrepid types itching to measure their skill and stamina against that of their mountaineering forefathers. To breathe in the thin air and be dazzled by the glacial glare and mind-blowing views from its peak is to taste once-in-a-lifetime adventure and top-of-Europe elation.

It was the enigmatic allure of 'what is up there' that prompted the first climbers – Jacques Balmat and Michel-Gabriel Paccard – to ascend Mont Blanc in 1786. A year later, British mountaineer Mark Beaufoy came nipping at their sprightly heels, complete with an entourage of guides and a duty-bound servant. Back in those pioneering days, there were no cable cars to ease the journey, no huts offering refuge snuggled on the mountainsides and definitely no paragliders. Imagine what those early explorers would have said if they had known that two centuries down the line you would be able to pull a lightweight paraglider out of your rucksack, strap yourself into your harness, spread your wings and fly – yes, fly! – 3800m from the summit to Chamonix. Today you can, with a good level of fitness, a little Alpine experience and a lot of guts.

Is Mont Blanc popular? You bet. But the fact that you won't have this mountain to yourself detracts nothing from the sweet sense of marvel and relief you will feel when the gruelling yet gorgeous ascent is over and you can sit back and glide among the ice and rock wilderness of the four-thousanders. And it's worth every gruelling, wind-battered, blister-inducing step and €1000-plus for the one-off chance to take a run and jump from the rooftop of Europe.

ESSENTIAL EXPERIENCES

✳ **Watching the sun set over mighty Alpine peaks from a mountain refuge, perched like an eagle's nest above the clouds.**

✳ Breathing a sigh of relief and amazement as you reach the summit after an obstacle-course of an ascent, traversing snowy gullies and dodging rock falls.

✳ **Glimpsing Chamonix far, far below as you soar among the glaciated heights and rock spires of the Mont Blanc massif.**

✳ Marvelling at 360-degree views of the French, Swiss and Italian Alps from the iconic spike of Aiguille du Midi.

✳ **Relaxing in Chamonix over a slap-up English breakfast or homemade brownies and coffee at La Petite Kitchen.**

122

ELEVATION 4810M | **LOCATION** CHAMONIX, HAUTE-SAVOIE, FRANCE | **IDEAL TIME COMMITMENT** ONE WEEK | **BEST TIME OF YEAR** JUNE, SEPTEMBER AND OCTOBER | **ESSENTIAL TIP** MOUNTAIN REFUGES ARE EXTREMELY POPULAR IN SEASON – BOOK WELL AHEAD

Climbers have a choice of three classic routes when ascending Mont Blanc. Voie Royale is a two-day ascent that begins with a tram ride from Saint-Gervais-les-Bains to the trailhead at Nid d'Aigle. The tough bit is crossing the Grand Couloir and dodging rock falls. One of the most technically challenging routes is Voie des 3 Monts, a three-mountain marathon that kicks off with a cable-car ride to the Col du Midi and a night at Cosmiques refuge. La Route des Aiguilles Grises is the classic route on the Italian side, involving a glacier crossing, some heavily crevassed sections and a long ascent on the second day.

▪ THE ADVENTURE UNFOLDS

The sky is crystal-clear, the Alpine air bracing and you are eager to tackle 'the big one' after four days of acclimatising and clambering up smaller neighbouring peaks. You spare a thought for those early explorers as you fast-forward the first 1000m to 2000m in the comfort of a cable car and then begin your ascent proper. Armed with crampons, ice axe, sling and paragliding gear, you climb past glaciers and moraine-strewn slopes where chamois hop nimbly from rock to rock. Arriving at your refuge set above 3000m, you have never felt so heartened by a simple meal, a cup of *chocolat chaud* and a dorm bunk.

In the predawn darkness, you slip on your headlamp and begin day two's challenging ascent. The first rays spotlight the peaks one by one and you are starting to understand what the guide meant by tough. The higher you go, the thinner and colder the air gets. Spurred on by your singular goal, you switch to autodrive and brave tough inclines, battering winds and rock-riddled couloirs. And then, finally, you reach the summit and triumph washes away your tiredness.

Standing in the footsteps of legends, you survey a sea of glacier-encrusted peaks – from pyramid-shaped Matterhorn to the jagged Italian Alps.

You climb into the harness of your paraglider – solo if you're experienced, otherwise accompanied by a pilot. Nothing has prepared you for the heart-fluttering, spirit-soaring sensation as you launch. Below you, the mighty peaks of the Alps unfold in beautiful slow motion and you play peek-a-boo with the fearsome faces of the Mont Blanc massif. You fly among rock turrets and spires, hanging glaciers, ice columns and shimmering ice fields – feeling at once tiny and huge – until you touch down with your heart pumping, your muscles aching and your head still spinning.

ARMCHAIR

* *Frankenstein* (Mary Shelley) Wild and remote, Mont Blanc is where Frankenstein meets his monster in this Gothic-Romantic novel.

* *Hugo et le Mont Blanc* (Colette Cosnier) An incredible account of Victor Hugo's journey over the Alps to Mont Blanc.

* *How to Climb Mont Blanc in a Skirt* (Mick Conefrey) An entertaining and insightful portrayal of the world of female explorers.

* *Mont Blanc* (Percy Shelley) A visit to the Chamonix Valley in 1816 inspired the English Romantic poet to pen this ode to Mont Blanc.

* *Storm over Mont Blanc* (1932) An Alpine black-and-white thriller zooming in on the raw beauty of the Mont Blanc massif.

KIT YOURSELF OUT

Be prepared with this checklist of equipment you should consider bringing or hiring:

* **Warm clothing: thermal underwear, waterproofs, a technical jacket, hat and mittens**

* A harness, sturdy mountain shoes and a headlamp

* **Gaiters, crampons and an ice axe for the snow; sunglasses or goggles for the glare**

* Lightweight flying equipment and a decent rucksack weighing a maximum of 10kg (a rescue parachute is also recommended)

MAKING IT HAPPEN

Ascending Mont Blanc is possible for anyone
with a good level of fitness and basic Alpine
experience. Though not considered difficult
by mountaineering standards, it's no walk in
the park either. Reputable companies like Les
Ailes du Mont Blanc and Absolute Chamonix
charge around €1030 for a mountain guide and
paragliding instructor. Budget extra for equipment
rental, cable cars, insurance, huts and meals.
The Office de Haute Montagne de Chamonix has
details on mountain refuges and flying locations.

AN ALTERNATIVE CHALLENGE

If time, expense or experience are an issue,
other paragliding opportunities abound in the
Chamonix Valley. For a buzz, little beats launching
yourself from the needle-thin pinnacle of Aiguille
du Midi (3842m). Tandem flights costing around
€220 are available year-round (July and August
aside). Preceded by a 20-minute walk along a
snow ridge, the flight involves a 2700m vertical
descent and affords phenomenal views of glaciers
and rock spires. For first-timers and children
wishing to cut their paragliding teeth, Planpraz is
an easier and cheaper (€100) alternative.

OPENING SPREAD Soaring above the Col de la Forclaz, Annecy in the Haute-Savoie region
of the Alps. **ABOVE** Cleared for take-off: paragliders queue to launch themselves into space
at Chamonix. **BELOW** A tandem paraglide in Chamonix is a great way to try the sport.

PLUNGE INTO THE CAVES OF BELIZE

PSYCHE YOURSELF FOR A JOURNEY INTO THE MAYAN UNDERWORLD – DELVE INTO THE VERY ROCK ON WHICH BELIZE IS FOUNDED, TO DISCOVER A DARK REALM OF GUSHING RIVERS, ANCIENT ARTEFACTS AND THE SKELETAL REMAINS OF SACRIFICIAL VICTIMS DISPATCHED A MILLENNIUM AGO.

To the ancient Maya, the caverns, sinkholes, lakes and underground rivers in Belize – which now offer such great opportunities for tubing, kayaking, swimming and abseiling – were not adventure playgrounds, they were gateways to Xibalbá, 'Place of Fear' – the Mayan underworld, ruled by death gods.

The geology, of course, is more prosaic. Many of the physical features that make Belize so beguiling – its picturesque karst outcrops, the barrier reef that skirts its shoreline and the caves pocking the northern interior – are manifestations of its porous limestone bedrock, repeatedly exposed then re-covered by rising and falling seas. Rain erosion created the fissures, potholes and pinnacles that now decorate the land and offshore reefs.

Most characteristic of these features are cenotes: sinkholes formed by the collapse of the roofs of caves carved out by underground rivers. To the Maya, these were sacred; the source of water and gateways to the underworld, they were places to bury the dead, perform religious ceremonies and make sacrifices. Intrepid travellers are reminded of past rituals by handprints, petroglyphs and pictographs etched or painted on rock walls, and by the bones and skulls that still litter some caves, possibly the remains of human sacrificial victims.

Only in the past 20 years have Belize's subterranean marvels been opened up for exploration. Now those with a head for heights (and depths) can abseil 91m into the jungle-filled Black Hole, or canoe or tube through Barton Creek Cave. Two Blue Holes offer contrasting aquatic experiences: take a cooling dip in the cerulean waters flowing through a vast inland cenote, or don snorkel or scuba equipment to explore the offshore sinkhole at Lighthouse Reef. And the hike, wade, swim and scramble to and through Actun Tunichil Muknal at the edge of Tapir Mountain Nature Reserve reveals a poignant sight: the skeleton of a young girl, sacrificed a millennium ago and now sparkling with calcite crystals.

ESSENTIAL EXPERIENCES

* **Trekking through steaming jungle and wading through waist-deep rivers to reach the sacrificial Crystal Maiden in Actun Tunichil Muknal.**

* Spotting tapirs, anteaters, monkeys, a dizzying array of birds and – if you're really lucky – a jaguar at Cockscomb Basin Wildlife Sanctuary.

* **Meeting the modern-day Maya in their villages in the southern Toledo district.**

* Chilling out on the Northern Cayes and snorkelling or diving the Western Hemisphere's longest barrier reef.

* **Taking the rough road to remote Caracol, the vast, jungle-clad Mayan city founded at least two millennia ago.**

* Abseiling 90m down into the rainforest-lined Black Hole.

LOCATION CENTRAL BELIZE | **IDEAL TIME COMMITMENT** THREE DAYS TO ONE WEEK | **BEST TIME OF YEAR** NOVEMBER TO MAY
ESSENTIAL TIP TAKE A LIGHTWEIGHT DRY BAG FOR CARRYING YOUR CAMERA AND ANYTHING ELSE YOU DON'T WANT TO GET WET

126

THE LIVING MAYA

As you gaze slack-jawed at crystal-encrusted skeletons or explore ancient, tumbledown temples, don't forget that, though the heyday of Classical Mayan civilisation ended some 11 centuries ago, Maya peoples still inhabit Belize today. In fact, over 10% of the country's population is Maya, divided into three linguistically distinct groups. The Yucatecs of the north originated over what's now the Mexican border, while the Kekchi migrated from Guatemala. The Mopan also arrived from Guatemala, though their roots were in Belize. An eye-opening stay in one of the Maya villages of the south can be arranged through the Toledo Ecotourism Association (TEA).

ANIMAL MAGIC

Belize boasts more than its fair share of natural
treasures; over 40% of the country's area is
protected by national or private organisations,
affording rich wildlife watching. Though named a
jaguar reserve, you'd be fortunate to spot Latin
America's biggest cat at Cockscomb Basin Wildlife
Sanctuary, but you could see howler monkeys,
Baird's tapirs, coatis, some of its 300 bird species
and perhaps even a selection of Belize's other cats:
ocelots, margays, pumas and jaguarundis. Elsewhere,
the lagoons of Crooked Tree Wildlife Sanctuary
attract profuse birdlife, while cats including jaguars
stalk the forests of Blue Hole National Park.

THE ADVENTURE UNFOLDS

Dawn's pink kiss is still fading from the sky as you set off through the jungle, wiping sleep from your eyes. Mist lingers in woolly tufts on the forest canopy ahead: moisture condensing in cold air, telltale signs of caves and streams, your guide tells you. A flash of movement sends your heart leaping into your mouth. That it's merely a coatimundi scampering down a tree brings both relief and disappointment – is a close encounter with a jaguar to be longed for or dreaded?

An hour's trek through dense forest is punctuated by waist-deep river crossings. You stop briefly at Actun Uayazba Kab – 'Handprint Cave' – to admire the eponymous stencils, and to boost the adrenalin with a short abseil past cliff niches holding pottery artefacts. But the real adventure begins at the hourglass entrance to the Underworld: Actun Tunichil Muknal, the 'Cave of the Stone Sepulchre'. The shiver as you slip into the shimmering turquoise pool can't be explained by the cool of the water alone. The ancient Maya believed this to be a gateway to Xibalbá, where the dead return and the jaguar retreats at night.

You flick on your headtorch and swim into the cave, scrambling a kilometre upstream, chest-deep in chilly water. Eventually, you clamber onto rocks coated with crystal flows; here you leave your shoes and pad on in stockinged feet through successive caverns, past wide pottery *ollas* (jars) and stelae carved to represent blood-letting tools, finally ascending into the Cathedral.

Though the soaring ceiling justifies the name, it could be called the Catacomb. Skulls sparkle with calcite and ahead lies the object of your mission: the Crystal Maiden, a young girl, resting where she was killed over a thousand years ago.

MAKING IT HAPPEN

Belize's caves dot the centre and west of the country; most are accessible only on organised tours. A couple of outfits are currently licensed to take visitors into Actun Tunichil Muknal; these tours, along with other caving adventures in the west of Belize, are best booked through your accommodation or the lodges in San Ignacio. The Black Hole abseil is run by Caves Branch Adventure Company, just off the Hummingbird Highway.

DETOUR

The world's second-longest barrier reef – a 300km limestone shelf topped with choice coral – skirts Belize's coast, in some spots within spitting distance of the shore, which makes for fine snorkelling. The country's Northern Cayes host scuba-divers, with dozens of fine dive sites easily accessible. The headline act is the Blue Hole, a vividly hued sinkhole on Lighthouse Reef, 305m across and 122m deep. Other sites offer opportunities for spotting whale sharks, manta rays, sea turtles, manatees and countless smaller species.

129

OPENING SPREAD The Mayans believed caves, such as this one in Belize, were gateways to the underworld. **ABOVE (L)** Stalactites are formed when dripping water evaporates and the dissolved limestone hardens. **ABOVE (R)** Rafters use Caves Branch River to travel between caves. **LEFT** A wild puma.

ARMCHAIR

* **The Maya** (Michael D Coe) An accessible, intelligent introduction to the dominant culture of ancient Belize.

* **Diving & Snorkeling Belize** (Tim Rock) A colourful guide providing detailed information on top dive sites and species to spot.

* **Time Among the Maya: Travels in Belize, Guatemala and Mexico** (Ronald Wright) This perceptive travelogue describes enlightening encounters with modern-day Maya among the lands of their ancestors.

* **Belize & Northern Guatemala: Travellers' Wildlife Guide** (Les Beletsky) Detailed introduction to the species to spot and where to see them.

* **The Mosquito Coast** (1986) Harrison Ford plays a fanatical inventor bent on creating a utopia in Central America. Paul Theroux's book was set in Honduras, but the steaming jungle in Peter Weir's film is Belize.

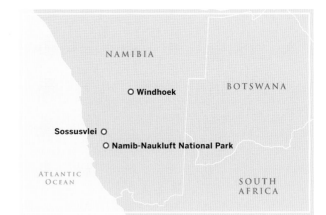

BALLOON OVER SOSSUSVLEI, NAMIBIA

THE BILLOW OF SILK, THE BURNER'S BLAZING ROAR, AN ANCIENT ORANGE EMPTINESS STRETCHING AS FAR AS THE EYE CAN SEE – FLOATING IN A HOT-AIR BALLOON OVER NAMIBIA'S PRIMORDIAL DESERT IS GREAT ADVENTURE AT ITS MOST ROMANTIC.

130

The first hot-air balloon passengers were not aeronautical engineers, they were a duck, a rooster and a sheep called Montauciel – or, in English, 'Climb-to-the-sky'. In 1783, French inventors Joseph-Michel and Jacques-Étienne Montgolfier elevated their farmyard brood in a basket suspended from an envelope of taffeta, on a flight that lasted eight minutes. Today, you might hope to stay aloft a little longer, but inflation-aviation basics haven't changed that much.

There's a romance to hot-air ballooning that snubs the advent of modern technologies. Though we can fly faster, higher and more predictably in other craft, there's a magic to its simplicity: balloon, burner, basket – all abiding by an elementary law of physics and the whim of the wind. Balloons need large open areas in which to land – which is one reason why the Namib Desert is ideal, encompassing around 80,000 sq km of predominantly empty space. But the main reason to ascend here is that it's so utterly astonishing: the iconic Sossusvlei area is a sensuous billow of orange sand, crafted by the breeze into ever-changing crests and swirls. Due to its scale, hostility, scorching temperatures and paucity of roads, it's difficult to appreciate from the ground.

There's no skill required to board a balloon – leave that to your flame-blasting pilot. A head for heights helps: there will be, after all, just a slither of wicker between you and the African air. But safety records are good; the biggest danger is landing, which can be a thrillingly bumpy affair – don't be surprised to get unceremoniously dragged before coming to a complete stop.

Hot-air balloon flights aren't cheap: a one-hour trip, in a balloon carrying six to 16 people, will cost around N$4000 (more than £300 or US$500). But this does include a hearty breakfast out at wherever-you-happen-to-land, during which you can raise a glass of champagne to, probably, the ride of your life.

ESSENTIAL EXPERIENCES

* **Feeling your flimsy basket begin to lift up off the dawn-cool desert floor.**
* Submitting to the vagaries of the wind and the blast of the burners – even your pilot has limited say on direction up here.
* **Watching the sun sneak over a ripple of apricot dunes and seem to set them on fire.**
* Following the bulbous shadow of your balloon as it creeps slowly across the landscape below.
* **Spying a long-horned oryx standing solo and imperious amid the vast sand sea.**
* Sipping champagne as you breakfast in the middle of nowhere, toasting your magical flight.

DISTANCE AS FAR AS THE WIND TAKES YOU (ON AVERAGE, 16KM) | **LOCATION** NAMIB DESERT, NAMIBIA | **IDEAL TIME**
COMMITMENT FIVE HOURS | **BEST TIME OF YEAR** YEAR-ROUND | **ESSENTIAL TIP** ENSURE YOUR INSURANCE COVERS BALLOONING

DADDY OF ALL DESERTS

The Namib Desert, which stretches along Namibia's Atlantic coast plain from Lüderitz in the south to the Uniab River, is the world's oldest desert. Vast and virtually uninhabited, it has existed for at least 55 million years, a stark but strangely beautiful ripple of gravel fields, craggy mountains and curvaceous sand dunes. Rainfall is low and unpredictable; that anything survives here (and it does, from tok-tokkie beetles and golden moles to 1000-year-old *Welwitschia mirabilis* plants) is thanks to the regular fogs that build over the ocean and drift inland, providing a miserly, but essential, drink.

DESERT GEM

Gemsbok, or oryx – large and handsome grey-coated antelopes with striking white-and-black faces – are found all over Namibia. But they're most iconic when seen standing before a Namib dune, their long, straight hornws piercing the orange sand behind. Although the desert is hot and hostile, gemsbok have adapted to survive here: if there's no shade, they'll orientate themselves so that as little of their body as possible is facing the sun. They can also allow their body temperature to rise by 6°C, reducing their water needs, while special capillaries in their nasal passages cool the blood before it enters their brains.

THE ADVENTURE UNFOLDS

As the pilot pulls down, the flame roars like an ill-tempered lion, breathing life into the silken balloon. The strange beauty of the Namib Desert lies in its pristine vastness, untouched by human meddling, and as those burners bellow another time, you feel yourself lift, wafting over this wonderfully weird world. The movement is gentle, like rising on an eagle's wings. The air feels still as you float with it, melting into the dawn sky. The rising sun is nudging all else awake, the dunes respond to those first sneaking rays by morphing from cool mauve to blood-red and burnished gold. As you gain height, more and more of this sand sea is revealed, a turbulent ocean of orange caressed into an artist's envy of sculptural forms.

The desert below is known as Sossusvlei. The name refers to a cracked-clay pan flanked by 300m-high dunes. You won't float that far – it's too deep into the desert – but that hardly matters. You and your basket-mates grin at each other. Save for the occasional fiery thrust, all is silent and still. The only movement you can detect is your balloon's shadow, which seems to be slow-motion racing you across the glowing land below. Vistas of equal magnificence drift off to the horizon in every direction, a sight so breathtaking you may cry.

Landing is an adventure – biff, bang, wallop – but as you crawl and giggle out of the basket, and take in your surrounds, you couldn't care less. Ahead, looking somewhat incongruous, is a linen-topped table, laden with breakfast. A waiter (where did he come from?) picks up a bottle of bubbly and uncorks it with the swish of a sword. Odd? A bit. But it's been that kind of morning.

MAKING IT HAPPEN

Namib Sky Adventures runs balloon trips from the Sesriem area of the Namib – the precise departure location is dependent on wind conditions. The company offers pick-ups from several local lodges; pick-up is 30 minutes before sunrise, weather permitting. Dress for the season: it may be chilly before lift-off but the burner keeps the basket warm in flight. Wear a hat. Take a camera, but little else – weight limits are strict.

AN ALTERNATIVE CHALLENGE

The Atlantic coast town of Swakopmund, 300km from Sesriem on the edge of the Namib-Naukluft National Park, is Namibia's extreme-sports hub. Here you can quad bike, sandboard, horse ride or land-yacht, then hit a German bakery for an *apfelstrudel* or a stein of beer. Ballooning is an option, but for more extreme air action, try a skydive. Operated by Ground Rush Adventures, usually after Swakopmund's morning fog has dispersed, daily tandem jumps from 3500m include 30 seconds of freefall and views of the desert.

OPENING SPREAD The world's tallest sand dunes slither across the Namib desert, some reaching 300m in height. **ABOVE** Ballooning above Sossusvlei. **LEFT** Running wild: gemsbok antelopes in the Namib desert can reach a top speed of 55km/h. Their horns can be more than 1m in length.

ARMCHAIR

* **Spectacular Namibia** (Tim O'Hagan) Tantalising images of the country's best bits, from searing orange dunes to the lush Caprivi Strip and eerie Skeleton Coast.

* **Sheltering Desert** (Henno Martin) Two Germans hide in the Namib during WWII – a true story of desert survival.

* **A History of Namibia: From the Beginning to 1990** (Marion Wallace) Comprehensive, scholarly study tracing the country's

evolution from its ancient civilisations to eventual independence.

* **The Purple Violet of Oshaantu** (Neshani Andreas) Novel set in a Namibian village, exploring the life of a local woman in a very traditional world.

* **The Fantastic Flying Journey** (Gerald Durrell) Magical children's book about Great-Uncle Lancelot's adventures in his balloon Belladonna; gorgeous illustrations by Graham Perry.

CAVING ENGLAND'S PEAK DISTRICT

CHANNEL YOUR INNER GOBLIN, GET OVER YOUR BOULDER CHOKE AND DIVE DEEP UNDER THE PEAK DISTRICT INTO A MYTHICAL WORLD WHERE EVERY HOLE'S A GOAL AND ROOF SNIFFING IS JUST ANOTHER WAY TO TRAVEL BETWEEN CAVERNS.

134

Let's be clear: if you suffer even a whiff of claustrophobia, caving is not your friend. While the reward of rich minerals was the incentive for Neolithic miners to dig their way under the Derbyshire hills, apparently it was purely the joy of exploring moist, dark spaces that led cavers and potholers to follow in their ancient tracks en masse from around the middle of the last century. Today, there's a vast network of underground tunnels to explore.

The Peak District National Park crosses into several counties, but it's under Derbyshire that you'll discover its most spectacular beauties. These include one of the jewels of the caving world, Titan Cave, the UK's tallest natural cavern, extending to a height of 141.5m. Carved over millions of years by water slowly eroding the limestone base, Titan features an enormous waterfall that plunges into the unknown deep. Incredibly, it was only in 2000 that local potholers discovered the cave, which occupies a space bigger than St Paul's Cathedral, giving an indication of just how much remains to be explored.

New tunnels are discovered every year and dug out by a committed hard-core group of local and visiting troglodytes – the ancient name for anyone lucky enough to live in a cave, although these days it has a strong association with being a bit weird. Not surprising, given that hanging around in caves has to be one of the more potentially hazardous activities people do for recreation. Thankfully, the specialist British Cave Rescue Council is always on hand to save trapped explorers, with fatalities a rare occurrence.

Still, never attempt to go caving on your own. There are plenty of local experts who can not only guide you through the bewildering labyrinths but will hire out the essential gear, such as a wetsuit, oversuit, helmet, lights, footwear and insurance, that will ensure you return to the surface safe and sound.

ESSENTIAL EXPERIENCES

* **Resting during an ascent of a particularly challenging rock face, knowing that your amazing buddies have got you safely secured.**

* Savouring every morsel of scroggin (energy food mix) as your body takes in the fuel you'll need to keep going.

* **Surfacing back at the start of the sump you just explored, only to realise you were minutes away from running out of oxygen.**

* Finally pulling your aching limbs out of a tight shaft and being able to stand totally upright in a cavern that has been waiting for you for millennia.

* **Knowing that you are part of a truly select group of lunatics brave enough to do this.**

LOCATION CASTLETON, DERBYSHIRE, ENGLAND | **IDEAL TIME COMMITMENT** SIX TO EIGHT HOURS | **BEST TIME OF YEAR** MAY TO SEPTEMBER | **ESSENTIAL TIP** IF YOU GO SOLO, DON'T FORGET PERSONAL LIABILITY INSURANCE BECAUSE IF YOU NEED RESCUING IT WON'T BE CHEAP!

SMOOTH TALK

As with most adventure sports, caving has produced a unique vocabulary to describe its peculiar experiences, sights and sounds. To cavers, foul air isn't just a fart in a tunnel, it signifies dangerously high levels of CO_2, which can affect cavers' concentration and motor function – not the kind of air you need while roof-sniffing, which is edging along a water-filled passage with just enough air space for your mouth and nose. Stuck in a tight spot? You'll probably wish you were a microbod: a tactfully tiny caver with the ability to seemingly dislocate your bones and overcome the most obstinate obstacles.

THE ADVENTURE UNFOLDS

After checking and rechecking your rope, it's time to push off and abseil into the abyss. Dropping into the darkness, you pivot and realise your headlamp is barely penetrating the shadows. Completely disoriented, you can hardly tell if you're moving up or down, and you begin to wonder how you got talked into doing this, when suddenly your light catches an enormous tract of limestone right beside you. It is utterly unlike anything you imagined, a giant wall of rock etched in prehistory, reaching out for you like some primeval memory. Your guide calls out for you to brace and suddenly you've reached the bottom.

All around you, spray from an unseen cascade hangs in the air like tiny moths dancing in your headlamp. And to think, all of this existed for millions of years before the first humans even had an inkling. That's the magic of the underworld: to penetrate the Earth is like being let in on a secret too big to comprehend and too important to share with anyone who hasn't had the experience.

We've all grown up trying to remember whether stalactites go up or down, but when you're intimately up against them, three hours into your exploration of a 10km cave network, all of a sudden geology starts to make sense. Soon your conversations will be interspersed with recollections of phreatic tubes and flowstones, as the caving bug bites and burrows into your soul.

You pull out your boob tube (a rubber hose that's long been standard-issue caving gear), carefully feed one end through a crack in a crevice into the clear pool of water you are told lies unseen behind the rock, put the other end to your lips and drink deep from the unsullied well of the underworld. Delicious.

MAKING IT HAPPEN

Castleton is an ideal town from which to launch your spelunking expeditions. It has a great range of accommodation, restaurants and caving shops, is the nearest town to Titan Cave, and is home to four of the other jewels in Derbyshire's caving crown: the Peak Cavern, Speedwell Cavern, Treak Cliff Cavern and Blue John Cavern. The latter is renowned for its Blue John stone that for centuries has been the chosen material used to make goblets for blue-blooded aristocrats.

AN ALTERNATIVE CHALLENGE

Snaking parallel with the River Wye, the 20km Monsal Bike Trail follows the old Midland Railway from Blackwell Mill to Coombs Viaduct. It not only offers some of the stunning scenery that has made the Peak District the second most visited national park in the world (after Japan's Mt Fuji), you can also get a taste of underground adventure, passing through several old railway tunnels. You can also walk or take a horse, although in winter, just like the caves, some of the tunnels are prone to flooding.

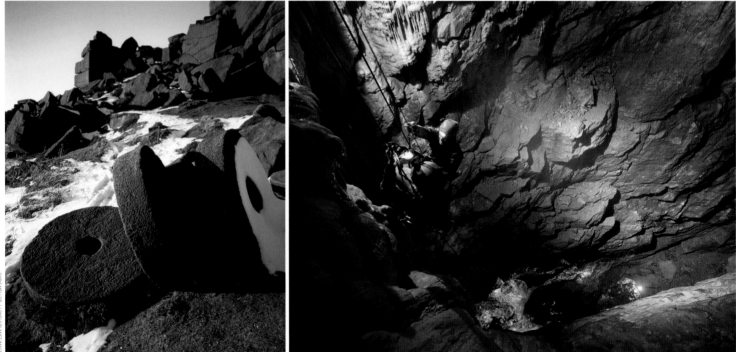

OPENING SPREAD Cavers in Britain wear specialist kit to keep warm and dry. **ABOVE (L)** Millstone Edge in the Peak District. Millstones from the local stone were used to grind grains. **ABOVE (R)** Ascending Titan, Britain's deepest cave shaft, in Castleton, Derbyshire. The shaft was discovered in 2000.

ARMCHAIR

* ***The Descent*** (2005) A movie about being trapped in a cave that will have you praying you don't get trapped in a cave.

* ***Sanctum*** (2011) Another movie about being trapped in a cave with the added fear factor of being co-produced by Andrew Wright, a survivor of the notorious Nullarbor Dreaming incident, when Australian cavers were trapped 80m below ground with radio their only means of contacting the surface.

* ***Caves of the Peak District*** (Iain Barker & John Beck) A complete guide to the Peak District's caves.

* ***Pride and Prejudice*** (Jane Austen) Jane Austen's classic includes several scenes set in and around Derbyshire.

* ***The Holding*** (2011) Get a taste of rural life inspired by screenwriter James Dormer's life on a local Peak District farm.

CLIMB

GREAT ADVENTURES

EXPLORE YOSEMITE'S WONDERS

Most visitors never leave the small area around Yosemite Village, save for short day hikes into the wilderness. But beyond the Ansel Adams Gallery and the tour buses, a vast wilderness awaits. Within the 3080-sq-km World Heritage Site, intrepid adventurers can backpack for days on end past roaring waterfalls and giant sequoia groves into a truly wild natural environment. The park is home to deer and bears, and has the tallest waterfall in California, Yosemite Falls. No wonder John Muir, the Scottish-born naturalist and activist instrumental to Yosemite's preservation, considered it 'by far the grandest of all the special temples of Nature I was ever permitted to enter'.

■ THE ADVENTURE UNFOLDS

One of the hardest elements of climbing the Nose is dealing with isolation and exposure. Imagine sleeping every night tied to the cliff. Picture yourself eating, drinking and dreaming in an environment that by its nature is hostile to life.

The rewards are great, but difficult to fathom for those who have never explored the vertical world. Every day you awake to a bird's-eye view of Yosemite's waterfalls and meadows. Tourists below look like ants, the towering trees blend together to form a rough carpet over the valley, and the only noises you hear are the constant rush of the wind and the occasional hoot from another climber. Silence itself attracts adventurers to this inhospitable realm.

While there are harder, longer and more exposed climbs in the world today, the 31 vertical pitches of the Nose are simply classic. There are giant pendulums with names like the King Swing, and unique formations like the Texas Flake and the Great Roof. Every pitch takes you through a little piece of climbing history, passing challenges that pushed the limits of climbing legends like John Long, Jim Bridwell and Royal Robbins over the years.

Life on a 'big wall' is odd. Doing your morning business into a tube becomes second nature. That can of spaghetti becomes a point of contention between you and your climbing partner. You start to imagine you're near the summit, only to realise you are still two days away; you consider going down, then remember you're too high up for an effective retreat. Your only way out becomes up. And with every step, each gear placement, you slowly burn down, concentrating every ounce of muscle and mind to making it to the top.

■ MAKING IT HAPPEN

Before you head up the Nose, you should spend several days getting a feel for Yosemite's signature granite. Most climbers stay in the walk-in Camp 4 camping ground; if you don't have a climbing partner, you can easily find one here. The Yosemite Mountaineering School has been guiding in the valley since 1969 – but if you don't know what to pack, or have limited climbing experience, then you shouldn't attempt the Nose, even with a guide.

■ AN ALTERNATIVE CHALLENGE

There are tonnes of adventures to be had in Yosemite National Park, from day hikes to waterfalls to multiday backpack treks in a park the size of Rhode Island. Across the valley from El Capitan, Half Dome beckons hard-core climbers and fit hikers alike. One of the best hikes on this iconic cliff is the cable route up the back to the summit. This 24km round-trip hike normally takes 10 to 12 hours, and ascends around 1440m. On the last 120m of the climb, two cables assist you up to the summit.

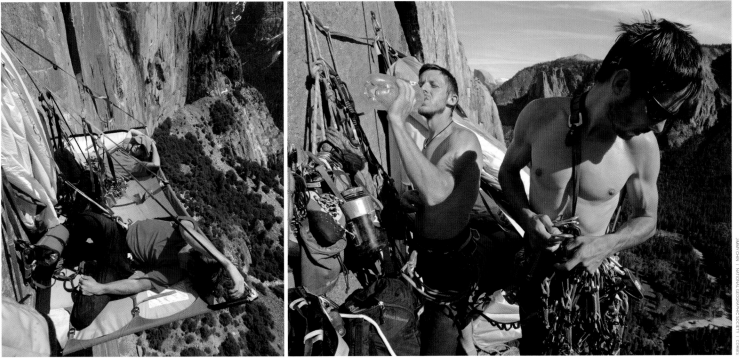

OPENING SPREAD Hanging out: climber and photographer Jimmy Chin at work on El Capitan. **ABOVE (L) AND (R)** Climbers conquering El Capitan eat, sleep and drink on the wall. But the quickest ascent has been recorded in just 2hrs 36mins. **LEFT** El Capitan rises above the Merced River in Yosemite.

ARMCHAIR

* **To the Limit** (2008) This feature-length German movie with English subtitles follows climbing legends Thomas and Alexander Huber on their attempt to break the speed record on the Nose.

* **Yosemite and the High Sierra** (Ansel Adams) This spectacular coffee-table book captures the best of Ansel Adams' photographic masterpieces.

* **Camp 4: Recollections of a Yosemite Rockclimber** (Steve Roper)

Chronicles the author's 10-year stay in Camp 4.

* **My First Summer in Sierra** (John Muir) Walden meets On the Road in this classic that combines transcendentalism with youthful wonder, with Yosemite as its mighty backdrop.

* **The National Parks: America's Best Idea** (2009) Six-disc Ken Burns documentary series that takes you through Yosemite and the rest of America's national parks.

CLIMB MT RORAIMA, VENEZUELA

HERE BE DRAGONS – AT LEAST, THAT'S HOW IT FEELS. FOR TO ASCEND VENEZUELA'S MIGHTIEST TABLETOP MOUNTAIN, VIA A TANGLE OF FOREST, AN ARMY OF SANDFLIES AND PUNISHINGLY SLIPPERY SLOPES, IS TO ENTER A PREHISTORIC, AND UTTERLY UNIQUE, LOST WORLD.

'Inaccessible, except by means of balloon.' That was the verdict on Mt Roraima in 1872. By the latter half of the 19th century, several Western explorers had set their eyes on the highest of Venezuela's strange table-shaped mountains, and all had determined it quite insurmountable – its foliage too dense, its situation too remote, its upper flanks too extraordinarily sheer.

In this era of pioneering and adventure, however, 'impossible' was just a challenge. In 1884, multitasking botanist, curator, author and photographer Everard Im Thurn and his assistant Harry Perkins finally made it to the top. Actually, it wasn't that hard. Roraima was, and still is, the simplest to climb of the 115 tepuis (flat-topped mountains) in Venezuela's sweeping Gran Sabana. A sloping ledge naturally hewn into Roraima's southern flank means that those of reasonable fitness willing to brave its humidity, downpours, slippery rocks and biting flies can negotiate the vertical cliffs of the upper reaches, and attain the summit, without recourse to climbing ropes or hot-air balloons. Hikers attempting to top this 2810m massif today still follow Im Thurn's historic route.

In 1912, Sir Arthur Conan Doyle, inspired by this alien realm, penned his non-Sherlock classic, *The Lost World*. In Doyle's imagination, this was a place where pterodactyls swooped and stegosauruses clomped. They don't, but you can believe they might. There's an eerie atmosphere on Roraima's singular summit – nightmarish rocks, strange sands and streamlets, a crystal valley and bug-eating plants that have evolved in lofty isolation from the land around.

Then there are the views – clouds permitting. Often the mesa is draped in a dramatic tablecloth of wispy white (it rains virtually every day). But when the linen is whipped off, the vastness is revealed; from here, you can look out over three countries – Roraima marks the meeting point of Venezuela, Guyana and Brazil – and across to other tepuis, which all have their own secret summits.

ESSENTIAL EXPERIENCES

* **Watching waterfalls tumble off the top of neighbouring tepui Kukenán – which, in Pemón, means 'Place of Death'.**

* Spending the night in a Roraima 'hotel', sandy areas sheltered by rock overhangs.

* **Scouring the tepui top for curious indigenous species – tiny black toads and unusual blooms.**

* Taking a dip in the jacuzzis – ice-clear, icicle-cold pools on Roraima's summit.

* **Waiting for the mist to clear, to give sweeping, international views of where Venezuela, Guyana and Brazil meet.**

* Nursing wobbly legs, a sunburned nose and myriad *jejene* (sandfly) bites with a cold beer back in Paraitepui, after a climb well done.

ELEVATION 2810M | **LOCATION** CANAIMA NATIONAL PARK, SOUTHEAST VENEZUELA | **IDEAL TIME COMMITMENT** FIVE TO SIX DAYS
BEST TIME OF YEAR NOVEMBER TO APRIL | **ESSENTIAL TIP** PACK OUT ALL WASTE

WEIRD WORLD

There may not be dinosaurs lurking on the tepuis, but they still feel prehistoric. These flat-topped mesas are two billion years old, formed when South America, Australia and Africa were still joined as the super-continent Gondwana. Over time the surrounding sandstone has eroded, leaving these tables to tower over the plateau. High and sheer-sided, each tepui has evolved in isolation, resulting in many unique species. Roraima has many endemic bromeliads, bellflowers and carnivorous heliamphoras, plus the *Oreophrynella quelchii* – a little black toad with an unusual defence mechanism: when faced with danger it doesn't hop away, but rolls into a ball.

CHINA

NEPAL

Sagarmatha National Park ○ △ Mt Everest
○ Kathmandu

INDIA

CLIMB MT EVEREST

EVEREST. REALLY, WHAT MORE NEEDS TO BE SAID? SIMPLY, TO CLIMB TO THE SUMMIT OF THE PLANET'S HIGHEST MOUNTAIN, THROUGH THE APTLY NAMED DEATH ZONE, IS TO TEST YOUR BODY TO ITS VERY LIMITS IN ORDER TO ATTAIN THE WORLD'S GREATEST PRIZE.

146

In 1852, the Great Trigonmetrical Survey of India declared that Everest – then catchily named Peak XV – was the highest mountain in the world. And from the first utterance of that fact, the race was on. If the pinnacle of the planet could be identified, it must be conquered. Take George Mallory's infamous answer to the question, why do you want to climb Everest? 'Because it's there.'

Mallory (probably) didn't make it up the mountain that so enticed him. He was last seen alive on 9 June 1924, ascending a rock step some 400 or so metres below the summit. It would be another 29 years before Everest was successfully scaled: on 29 May 1953, New Zealander Edmund Hillary and Nepali Sherpa Tenzing Norgay stood on the top of the world.

The mountain may have entered Western consciousness only in the 1850s, but it has far greater provenance. The people living in its shadow have long appreciated its significance: the Nepalese call Everest Sagarmatha (Head of the Sky); the Tibetans call it Chomolungma (Goddess Mother of the Mountains).

Everest is indeed the head honcho, the mother of all peaks – and should never be underestimated. The number of climbers who've reached the top has grown exponentially in recent years; around 80% of the 3200-odd summiteers have done so since 2000. But even with modern improvements in kit and logistics, it's still a daunting prospect. With oxygen levels too low to long sustain human life, they don't call the area above 8000m the Death Zone for nothing. Those venturing here need not only cash (this is a very expensive undertaking) but technical climbing know-how and high-altitude experience. Not to mention guts and determination.

But though it's hard, cold, pricey and downright dangerous – there's one death for every 10 successful ascents – adventurers will always flock to this mighty mountain. Because it's huge, because it's beautiful, because it's there.

ESSENTIAL EXPERIENCES

* **Stopping off in Namche Bazaar, en route to Base Camp, for apple pie and cappuccinos – your last taste of civilisation for many, many weeks.**

* Watching your Sherpas perform a *puja* (prayer) ceremony, during which they ask the gods' permission to climb the mountain.

* **Mastering the sparkling seracs and deadly crevasses of the legendary Khumbu Icefalls.**

* Pausing on the Balcony (at 8400m), a small ledge with big views.

* **Standing, quite literally, on the very top of the world.**

* Keeping your head and watching your feet, to ensure you descend safely (and get to gloat to everyone back home).

ELEVATION 8850M | **LOCATION** EASTERN NEPAL | **IDEAL TIME COMMITMENT** 70 DAYS | **BEST TIME OF YEAR** MARCH TO MAY
ESSENTIAL TIP EAT LOADS – YOU'LL LOSE 20% OF YOUR BODY WEIGHT ON THE CLIMB

EVEREST IN THE RECORD BOOKS

The prize for being first goes to Hillary and Tenzing Norgay. But Everest has spawned many more record breakers. In 1975, Junko Tabei of Japan became the first woman to ascend the mountain. In 1978, legendary climber Reinhold Messner made the first ascent without supplementary oxygen; in 1980 he was back for the first oxygen-less solo ascent. Pemba Dorje Sherpa reached the top in only eight hours 10 minutes in 2004 – the fastest climb. The oldest summiteer is 76-year-old Nepali, Min Bahadur Sherchan; the youngest is 13-year-old Californian Jordan Romero. Apa Sherpa, who has summitted 21 times, has climbed Everest the most.

THE SUPER SEVEN

The Seven Summits challenge is the quest to conquer the highest peak on every continent: Everest (Asia: 8850m), Kilimanjaro (Africa: 5895m), Aconcagua (South America: 6962m), Elbrus (Europe: 5642m), McKinley (North America: 6194m), Vinson (Antarctica: 4892m) and Carstensz Pyramid (Oceania: 4884m). The degree of difficulty varies wildly. Elbrus is relatively simple, with some glacier-walking, though it's located in a rather fractious region. Kili and Aconcagua are basically treks, made more testing by their altitudes. Carstensz is a moderate, exotic climb; McKinley and Vinson are technically tougher, and very cold. Then there's Everest... Only around 100 people have ticked off all seven.

■ THE ADVENTURE UNFOLDS

It's hard to explain what life feels like above 8000m. The air is so thin that every footstep feels like a marathon. Instead of inhaling 30 or so times a minute, you're panting at a rate of 80. Just breathing takes every ounce of energy you have. And after weeks of exertion, you don't have much to spare.

You know the symptoms of altitude sickness: fatigue, headaches, nausea, disorientation. If anything, you feel drunk. You're hallucinating. Is this how yeti stories begin? You've spent years getting your mind and body ready for this challenge but, cruelly, when you most need to be operating at 100%, when one error could send you tumbling to your death, you feel like you've had 10 tequilas.

From that first white-knuckle flight into Lukla airport, you fell in love with the Himalayas, a soaring, stretching dragon's back, unmatched elsewhere on the planet. But that was an age ago now. After settling at Base Camp, you've spent weeks making up-down forays, acclimatising slowly, establishing higher camps, descending to lower ones. Repeat. Repeat again. You've struggled across ladders spanning bottomless crevasses. You've fought Arctic blasts and blazing sun. You've lugged your heavy pack around seracs, dug your crampons into ice walls and had moments when you'd rather be anywhere else. You've also come to rely on your Sherpas, without whom you'd never have made it this far.

But made it you have. Ahead: a flutter of prayer flags, and a couple grinning like they've won gold. You stumble to join them, looking out on the ultimate panorama – no impediments, nothing higher. You are king of the world. Now all you need to do is get back down…

■ MAKING IT HAPPEN

Specialist companies arrange Everest climbs. You'll need lots of specialist kit, including harness, helmet, ice axe and ropes; the operator will provide items such as tents, food and supplementary oxygen as well as organising expensive permits. Most expeditions start in Kathmandu, fly to Lukla, trek to Everest Base Camp, then begin a lengthy period of acclimatisation before attempting the summit after several weeks, weather dependent.

■ AN ALTERNATIVE CHALLENGE

If you don't have any climbing experience, or a spare $50,000, consider finishing your hike at Base Camp rather than the summit. The classic return trek from Lukla takes around 14 days. It follows the Kosi River to bustling Namche Bazaar, then heads along the Khumbu Valley to Base Camp (5340m). Accommodation is in tents or, better for the local economy, teahouses. The best views of Everest are from Kala Pattar (5545m), a lookout reached via a steep two-hour climb from Base Camp.

OPENING SPREAD In 1924 George Mallory and Andrew Irvine attempted to summit Everest. Mallory's body was found 618m below the summit in 1999.
ABOVE (L) Leave the tweed at home: bring oxygen and high-tech kit. **ABOVE (R)** Cross crevasses on ladders. **LEFT** Everest's weather dictates your fate.

ARMCHAIR

❋ ***Into Thin Air*** (Jon Krakauer) The journalist/mountaineer recounts his first-hand experience of the disastrous 1996 expedition.

❋ ***Everest: A Trekker's Guide*** (Cicerone) A manual of more manageable routes in the region.

❋ ***Climbing Everest: George Mallory's Writings on Mountaineering*** (edited by Peter Gillman) Mallory's musings, pulled together from disparate archives, culminate in his attempts to be first up Everest,

which ultimately cost him his life.

❋ ***Dark Summit: The Extraordinary True Story of Everest's Most Controversial Season*** (Nick Heil) The year 2006 was a bad one on Everest: Heil investigates what went wrong, and whether too much is being sacrificed in pursuit of mountaineering's greatest prize.

❋ ***Everest: Beyond the Limit*** (2006–09) The three Discovery Channel reality series, available on DVD, follow climbers on the mountain.

TAKE THE THREE PEAKS CHALLENGE

BEN NEVIS, SCAFELL PIKE AND SNOWDON – THE HIGHEST PEAKS IN SCOTLAND, ENGLAND AND WALES – ARE ALL LOVED AS MUCH FOR THEIR WILD BEAUTY AS FOR THEIR ALTITUDE. TACKLING ALL THREE IN ONE EPIC DAY IS A CHALLENGING WAY TO SEE SOME OF THE VERY BEST OF BRITAIN.

150

Biggest, as we all know, is not always best. So why tackle a challenge that involves tramping up the three highest mountains of Scotland, England and Wales in under 24 hours? As George Mallory might have answered: 'Because it's there...and there...and there.' But while it's true that some of the 30,000 or so three-peakers who hurtle across Britain every year do so merely to say that they've bagged it, many are partaking in organised charity events.

It shouldn't be assumed that, just because so many people undertake the challenge, it's easy. In global terms these peaks aren't huge, but neither are they simple strolls. Bank on at least four hours up and back for Scafell Pike and Snowdon, and five hours for Ben Nevis (1344m), the UK's highest peak.

Then there's the driving. Expect to cover about 800km in total, a good chunk of it at night. And of course the weather is notoriously fickle, especially up high; snow often lingers into summer on the peak of Ben Nevis, where temperatures can be almost 10°C colder than at the base of the mountain.

Not only is a good degree of fitness a prerequisite, but map-reading skills are important, particularly – again – on Ben Nevis, where navigating the descent from the summit can be tricky.

But the payoff isn't just in tales told in the pub at the end. These mountains are all truly magnificent, with wonderful walking. Snowdon lords it over Wales' northwest, where vistas sweep over the sharp ridges and verdant valleys towards the coast. The ascent of Scafell Pike from Wasdale Head takes hikers into the heart of the Lake District, with dramatic views across the iconic waters from the pinnacle peak. And Ben Nevis is truly the roof of Britain, affording panoramas of Scotland's west coast and the islands of Mull, Rum and Skye.

ESSENTIAL EXPERIENCES

* **Adding a stone to the cairn atop the summit of Britain, Ben Nevis.**

* Swivelling on your heels to absorb a 360-degree panorama of Scotland's coast, islands, glens and peaks.

* **Drinking in the views of the lakes from the summit of Scafell Pike: Derwent Water, Windermere and Buttermere.**

* Watching buzzards soar overhead as you tread the stone slabs of the Pyg Track on your final ascent up Snowdon.

* **Settling into the bar at the Pen-y-Gwyrd Hotel at the end of the challenge, sipping a well-earned pint among climbing mementos left by Everest-topper Edmund Hillary.**

DISTANCE 800KM DRIVING, 42KM WALKING | **ELEVATION** 1344M (BEN NEVIS) | **LOCATION** SCOTLAND, ENGLAND AND WALES
IDEAL TIME COMMITMENT 24 HOURS | **BEST TIME OF YEAR** MAY TO SEPTEMBER | **ESSENTIAL TIP** TAKE THE MOST ACCURATE MAPS YOU CAN FIND – AND KNOW HOW TO USE THEM

ALFRED WAINWRIGHT

The writer and illustrator 'AW' became irrevocably linked with his beloved Lake District on publication of his seven-volume Pictorial Guide to the Lakeland Fells. Describing 214 of the Cumbrian fells, these books – first printed between 1955 and 1966 as replicas of his painstakingly hand-lettered and illustrated manuscripts – were both charming and practical, quickly becoming the quintessential walking guides to the region. He was also an innovator, devising the 308km Coast to Coast Path, and in the 1980s became known as a television personality, recognisable for his ever-present pipe and flat cap. AW died in 1991, aged 84.

SUSTAINABLE SUMMITS

Concerns have been raised about the environmental impact of the Three Peaks challenge, particularly the results of very large groups flooding these wild places. Aside from the carbon footprint of so many individuals driving hundreds of kilometres in 24 hours, paths suffer from heavy erosion, and local businesses receive little benefit thanks to the dash-in dash-out nature of the endeavour. Consider avoiding busy weekends, car sharing, keeping group numbers small and extending the challenge over a few days, staying overnight near each of the peaks. Also stick to paths, carry out litter (that includes the empty foil wrappers of energy gels) and don't speed while driving between mountains.

■ THE ADVENTURE UNFOLDS

It seems topsy-turvy to begin your trek by taking off your walking boots, but that is the rule: your 24-hour adventure only counts if you dip your toes in the sea at either end. So (gingerly, reluctantly) your bare foot is dunked in the waters of Loch Linnhe at Fort William – and the clock starts ticking.

Dash to car. Drive to Ionad Nibheis Visitor Centre. Leap from car, stop for photo alongside 'Ben Nevis Path' signpost, gaze up at mountain. Despite the rush, you pause and memory-mark the key spots: catching your first glimpse of the waters of Lochan Meall an t-Suidhe; crossing Red Burn; looking back over the mountain's shoulder to Fort William; topping the zigzag path onto the rounded summit; and touching the cairn that marks the very top of Britain.

A quick look around – hurry, the light's fading – and down. Into the car. Slumber fitfully during the drive to Seathwaite. Rub eyes, tighten bootlaces, turn on head torch, start again. Scafell Pike and its craggy companions reveal themselves as dawn breaks; you're hiking through a broken world, among battalions of shattered rocks. The final haul to the summit is dramatic, unforgiving and – fortunately, given your weariness – inspiring. Time for a quick 360° pirouette to absorb the panoramic views before the descent.

Now you're on the last leg – and, you fear, your last legs. Fortunately, Snowdon, with its well-trodden trails, is a gentler test; the stone slabs of the Pyg Track ease you into the climb before the tightly winding final ascent past the Fingerstone and to the summit. Run down, knees creaking, to the car and the final scoot to Caernarfon to baptise those sore toes. Mission accomplished.

■ MAKING IT HAPPEN

Recruit a dedicated driver (ideally two) so that hikers can rest between peaks, and allow at least 10 hours total for the 800km on the road between ascents. In summer, with careful timing, it's possible to achieve most of the walking in daylight. Set off up Ben Nevis around 5pm, reach Wasdale Head or Seathwaite and start up Scafell Pike just before dawn the following day, and tackle Snowdon just after midday to finish late afternoon.

■ AN ALTERNATIVE CHALLENGE

A more local alternative to the 'National' challenge is its Yorkshire namesake, tackling the three highest peaks in the Dales: Whernside (736m), Ingleborough (723m) and Pen-y-ghent (694m). A circular route touching the summits of all three is a classic walk, first completed in 1887. The traditional start and end point is the Pen-y-ghent Café at Horton in Ribblesdale, which operates a clocking-out and -in system, partly for safety, but also so hikers who complete the circuit in under 12 hours can join the Three Peaks of Yorkshire Club.

153

OPENING SPREAD Looking along Wastwater towards Scafell Pike in the Lake District National Park. ABOVE Numerous routes exist for ascending Ben Nevis, from basic hikes to highly challenging rock and ice climbs. LEFT Scaling Snowdon in winter requires experience and warm, windproof kit.

VISITBRITAIN | BRITAINONVIEW | GETTY

ARMCHAIR

* *A Pictorial Guide to the Lakeland Fells: The Southern Fells* (Alfred Wainwright) The fourth in Wainwright's beautiful hand-lettered, meticulously illustrated love letters to his cherished Lake District.

* *The First Fifty: Munro-Bagging Without a Beard* (Muriel Gray) The notable arts broadcaster, renowned in the 1980s for her spiky wit (and hair), reveals a flair for humorous, inspiring descriptions of hill-walking in her native Scotland.

* *The National 3 Peaks* (Brian Smailes) This compact but comprehensive guide to the challenge includes tips on equipment, timings and routes.

* *The National 3 Peaks: Taking Up the Challenge* (Steve Williams) A more personal tome, this practical guide also describes the author's experiences and provides suggestions for planning and training.

SUMMIT MT KILIMANJARO

WELCOME TO THE ROOF OF AFRICA. IT'S NOT OFTEN MERE MORTALS GET TO RISE ABOVE THE CLOUDS AND STARE DOWN ON AN ENTIRE CONTINENT. BUT THIS 5895M PEAK OFFERS THAT CHANCE, VIA A MAGNIFICENTLY MANAGEABLE CHALLENGE – BUT DON'T UNDERESTIMATE TANZANIA'S MIGHTY MOUNTAIN.

154

Snow on the equator? When Swiss-German missionary Johannes Rebmann first reported such things in 1849, scholars scoffed; the Royal Geographical Society's president declared it 'a great degree incredulous'. But Kilimanjaro, the highest peak in Africa, sitting just 3 degrees south of the earth's sunbaked middle, was then (and still is...just) topped by a yarmulke of white.

Rebmann was the first European to see Kili, but he didn't scale it. Tanzania's dormant 5895m volcano remained unclimbed until 1889, when German geology professor Hans Meyer mastered its ice fields, inclement climes and hostile tribes to reach the summit of Kibo, the loftiest of the mountain's three cones.

Many, many hikers have since followed in Meyer's footsteps. It's just too tempting. Unlike bigger peaks that are near-hidden amid towering ranges, Kilimanjaro stands alone, a Rift Valley beacon calling out to be climbed. From 58 souls in 1939, to 1000 in 1965 and 28,000 in 2003, it's reckoned that now over 40,000 people a year attempt this climb. 'Attempt' being apposite: many of those who embark on one of the five main routes up the mountain do not summit.

It's not lack of fitness that prevents a successful bid for Uhuru Peak – Kili's highest point. Couch potatoes should not apply, but you don't need to be Superman, nor do you need technical climbing skills. No, it's usually altitude that scuppers hikers here, insufficient acclimatisation causing dizziness, headaches, nausea – and worse. Most trekkers feel some symptoms; some are forced to descend.

And that's how it should be. People haven't completely tamed this mountain and the popularity of the hike doesn't make it any easier. This is a slog – albeit a spectacular life-changing one – up to almost 6000m, where rain, snow, freezing temperatures, unforgiving slopes and breath-stealing altitudes don't care how many trekkers have passed by before. Forget lions – in Africa, Kili is king.

ESSENTIAL EXPERIENCES

❋ **Looking out for red-hot poker plants and colobus monkeys as you ascend through the mountain's lush lower rainforest zone.**

❋ Devouring porridge, pasta and popcorn in large quantities, to power you up the mountain – generally served in dining tents accompanied by hot chocolate and Swahili singing.

❋ **Brushing your teeth alfresco, under the most incredible sweep of stars – light pollution: zero.**

❋ Standing on the roof of Africa, next to that iconic wooden sign, not knowing whether you'll laugh, cry or vomit, but loving it anyway.

❋ **Raising a chilled Kilimanjaro beer with your trek-mates at the trip's (hopefully successful) end.**

ELEVATION 5895M | **LOCATION** NORTHERN TANZANIA | **IDEAL TIME COMMITMENT** SIX TO EIGHT DAYS | **BEST TIME OF YEAR** JANUARY TO MARCH, JUNE TO OCTOBER | **ESSENTIAL TIP** WALK *POLÉ POLÉ* (SLOWLY SLOWLY)

WILD KILI

There are tales of leopards stalking Kilimanjaro. But though the peak sits near some of Africa's top safari spots (Amboseli, Ngorongoro), you'll see few big animals. The lower slopes are leafy with redwoods, eucalypts and podocarps, and coloured with gladioli and red-hot pokers. Elephants are present, but sightings are rare; you're more likely to spy colobus monkeys, plus Hartlaub's turaco, malachite sunbirds and other avifauna. As you climb, the landscape turns to heath, where the most striking survivors are lobelia plants – phallic and cabbage-shaped. Above 4000m, a few everlastings dot the moonscape; over 5000m, it's lichen, glaciers and little else.

■ THE ADVENTURE UNFOLDS

It's like someone hit you with a mallet. And your head was throbbing anyway, thanks to the stingy oxygen levels up here. The words gasped by a bloke with an altimeter, from somewhere in the abyss behind, register with a thunk: 'We're at 4900m.' Which means over 1000 more to go. It's 2am, and you've already been climbing – well, shuffling – for two hours. Alas, Uhuru Peak is still a good five hours hence. You focus on the circle being beamed by your head torch, rally your weary brain and take another fatigued step forwards.

You've been hiking up this mountain for four or five days now: you've been rained on in the forest zone, sunburned on the higher moon-like slopes; you've endured rancid long-drop loos and bouts of flatulence, an embarrassing side effect of adapting to altitude. You're nauseous, shivering and rather smelly. But, regardless, you've been having the time of your life. Until now.

Summit night – a vertical mile up from last night's camp – is not about enjoyment. It's about getting to your prize. The lower flanks are where you saw monkeys, admired views, sang Swahili songs, enjoyed the ride. Now you're digging in.

Then you see it, just ahead: the wooden sign, the magic numbers – 5895m. Your body is beat, but you've made it! All that walking *polé polé* (slowly slowly), like your guide advised; all that gorging on pasta (and still losing half a stone); all that grit and determination, mean success is yours. You're grinning like you've won Olympic gold. Or that could be altitude delirium setting in...

Either way, it's overwhelming. The towering glaciers – much receded, still staggering – start to sparkle as the sun breaks over the horizon, heralding a new day. And what a day: the one when you stood on top of Africa.

ARMCHAIR

* *The Shadow of Kilimanjaro: On Foot Across Africa* (Rick Ridgeway) Worthwhile travelogue following the author's walk from Kili's summit to the Kenyan coast.

* *Kilimanjaro: The Trekking Guide to Africa's Highest Mountain* (Henry Stedman) Excellent Trailblazer guide to the mountain, with practical info on the routes, plus history, health, and flora and fauna.

* *The Snows of Kilimanjaro* (Ernest Hemingway) Haunting short story involving tragedy on the mountain's slopes. It was made into a film in 1952, starring Gregory Peck.

* *Kilimanjaro: Mountain at the Crossroads* (Audrey Salkeld) Beautiful book of the 2002 IMAX film, packed with breathtaking shots and fascinating facts.

* *Swahili Phrasebook* (Lonely Planet) Pocket-size guide to the local language, full of sentences to ease trekker–porter conversation.

PORTER POWER

No trekker would manage Kilimanjaro without their local support team: 10 hikers might have 30-plus staff, including a lead guide, assistant guides, cooks and porters – superheroes who carry tables, tents, gas canisters and more up the mountain so you don't have to. It's a tough way to make a shilling, and they're often exploited. The Kilimanjaro Porters Assistance Project (KPAP) aims to stop this. Its best-practice guidelines include: limiting porter loads to 25kg; instigating transparent tipping procedures, so porters aren't short-changed; and supplying porters with adequate clothing, shelter and food. If you suspect your porters are ill-treated, notify KPAP.

■ MAKING IT HAPPEN

Kilimanjaro International Airport is between
Moshi (42km) and Arusha (50km). Tour
companies in both towns offer trips up the
mountain. The most popular routes are Marangu
(hutted) and Machame (camping); other options
are Rongai, Shira/Lemosho and Umbwe (all
camping). Alternatively, book a trip via an
operator in your home country; many combine
Kili climbs with a Serengeti safari or beach time
on Zanzibar. Independent climbing is not allowed.

■ AN ALTERNATIVE CHALLENGE

Mt Kenya, Africa's second-highest peak, is an
impressive 5199m – though it's often overlooked,
lacking quite the same bragging rights of
nearby Kilimanjaro.

But Kenya is a fine climb. Of its three peaks,
4985m Point Lenana is conquerable in a three-day
hike, easier than Kili but a challenge nonetheless.
The route rises through wildlife-rich national
park; the lower slopes are rife with elephants and
ungulates, while the eerie upper realm is home
to rock hyraxes, cartoonish senecio plants and
few other hikers. Mt Kenya's two more fearsome
summits – spiky Batian (5199m) and Nelion
(5188m) – are for technical climbers only.

R TYLER GROSS | AURORA OPEN | CORBIS

OPENING SPREAD In Mt Kilimanjaro's shadow: Masai tribespeople in Ngorongoro, Kenya.
ABOVE Make an early start to see dawn at the summit. There are six different routes up,
including the Northern Circuit traverse. **BELOW** The view of Mt Mawenzi from Stella Point.

CLIMB VOLCANOES IN KAMCHATKA

MYSTERIOUS. PRISTINE. REMOTE. TRAVEL BEYOND SIBERIA TO THIS PRIMEVAL LAND OF FIRE AND ICE, WHERE BEARS ROAM FREELY, THE STREAMS ARE FULL OF SALMON AND THERE'S A *SOPKA* (VOLCANO) FOR EVERY COMFORT ZONE. JUST GETTING THERE IS AN ADVENTURE.

158

Sitting on the Pacific Ring of Fire, the Kamchatka Peninsula, in remote far eastern Russia, boasts one of the greatest collections of active volcanoes on earth. Geysers, birch forests, river valleys and tundra riddle this primordial, oft snow-covered landscape that in summer curiously mottles blue and white. Nature here is vibrant and unfettered, wildlife varied and abundant, and the environment so fragile that the peninsula boasts six biodiversity hot spots, five Unesco World Heritage Sites, and more brown bears than anywhere else.

Part of Russia since invading Cossacks suppressed the indigenous Koryak, Chukcha and Itelmen tribes in the early 18th century, cruelty, tragedy and secrecy dog Kamchatka's history. Closed during the Cold War, it's only been possible to visit since the collapse of communism. Infrastructure is low-key and haphazard, though this is gradually changing as Kamchatka's profile is rising, especially among Russians after Vladimir Putin waxed lyrical on its beauty.

Volcanoes range from modest single-day climbs simply requiring reasonable fitness, to serious multiweek expeditions where mountaineering skills are mandatory. With minimal public transport, Kamchatka isn't ideal for independent travel, and most time-poor visitors take a packaged trip from a local tour operator, which commonly include helicopter access, guides, rudimentary accommodation, and other activities such as rafting, horse riding, cross-country skiing or a visit to the famous Valley of the Geysers. Such trips can be almost prohibitively expensive and their ecological footprint sometimes questionable. By avoiding helicopters, engaging local guides (or going alone), staying in local homes and using the few public buses (and your legs and thumbs), you can minimise costs and your environmental impact. Several of the easiest, yet still stunning climbs are quite close to the capital Petropavlovsk-Kamchatsky (PP) and are accessible using public transport.

ESSENTIAL EXPERIENCES

✳ **Bagging your first volcano and gawking awestruck at the incredible views of a landscape unlike any other in the world.**

✳ Peering deep into a caldera, while trying not to gag on the noxious sulphur fumes.

✳ **Wrapping your taste buds around that mouth-watering hunk of salmon you just haggled over in the market with your newly acquired knowledge of Russian numbers.**

✳ Being humbled by the amazing hospitality of the locals as they share their food, homes and cars – but watch out for that vodka!

✳ **Soaking away your climbing aches in one of the plentiful hot pools.**

ELEVATION 900M TO 4688M | **LOCATION** KAMCHATKA PENINSULA, RUSSIAN FAR EAST | **IDEAL TIME COMMITMENT** TWO TO THREE WEEKS | **BEST TIME OF YEAR** JUNE TO SEPTEMBER | **ESSENTIAL TIP** BRING A HEAD NET FOR THE INSECTS!

FURTHER NORTH

The Klyuchi group of volcanoes (Klyuchevskaya 4688m, Kamen 4580m, Ushkovsky 3943m and Tolbachik 3682m) contains the highest volcanoes on the peninsula, as well as some of the most active (Tolbachik). They should only be attempted by those with strong mountaineering skills; climbers have died here. Bus to Kozyrevsk or Klyuchi village, then arrange private transport; do not try to walk through the bear-infested woods. Alternatively, get a chopper to base camp. For a more relaxing time, hop on a bus to the laid-back Eveni town of Esso, where hot springs, homestays, horse riding and rafting are on offer.

KRONOTSKY NATURE RESERVE

Kronotsky Nature Reserve is one of the peninsula's biodiversity hot spots and Unesco sites. It includes the perfectly symmetrical cone of Kronotskaya Sopka (3527m), the otherworldly geothermal Uzon Caldera and the spectacular Valley of the Geysers. The latter, only discovered in 1941, is arguably second only to Yellowstone National Park for geothermal activity. The environment here is particularly fragile, and in 2007 a mudslide buried a large chunk of the valley. Many endangered species find refuge in the reserve, and brown bears (right) are found here in large densities. Unless you're a scientist, you can only visit on an expensive helicopter day trip.

THE ADVENTURE UNFOLDS

The bus drops you at '25km', an intersection on the Yelizovo–PP road, and you applaud your resilience for not giving into the taxi mafia. The rough road to Avachinskaya and Koryakskaya base camp (PP's 'backyard volcanoes') heads northeast, through fields, dachas, veggie patches and taiga before turning into a dry creek bed. After 22km in the July heat, you're regretting vetoing that taxi.

Base camp, a motley collection of shipping containers and portables, sits in the saddle between the two peaks. You search for a quiet camp site away from the crowds, near some snowmelt. The mosquitoes are insane, but you have a head net and industrial-strength DEET. Someone hassles you for your permit and/or money. Take a deep breath, sit down, smile. Your smoked salmon from the PP market, washed down with vodka, is fantastic. Avachinskaya (2741m) turns molten gold in the setting sun and you're humbled by the beautiful, volcano-studded vista back towards the coast. Already the struggle is worth it.

Early the next day, on Avachi's ridge, a long, steep plod leads to a plateau with permanent snow patches. Traverse this for fantastic views of Koryakskaya (3456m, a serious climb) and the Nalychevo River valley (a two-day hike from base camp, with thermal springs and volcanoes). Next, the summit cone beckons, and it's two hours of very steep, loose scree before you finally top out, six hours from camp. Kamchatka lies spread out beneath you like a patchwork quilt. You're awestruck and elated – until you start choking on the sulphur fumes from the caldera. Quick photos, then a boot-skiing descent through the scree has you back in base camp in half the time.

MAKING IT HAPPEN

June–September is the best time to visit, but some volcanoes are climbable year-round with the right gear. In Petropavlovsk-Kamchatsky (PP), the only real town on the peninsula, you'll find supplies, maps, permits, outdoor equipment, transport, tour companies and accommodation. Khabarovsk offers the best air connections to PP. Bring camping gear, a petrol-burning stove and vats of insect repellent.

AN ALTERNATIVE CHALLENGE

The Mutnovsky group of volcanoes (Mutnovskaya 2322m, Gorely 1892m and Vilyuchinskaya 2173m) across Avacha Bay from PP are easier to climb than the Avachi group, due to their lower altitude; they can attract a lot of snow, though, and avalanches can occur. Popular with tour groups, they are accessible independently if you have the time. Catch a bus to Termalnyj (via Paratunka), then walk or hitch up the road to the geothermal power station. You can camp in the valley behind the power station or at the individual base camps. Look out for the Malaya Valley of Geysers.

SERGEY GORSHKOV | GETTY

SERGEY GORSHKOV | GETTY

OPENING SPREAD A 2010 eruption of Klyuchevskaya Sopka stratovolcano, the highest in Asia at 4750m, was visible from the space shuttle Endeavour. **ABOVE** Share Kamchatka with brown bears and Steller's sea eagles. **LEFT** Climbing Avachinskaya Sopka, one of Kamchatka's most active volcanoes.

ARMCHAIR

* **The Russian Far East** (Josh Newell) Reference guide highlighting development and conservation issues.

* **Kamchatka: Land of Fire and Ice** (Vadim Gippenreiter) Exceptional images from the veteran Russian photographer, focusing on volcanic eruptions and premudslide Valley of the Geysers.

* **The Bear Man of Kamchatka** (2006) Scenically rich BBC doco on Charlie Russell, self-appointed brown bear saviour.

* **Trekking in Russia & Central Asia** (Frith Maier) Classic guide for Russian wilderness adventures, with a short chapter on Kamchatka, but don't expect step-by-step directions.

* **Kamchatka: A Journal and Guide to Russia's Land of Ice and Fire** (Diana Gleadhill) Two 'mature' Irish women on the loose in this quirky part travelogue, part guidebook.

SCALE VIE FERRATE IN THE DOLOMITES

THE THRILLING *VIE FERRATE* ('IRON ROADS') ARE ANTLIKE TRAILS ACROSS ITALY'S ROCKY DOLOMITES. THESE NETWORKS DATE FROM WWI, WHEN THE MOUNTAINS WERE THE SETTING FOR FURIOUS BATTLES. TODAY, THE CABLES AND STAIRWAYS PROVIDE EXHILARATING PROTECTED CLIMBING.

162

The Dolomites are not surrounded by gentle foothills. These vertical limestone stacks appear to thrust themselves directly out of the ground. This is savage terrain: great toothy crags rear up into the sky, their exposed cliffs, jagged gullies and tiny ledges teetering above yawning chasms of ragged rock. Just imagine trying to cross these mountains amid the combat of WWI, when the Dolomites were the scene of heavy fighting between the Austro-Hungarians and the Italians.

To ease their way across the terrain, soldiers on both sides built tiny spidery supports into the rock face. Consisting of ladders, cables and bridges, they formed a fine web of *vie ferrate*. Some of these iron roads still exist today, monuments to the hardship suffered here, with memorial plaques punctuating the routes. Others have been renewed, extended and given an entirely new life as an incredible way to climb across this challenging and thrilling landscape – allowing you to clamber across otherwise unthinkable routes.

Although a good level of fitness is required, there is a great variety of difficulty on these routes. There are easier sections to suit less-experienced climbers, and some which only the extremely proficient should attempt.

Other than on broader, unprotected sections along the routes, the basic safety rule is that you use the belaying technique, climbing with two lines. This means that when you move onto a new section, you unclip one line at a time and are never completely unsecured. You'll need a head for heights, though, as you inch along narrow ledges with seemingly nothing but cloud swirling beneath you.

Crossing this out-of-this-world landscape is an incredible experience, where pinnacles and sheer walls alternate with lush green valleys of forests, meadows, canyons and thundering waterfalls.

ESSENTIAL EXPERIENCES

* **Creeping your way across the vast vertical stacks of the Dolomites.**

* Seeing the relics of WWI, including the original settings of the *vie ferrate*, reminders of the fierce battles fought in this mountainous landscape.

* **Managing to climb places that would be technically far out of your reach without the assistance of the iron roads.**

* Glimpsing the craggy bared teeth of the mountains through the mist.

* **Ending your day at a remote mountain refuge, and enjoying a well-earned Italian meal washed down with wine.**

* Waking up to watch the dawn over the Dolomites.

ELEVATION 2800M | **LOCATION** BOCCHETTE CENTRALE, BRENTA DOLOMITES, ITALY | **IDEAL TIME COMMITMENT** ONE WEEK
BEST TIME OF YEAR JUNE TO OCTOBER | **ESSENTIAL TIP** YOU'LL NEED A HELMET, GLOVES, HARNESS, ROPE AND BELAYS

The Brenta Dolomites lie within the protected area of the Parco Naturale Adamello Brenta, which covers 620 sq km and encompasses more than 50 lakes. The park altitude ranges from a lowly 400m to the 3500m of Cima Presanella, and thus alternates woodlands, pastures, grasslands, rocky areas and glaciers. It's home to a few brown bears, ibexes, red deer, marmots, chamois and 82 bird species, as well as 1200 different types of mountain flowers. To the west is the imposing Adamello-Presanella mountain group (Trentino section), while the pinnacles and towers of Dolomiti di Brenta lie to the east.

THE HIGH-ALTITUDE WAR

For three years during WWI, the Italian and Austro-Hungarian armies fought ferocious battles in these mountains. The armies not only constructed the first *vie ferrate*, but dug a network of tunnels and trenches to try to surprise and overtake the enemy; you can still see these at Lagazuoi and Castelletto della Tofana. Natural dangers were even more fearsome than snipers; thousands died from hypothermia or exposure, and around 50,000 from avalanches. In late 1917, the Italian army withdrew to the River Piave, where the Battle of Caporetto marked the beginning of the end for the Italian forces.

■ THE ADVENTURE UNFOLDS

Via Bocchette ('the Way of the Passes') is the most famous of the iron roads of the Dolomites. One of the first trails to be developed, it offers an experience closer to real mountaineering, with several sections that are completely exposed.

You're heading for the more approachable part of the route, the Bocchette Centrale section. The route snakes across the Brenta Dolomites, a jagged and imposing group that's slightly separate from the main range. The approach is via a wide forested path, which gradually climbs above the tree line. You pass the grey-stone refuge, Rifugio Alimonta, a climbers' guesthouse that sits, wildly remote, just below the start of the *via ferrata* (*vie ferrate* is plural).

At the top of the frozen splurge of the ancient Sfulmini Glacier, the Bocca di Molveno section of the Bocchette Centrale route starts. Fixing yourself onto the first of many metal sections, you begin to climb a long ladder that clings to a bulbous, vertical rock face. At the top, you clip yourself in again, and cross a thrillingly exposed narrow ridge, from where there are brilliant views across a forest of sculpted peaks. From here, you carefully edge along a profoundly dangerous lip of rock. Below is a vertical drop; above is a vertical wall. Your safety depends on your connection to the fine wire that runs along the cliff face. In places this looks a little rusty, but mostly it's in good repair; a reassuring thought, as you are trusting it with your life. You are also glad of your gloves, which protect your hands against the sharp rock and fine, cold wires.

The combination of ledges and ladders on the Bocchette Centrale makes it a perfectly manageable challenge, offering mist-swathed views of a terrifying moonscape and routes over dizzying pinnacles that are usually only accessible to world-class climbers.

■ MAKING IT HAPPEN

Trento is the best base for the Brenta Dolomites, and is well connected by train to Bologna, Verona and Venice. The tourist office will help with accommodation, and you can buy or hire the necessary equipment from local shops. To find guides, maps and information on refuges, head to the visitors centre at Sant'Antonio di Mavignola or the park headquarters in Strembo.

■ DETOUR

To learn about the war in the mountains, visit the open-air Museum of the Lagazuoi, Passo Falzarego. During WWI, Italian and Austro-Hungarian soldiers dug shelters into the rock of Mt Lagazuoi, turning the mountain into a natural fortress. It's fascinating to see the restored tunnels, trenches, machine-gun posts and rock-hewn turrets. Entry to the museum is free. It can be reached via a steep climb or by the Lagazuoi cable car.

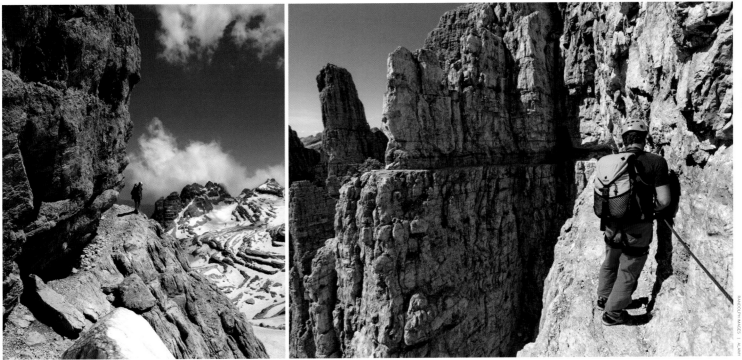

OPENING SPREAD By clipping into steel cables, amateur climbers tackle the Brigata Tridentina route. **ABOVE (L)** On the Sentiero Alfredo Benini. **ABOVE (R)** You'll need a head for heights and a helmet on the Bocchette Centrale. **LEFT** Walking to the Brentei refuge in Parco Naturale Adamello Brenta.

ARMCHAIR

* ***Via Ferratas of the Italian Dolomites*** (Graham Fletcher & John Smith) Volumes 1 and 2 are essential reading for anyone wanting to attempt the *vie ferrate*, with gradings for all routes taking into account level of exposure and technical difficulty.

* ***Shorter Walks in the Dolomites*** (Gillian Price) A selection of shorter walks in the Dolomites, if you don't fancy belaying yourself to the rock.

* ***The White War: Life and Death on the Italian Front 1915–1919*** (Mark Thompson) Fascinating account of the fierce fighting in the Italian Dolomites, and how the battles paved the way for the rise of Mussolini.

* ***Asiago Plateau: Battle in the Woods and Clouds – Italy 1918*** (Francis MacKay) Provides a sense of how it was to fight in this beautiful mountainscape.

CLIMB ARGENTINA'S MT ACONCAGUA

QUITE SIMPLY, THIS IS THE HIGHEST HIKE IN THE WORLD. ARGENTINA'S 6962M MOUNTAIN, LOFTIER THAN ANY SUMMIT OUTSIDE THE HIMALAYAS, IS IMMENSE BUT CONQUERABLE BY THOSE WITHOUT TECHNICAL CLIMBING SKILLS – IF YOU'RE UP FOR THE BREATHLESS BUT ULTIMATE CHALLENGE…

166

The Himalayas are greedy. Every 7000m-plus peak on the planet lies in this lofty range or in the neighbouring Karakorams. Just. Aconcagua – at 6962m, the highest mountain outside Asia – comes tantalisingly close. (Indeed, the idea of erecting a 40m-high tower on the summit was once proposed.)

But Aconcagua (whose name is possibly derived from the Quechuan *ancho cahuac*, or 'white sentinel'), remains an intimidating prospect. Its air-depleting altitude, and the katabatic winds that lash and freeze the slopes, kept climbers from the top until 1897, when Swiss mountaineer Matthias Zurbriggen became the first to gaze down on all of the Americas. After a bit of trial and error, Zurbriggen ascended Aconcagua via the Horcones Valley. Today, most would-be summiteers follow his pioneering footsteps, along what has become known as the Normal Route. And several do indeed follow: around 3700 people a year attempt the mountain, which, despite its gargantuan proportions, is not considered a 'proper' climb but is essentially a really tough walk.

Unbelievably, Aconcagua requires no real technical skill. Both the Normal and slightly longer and less-used Vacas Valley routes can be attempted by trekkers – albeit physically and mentally super-fit ones. The final push may entail some crunching in crampons, but it's the extreme altitude, which makes every movement require momentous effort, that provides the biggest challenge.

There are prettier peaks. Much of the land here is bleak and dusty, the air is thin, those winds unremitting. But the prospect of such a trophy – the world's highest trekking peak! – is, for many, worth the cons. And if you do make it to the top (it's purported that only around 30% of hopefuls do), and when you're standing – or staggering – around the summit, looking across an ocean of other icy crests to the Pacific Ocean glittering in the distance, you'll feel on top of (most of) the world.

ESSENTIAL EXPERIENCES

❋ **Hiking from Confluencia camp and back, to acclimatise – and to glimpse Aconcagua's terrifying south face.**

❋ Staring out from Nido de Cóndores to the central valleys, endless mountains and the twin peaks of Aconcagua.

❋ **Looking out for herds of wild guanacos on the Vacas Valley route.**

❋ Walking amid the mountain's *penitentes*, spikes of snow sculpted by the chill winds – like walking through oversized sharks' teeth.

❋ **Mastering La Canaleta, the infamously punishing 300m-high scree slope that must be faced at 6500m.**

❋ Standing atop the highest mountain outside of the Himalayas, with views across glaciers and mountains to the Pacific Ocean.

ELEVATION 6962M | **LOCATION** MENDOZA PROVINCE, ARGENTINA | **IDEAL TIME COMMITMENT** THREE WEEKS | **BEST TIME OF YEAR** DECEMBER TO FEBRUARY | **ESSENTIAL TIP** ACCLIMATISE, ACCLIMATISE, ACCLIMATISE

MAN & MULE

Aconcagua's barren slopes are not conducive to wildlife – but one creature is found here in abundance. Hardy mules transport supplies up and down the mountain, capable of carrying 60kg loads (and weary trekkers if necessary). Their *arrieros* (drivers) are an icon of rural Argentina, hardworking and loyal men who each handle three mules, and guard them fiercely; learn a little Spanish and you'll have some interesting conversations. Every *arriero* carries a satchel containing his maté-making kit: a pouch of yerba maté tea leaves, a drinking vessel or gourd, and a *bombilla* (metal filter straw) through which to sip.

THE ADVENTURE UNFOLDS

Up. Down. Up again. Down again. Such is life on Aconcagua. Some record-seeking madman might have made the summit and back in a dumbfounding 20 hours but you'll be hiking on this Andean behemoth for almost 20 days.

Acclimatisation – trudging higher, sleeping lower – is essential if you're to reach the top. Even so, the escapade is perilously oxygen-parched from the start, with Confluencia, the very first camp, teetering at 3390m. At the medical centre at Plaza de Mulas (4250m), you've had your own oxygen levels tested – so far so good. You've researched the symptoms of acute mountain sickness: fatigue, headaches, disorientation. Fatigue seems inevitable, but you plan to climb slowly and eat like a mule to avoid the onset of the other symptoms. That way you have the best shot of making it to the top, wild weather willing.

You make friends fast on such a gruelling shared mission. You've tried your pidgin Spanish on the muleteers and sipped their maté tea. You've embarked on day hikes with your trek-mates, to see pinnacles of ice and terrifying views of your distant goal. As the days pass, anticipation grows: now you just want to get there.

Eventually you bed down in Camp Berlin, the Normal Route's final pause before the summit. It sits at 5850m, almost the height of Kilimanjaro. You try to sleep, praying it doesn't snow...

The next day's a blur. Setting off in the chill predawn, you huff and stumble up and up. On the callous scree of La Canaleta, two steps forward mean one step back. Your crampons scrape the ice; nausea scrapes your throat.

Finally, after 10 hours, you've reached the North Peak – Aconcagua's highest point. The understated cross that marks the spot is dressed up like Christmas, bedangled by the flags and

ARMCHAIR

※ **Aconcagua: Summit of South America** (Harry Kikstra) A practical guide to getting up the mountain, including planning tips and packing lists, historical background and route info.

※ **Altitude Illness: Prevention and Treatment** (Stephen Bezruchka) Invaluable mountaineers' handbook, containing info on how to avoid AMS (acute mountain sickness), and how to spot the symptoms.

※ **Seven Years in Tibet** (1997) Though Brad Pitt was supposedly hiking in the Himalayas, many of the mountain scenes in this Hollywood epic were filmed amid the peaks of Mendoza.

※ **Aconcagua: The Invention of Mountaineering on America's Highest Peak** (Joy Logan) Easily readable examination of the social and cultural history of Aconcagua.

※ **In Patagonia** (Bruce Chatwin) Travel classic; pretty much required reading for anyone travelling anywhere in Argentina.

MUMMIES ON THE MOUNTAIN

The first confirmed ascent of Aconcagua may have been in 1897, but the Inca at least part-scaled these mighty mountains much earlier, climbing them to make sacrifices to their gods back in the 15th and 16th centuries. In 1985 a well-preserved 500-year-old mummy was discovered at 5200m, on the southwest ridge of Cerro Pyramidal, one of Aconcagua's surrounding peaks. The mummy – a young boy, believed to be aged around seven – was wrapped in folds of cloth, the outer layer embroidered with yellow feathers. Buried with him were sandals, Inca statuettes and some bags of cooked beans.

bandanas of those who've been before. You add your own 'bauble' – proof, if only until the wind whisks it off into oblivion, that you mastered this mighty mountain.

■ MAKING IT HAPPEN

It's permissible to climb Aconcagua without a guide; you could just hire mules to carry your kit (or carry it yourself). However, you must be an experienced mountaineer to attempt a 6962m peak alone. All climbers need a permit, available from the Aconcagua National Park Office in Mendoza. If you book an organised trek (either with a local company or back home), they will most likely arrange this, as well as the other logistics.

■ DETOUR

Raise a glass of rich red to your high-altitude achievements in Mendoza Province, Argentina's wine heartland, blessed with year-round sunshine thanks to the rain shadow provided by the mountain you've just climbed. Malbec is the grape of choice; pick up the Caminos del Vino maps (available from hotels and wine shops), which will help guide you down the area's winding, vine-flanked roads to bodegas offering tours, tastings and, increasingly, boutique accommodation.

OPENING SPREAD Climbers at 6800m on Aconcagua's Upper Canaleta. Due to its relative technical ease, Mt Aconcagua is potentially dangerous for novice climbers. **ABOVE** Be prepared: weather changes rapidly on the mountainside. **BELOW** Sunset on Mt Aconcagua.

ROCK CLIMB AT RAILAY, THAILAND

SCALE LIMESTONE CLIFFS HIGH ABOVE SOME OF ASIA'S FINEST AND MOST SCENIC BEACHES, STARING OUT OVER THE ANDAMAN SEA AS YOU CLING TO WALLS OF ROCK HIGH ABOVE SUN-SEEKING BEACHGOERS.

Thailand is framed with great beaches, but it's not often you can enjoy a bit of postcard-perfect paradise while grunting your way, finger hold by finger hold, to the top of a rock wall. Welcome to Railay, a jagged peninsula of lush limestone cliffs west of the city of Krabi.

Once considered to have the best beaches in Asia, Railay has also become one of the world's best-known rock-climbing destinations. First discovered by climbers in the late 1980s, its cliffs are now laced with more than 800 sport-climbing routes, offering everything from grade 4 stepladders to grade 8c epics (the French rating system is used at Railay). The climbing is world-class, with the added bonus that you can hang on the rope and enjoy some of the finest coastal scenery on Earth as you rest your weary limbs.

The peninsula is edged by four beaches – Hat Rai Leh East and West, Hat Phra Nang and Hat Ton Sai – with most of the climbing walls concentrated around Ton Sai and the headlands at the southern ends of Rai Leh East and West beaches. Most surfaces provide high-quality limestone with steep, pocketed walls, overhangs and the occasional hanging stalactite.

Novices often begin at Muay Thai, a 50m-high wall with around 17 climbs at the southern end of Hat Rai Leh East, including three climbs rated at grade 5. Railay's most challenging climbing areas are arguably the high cliffs of Dum's Kitchen and Andaman Beach at the southern end of Hat Ton Sai – if nothing else, it's possible to simply grab a beer from one of Ton Sai's beachfront bars and watch the more talented rock rats tackle the overhanging rock.

For sheer spectacle, Thaiwand Wall, the incisor of rock that dominates Rai Leh West beach, may be the most stunning climbing area...though it's all degrees of stunning at Railay.

ESSENTIAL EXPERIENCES

* **Lounging about in Ton Sai, where climbers drop in to drop out from the world.**

* Hanging out – literally – on Thaiwand Wall, with Thailand's Andaman coast stretched out below.

* **Walking to Sa Phra Nang, a hidden lagoon inside the cliffs between Rai Leh East and Phra Nang.**

* Sipping an evening beer on the sand in front of a beach bar in Ton Sai as the sun sets over the Andaman Sea.

* **Deep-water soloing on a cliff overhanging the ocean.**

DISTANCE 5M TO 125M | **LOCATION** RAILAY, PHRA NANG PENINSULA, KRABI, THAILAND | **IDEAL TIME COMMITMENT** THREE DAYS TO THREE WEEKS | **BEST TIME OF YEAR** NOVEMBER TO FEBRUARY | **ESSENTIAL TIP** TO AVOID DEHYDRATION, SEEK OUT SHADED CLIMBING AREAS

A DAY OFF

Railay is a laid-back place, inviting plenty of time away from the climbing walls. For many, that means time in the sun on Phra Nang beach, but there are a couple of active opportunities in easy reach. From the resort town of Ao Nang, a short long-tail boat ride from Railay, sea-kayaking trips head out to mangroves in Phang Nga Bay or offshore to the sea lagoon on the island of Ko Hong. Landlubbers can opt for elephant treks from Ao Nang, lumbering into the surrounding forest filled with monkeys and birdlife.

THE ADVENTURE UNFOLDS

On the wall of One Two Three, at the southern end of Hat Rai Leh East, you're spreadeagled against the cliff, looking like a star jump half completed. Your fingers are jammed into tiny holes and your eyes flicker about in search of the next ledge for your foot. Located next to Muay Thai, One Two Three is among the easiest of Railay's rock faces. Ropes hang from bolts like spaghetti, and local climbing guides scurry barefoot up the cliff's jagged edges, making it look simple. In comparison, you feel about as smooth as the choppy ocean below.

You follow a route that funnels into a cave, looking so intently at your hands and feet that you bump your head on a stalactite. Still, further along the wall, you hear a call to another climber, and you realise you aren't doing so badly.

Later, as the waning tide drains the bay to a rocky seabed and you bed down among the smattering of resorts behind Hat Ton Sai, the silhouettes of other climbers edge up the cliffs even as the sun is falling into the sea.

Next morning you wander along Hat Rai Leh West, the most perfect strip of sand on the peninsula. Today the 200m-high tower of rock that looms above its southern end – Thaiwand Wall – is your climbing goal. From behind the wall, you wander up into a cave, from where a view of Hat Phra Nang stretches out below, long-tail boats selling drinks and snacks nosed up against its sands. At its other end, the cave overlooks Hat Rai Leh West, the peacock-blue sea here resembling a highway of long-tail boat traffic.

Thaiwand Wall is now below. You abseil 30m down from the cave, configure your ropes and begin to climb a buttress. It seems easier today, but still you let go occasionally, to lean back on the rope and absorb the only-in-Thailand view.

MAKING IT HAPPEN

The simplest way to reach Railay is by long-tail boat from either Krabi or Ao Nang, further north along the coast. Most climbers stay in the backpacker commune of Ton Sai. Hat Rai Leh West and Hat Phra Nang offer more upmarket stays. Climbing guides and schools abound – King Climbers and Basecamp Tonsai are among the more established and respected.

DETOUR

About 40km offshore from Krabi are the twin islands of Ko Phi-Phi, the birthplace of climbing in Thailand. Discovered by climbers in 1988, and hit hard by the 2004 tsunami, they are today better known as a hedonistic paradise for tanned beachgoers, though a climbing subculture remains. The islands' topography is similar to Railay, featuring around seven climbing areas on limestone cliffs. Ton Sai Tower, on Ko Phi-Phi Don, is the main climbing site, offering routes up to 100m in length. On Ko Phi-Phi Leh, Maya Bay – the famed location for the movie version of Alex Garland's *The Beach* – has a few climbs.

OPENING SPREAD For fanatical climbers chasing the seasons, Railay is a tropical treat. ABOVE (L) Climbers on Railay's karst cliffs are belayed by partners on the ground. First-timers can book three-day courses. ABOVE (R) Rent long-tailed boats to explore Krabi. LEFT Railay Bay.

ARMCHAIR

* ***King Climbers Route Guide Book*** (Somporn Suebhait) The classic climbing guidebook to Railay, now into its seventh edition.
* ***Thailand: A Climbing Guide*** (Sam Lightner Jr) Features more than 350 routes in Thailand, with Railay the major focus.
* ***A Guide to Rock Climbing in Northern Thailand*** (Josh Morris & Khaetthaleeya Uppakham) If you want to spread your climbing wings to northern areas such as Crazy Horse Buttress.

DEEP-WATER SOLOING

To combine Railay's cliffs and the sea into one adventure, try deep-water soloing, where you climb onto a cliff overhanging the sea direct from a boat. You wear no harness, only your shoes and a chalk bag. You climb, without the security or hindrance of a rope, until you can climb no more – it's rock climbing at its purest – leaping or falling from the cliff into the sea when you're done or exhausted.

BOULDERING AT FONTAINEBLEAU

TREES, SERENITY AND 30,000 BOULDERS, CALLING LIKE A SIREN TO ROCK CLIMBERS WHO RATE TECHNIQUE FAR ABOVE ALTITUDE. FONTAINEBLEAU – FONT OR BLEAU TO ITS FRIENDS – IS FRANCE'S OWN NATURAL ADVENTURE PLAYGROUND.

174

Picture the scene: a sculpture garden of sandstone boulders, carved into surreal shapes by millions of years of erosion, scattered across a prehistoric forest dusted with white sand. Trapped by a pack of wolves, an early forest dweller sets one hairy foot against the rock and launches into an awesome dyno leap, to hang, one-handed, from a two-finger pocket. The rest of the hunting party look on in awe. 'Dude, that was at least a 7c.'

OK, maybe that isn't how bouldering at Fontainebleau started, but climbers have been training here since the 19th century, preparing for tough expeditions to the Alps. The first Bleausards, the favoured tag for French Font veterans, concentrated on the boulders at Bas-Cuvier and Gorges d'Apremont, but modern climbers have expanded the focus to Franchard, Trois Pignons, L'Elephant and a dozen other boulder fields scattered across the Fontainebleau forest.

This is rope-free climbing at its best – from the first warm day of spring, the forest comes alive with climbers testing themselves against more than 10,000 circuits and routes, known as 'problems', marked on the rock with coloured paint. Learning the meaning of these pictographs is an integral part of the Font climbing experience. In terms of climbing prowess, you don't need to be able to climb 8c to enjoy Font, but the best problems are in the upper grades.

While the sand provides a natural landing pad, most people back this up with a bouldering mat and some attentive assistance, known as 'spotting'. Chalk for sweaty palms is acceptable; *pof* (tree resin) is popular with French climbers, but loathed by everyone else. Climbs at Font are famously technical – some of the biggest names in climbing have tumbled off routes well within their grade – so come prepared for sudden dismounts and aches in muscles you never realised you had.

ESSENTIAL EXPERIENCES

* **Stepping into the forest for the first time and gripping your first hold.**
* Soaking up the kudos after conquering one of the great Font problems.
* **Making up your own classic route on a virgin Font boulder.**
* Swapping forest serenity for Louis XIV splendour in the Palace of Fontainebleau.
* **Swigging a beer at day's end and comparing problems and skinned knuckles.**

DISTANCE FROM PARIS 56KM | **ELEVATION** 150M | **LOCATION** FORÊT DE FONTAINEBLEAU, FRANCE | **IDEAL TIME COMMITMENT** A WEEKEND TO A WEEK | **BEST TIME OF YEAR** SPRING AND AUTUMN | **ESSENTIAL TIP** BRING AN OLD TOWEL TO WIPE OFF THE SAND BEFORE YOU CLIMB

FAMOUS FONT FACES

Every climber worth their boots has put hand to rock at Fontainebleau at some stage in their career. Indeed, some of France's greatest Alpinists have left their names on problems scattered around the Forêt de Fontainebleau. But one climber is associated with Font above all others – Pierre Allain, the pioneer who invented the soft-soled climbing shoe in 1935, transforming climbing from a plodding struggle in hobnail boots to a graceful ballet in three dimensions. If you climb at Font today, keep an eye out for Jacky Godoffe, route-setter extraordinaire and author of the definitive guide to the Bleau.

BRAZIL
PARAGUAY
CHILE

URUGUAY
PACIFIC
OCEAN
○ Buenos Aires
ARGENTINA

SOUTH
ATLANTIC
OCEAN

○Los Glaciares National Park
Moreno Glacier ○ ○ El Calafate

ICE TREK ARGENTINA'S MORENO GLACIER

DON'T JUST OGLE THE WORLD'S MOST FAMOUS GLACIER – STRAP ON
SOME CRAMPONS AND WALK ATOP IT. SO-CALLED 'MINI TREKS' WILL
HAVE YOU CRUNCHING ACROSS THE ICE, DISCOVERING A WORLD OF
SERACS, CREVASSES AND SINKHOLES.

178

Spilling down from the Chilean border on Cerro Pietrobelli, in the chilly heights of the Patagonian Andes, Perito Moreno Glacier is a pin-up of world ice. In tourism terms, it is a phenomenon, drawing thousands of people every summer's day, who arrive from the nearby gateway town of El Calafate. Most of them simply wander around the maze of walkways and viewing platforms on Peninsula Magallanes, watching and hoping for calving ice, but a few of the more adventurous types among them boat across to Lago Argentino's opposite shore, to explore the glacier at much closer quarters.

Among the rock rubble at the edge of the glacier you'll be equipped with crampons – a set of spikes that are fitted to your shoes to give you grip and traction while hiking on the ice. If you have never used crampons before, this is the perfect adventure to trial them, with treks following smooth and safe lines across the ice. At this level, it's as simple as remembering to walk with your legs slightly further apart than normal, to avoid catching a spike in your trousers or leg.

Once crampons are fitted, trekkers spend around 90 minutes on the ice, exploring just a tiny sliver of this remarkable glacier. Around 23km in length and up to 700m deep, Moreno advances at an average of about 2m per day at its centre, pushing inexorably forward, issuing thunderous booms as ice topples from its snout into Lago Argentino seemingly every few minutes.

The trek across the ice provides a showcase of glacial features as you wander past crevasses, seracs and sinkholes, with views back over the glacier to the grey surface of Lago Argentino. At trek's end you'll even get to taste the glacier, with a final stop at a makeshift bar for a gut-warming whisky on ice... ice that's been chipped straight from Moreno Glacier.

ESSENTIAL EXPERIENCES

❋ **Watching seracs crash and splash down from the glacier into Lago Argentino.**

❋ Peering into the depths of a sinkhole as you wonder just how deep this glacier really is.

❋ **Standing in a shower of ice as the guide ahead of you cuts steps into the glacier with his ice axe.**

❋ Toasting your glacial prowess with a whisky and an alfajores biscuit at trek's end.

LOCATION PERITO MORENO GLACIER, LOS GLACIARES NATIONAL PARK, ARGENTINA | **IDEAL TIME COMMITMENT** ONE DAY
BEST TIME OF YEAR NOVEMBER TO MARCH | **ESSENTIAL TIP** WEAR BOOTS WITH RIGID SOLES, AS THESE FIT BEST INTO CRAMPONS

GLACIARIUM

The Argentinean town of El Calafate thrives on glacier tourism, with buses radiating out each morning to the various glaciers that surround it. In 2011, El Calafate took the icy relationship another step, with the opening of the Glaciarium museum on the outskirts of town. Featuring displays about glaciation and glaciers around the world, the well-designed museum places particular focus on the many glaciers of Patagonia and nearby Los Glaciares National Park. When you're done browsing the displays, head downstairs to the Glacio Bar, with its chairs, tables and bar carved from a Moreno Glacier iceberg, for a drink in subzero temperatures.

■ THE ADVENTURE UNFOLDS

At Bajo de las Sombras on Lago Argentino you board the *Perito Moreno*, the boat threading between icebergs as it sails across the lake. As you climb out onto the rocky shores, there's an explosion that you seem almost to feel rather than hear. A serac has calved from the front of the glacier, creating a mighty splash like fireworks.

A short walk through the forest and along the pebbly beaches brings you to the front edge of the glacier. Here, you're fitted with your crampons, and you waddle out like a duck towards the ice. At first you wonder how you're going to walk on something as slippery as ice, but immediately you feel the bite of the crampons into the glacier. It's as though you've been velcroed to the thing.

In a line of trekkers you snake across the glacier, climbing slowly higher. What strikes you most is the colour of the ice. It doesn't have the transparency of water or other ice. Instead, it's blue, having been so tightly compressed that only the blue photons of light penetrate to its depths.

You look up at the mountains around you. A condor circles a summit, and the nearest rock face is scarred and scratched by the movement of the glacier millennia ago. You are standing atop a natural powerhouse – a bit of ice so strong and relentless it has all but shaped this mountainous land – and yet it seems so remarkably peaceful.

As you become more confident on your crampons, you also grow bolder. You lean into a sinkhole, a guide anchoring you by the arm as you watch meltwater pour deep into the hole, disappearing into a blue abyss. You have no wish to follow it. This hole looks like it goes on forever, and yet you know you can only see a part of it. You step back and feel your nerves resettle,

ARMCHAIR

⁕ *Handbook of Lago Argentino & Glaciar Perito Moreno* (Miguel Angel Alonso) Guidebook specific to the Los Glaciares National Park region and Moreno Glacier in particular.

⁕ *The Physics of Glaciers* (Kurt Cuffey & WSB Paterson) Definitive book on the what, why and how of glaciers.

⁕ *Perito Francisco Pascasio Moreno, Un Heroe Civil* (Hector Fasano) If you read Spanish, and can track it down, this biography tells the life of the eponymous Argentinean explorer and surveyor.

⁕ *Los Glaciares National Park Travel & Trekking Guide* (Colin Henderson) A regional guide that includes Moreno Glacier as well as nearby trekking routes.

⁕ *Alpine Climbing: Techniques to Take You Higher* (Mark Houston & Kathy Cosley) If the feel of crampons has you thinking about bigger mountaineering challenges, start here.

THE ADVENTURE UNFOLDS

Most skiers go from west to east, starting in Chamonix, France, and ending in Zermatt, Switzerland. Throughout the six-day journey, you'll find yourself in the shadow of imposing peaks, traversing glaciers, cols and high plateaus, with stretches of sustained climbing punctuated by exhilarating downhill runs. Nights are spent in Swiss Alpine Club huts, windswept oases perched on high ridges that greet travellers with down-quilted beds, beer, wine and hot meals.

On Day 1, you climb into the mountains, snake across glaciers at the foot of Mont Blanc and cross the French-Swiss border to Trient Hut (3170m). Next morning, an invigorating descent through the Val d'Arpette leads to the Swiss village of Champex (1477m), and transport to Verbier.

From Mont Fort Hut outside Verbier, plunge back into the snowy wilderness on Day 3, crossing the Grand Désert glacier, then climbing over 3336m Rosablanche to Prafleuri hut. Day 4 is largely spent circumnavigating the western edge of Lac des Dix (2364m), before a mid-afternoon ascent to Dix Hut (2928m).

Day 5 involves a strenuous climb to the route's highest point, the 3790m summit of Pigne d'Arolla, followed by an overnight at spectacularly sited Vignettes Hut (3160m), which clings to a lonely spur of rock astride the Vuibé Glacier. The trip's long final day traverses three more passes along the Swiss-Italian border before reaching the ultimate reward: full-on Matterhorn views and a dizzying descent into Zermatt, a historic mountain resort whose idyllic end-of-the-road location offers a gentle re-entry into 'normal' life.

MAKING IT HAPPEN

Chamonix is accessible from Geneva's airport. From Zermatt, trains run to Zürich and Geneva.

You'll need extreme backcountry gear, including: *randonnée* or telemark skis fitted with skins; a shovel, probe and beacon for avalanche safety; an ice axe, rope, harness and crampons. Compagnie des Guides de Chamonix (and others) offer Haute Route excursions with IFMGA-certified guides.

Celebrate trip's end at Zermatt's Hotel Monte Rosa, where the first climbing party to scale the Matterhorn rendezvoused in 1865.

AN ALTERNATIVE CHALLENGE

The longer 'Grande Lui' route avoids motorised transport on Day 2 by veering southeast between 4314m Grand Combin and the Swiss-Italian border, overnighting at La Fouly, Grand St Bernard Hospice, Vélan Hut and Chanrion Hut before rejoining the main route at Vignettes Hut.

Alternatively, trek the high country in summer on the 12-day hiker's version of the Haute Route; huts are open from mid-June to early September.

OPENING SPREAD Rooms with a view: cabins at the foot of the Matterhorn. **ABOVE (L)** Ski-tourers can slip scaly 'skins' over their skis to shuffle up gentle slopes. **ABOVE (R)** Reservations are essential for the Cabane du Mont-Fort refuge on the Haute Route near Verbier. **LEFT** Skiing the Haute-Savoie.

ARMCHAIR

* *The First Ascent of the Matterhorn* (Edward Whymper) The classic account of Whymper's pioneering 1865 expedition.

* *Two Planks and a Passion* (Roland Huntford) A history of skiing, from early mentions in the Norse sagas to the first Winter Olympics in Chamonix.

* *Haute Route Chamonix-Zermatt* (Peter Cliff) The best English-language guide to skiing this route.

* *Mountains of the Mind* (Robert Macfarlane) Never less than enthralling, Macfarlane explores science, art and philosophy to explain our fascination with mountains in this award-winning book.

* *Backcountry Skiing: Skills for Ski Touring and Ski Mountaineering* (Martin Volken, Scott Schell, Margaret Wheeler) Acquire the skills to travel safely in the mountains, including techniques and navigation. Suited to intermediate skiers and above.

ICE TREK ZANSKAR IN INDIA

JOURNEY INTO THE ICY LANDSCAPES AND HIDDEN VALLEYS OF INDIA'S ZANSKAR REGION WITH A WALK ON THE FROZEN CHADAR RIVER. THIS IS AN EXHILARATING TREK THROUGH AN EXQUISITE NATURAL ENVIRONMENT – AND A PASSAGE BACK IN TIME TO A PLACE AND A CULTURE RARELY SEEN BY OUTSIDERS.

190

Every winter, the inhabitants of Zanskar, in the Indian Himalayas, make the dangerous journey from their snow-bound alpine villages to the town of Leh in Ladakh. They do this as they have for centuries: by walking on the icy Chadar River. Zanskar is encircled by 7000m-high peaks, and in the eight-month-long winter, it's all but cut off from the outside world. It's then that the partially frozen Chadar becomes a lifeline for Zanskaris: their only physical connection with the rest of the planet. For Zanskaris, this precarious 200km journey is a way of life. The frozen Chadar is their winter trade route: along it they bring wares to sell in Leh; then haul their purchases back to Zanskar, on the ever-shifting Chadar ice. It's a bone-chilling trip that demands sound knowledge of the river and the stamina to endure cold days – and freezing nights.

Zanskar's isolation has attracted adventurous outsiders to this ancient route. Hungarian scholar Alexander Csoma de Körös may have been the first Western visitor. He spent the winter of 1823 here, studying Tibetan language. In the late 1990s, trekkers began to make their way to the Chadar. Today, Zanskaris share the route with Western trekkers. Few visitors carry the heavy loads that locals do, but a Chadar ice trek is a tough undertaking. A return trip takes 14 to 18 days, with daytime temperatures averaging -10°C, dropping to -20°C at night. Most walkers sleep in tents; Zanskaris build campfires and hunker down in their woollen *gonchas* in riverside caves. To do this trip, you need to be a fit, experienced walker, and be kitted out for the cold. Despite the hardships – or maybe because of them – an ice trek to Zanskar is a bewitching journey. You'll marvel as much at the beautiful frozen landscapes as you will at the tough and ever-smiling Zanskaris for whom this difficult route is the only path home.

ESSENTIAL EXPERIENCES

* **Surrounding yourself with the pure, natural beauty of the Zanskar winter.**

* Meeting the tough, resourceful Zanskaris, and marvelling at their culture and spirituality.

* **Spotting wildlife: perhaps an elusive snow leopard – or perhaps only its tracks.**

* Overnighting (at least once) in the flickering orange firelight of a riverside cave, while your Zanskari companions chat late into the night.

* **Visiting the Buddhist *gompas* (monasteries) and *chortens* (stupa) and passing intricately carved *mani* walls that are expressions of the strong Buddhist faith here.**

* Coming in from the snowy cold to the delicious warm of your Zanskar village homestay.

DISTANCE 200KM | **ELEVATION** 3500M | **LOCATION** LADAKH AND ZANSKAR, JAMMU AND KASHMIR, INDIA | **IDEAL TIME COMMITMENT** THREE TO FOUR WEEKS | **BEST TIME OF YEAR** FEBRUARY | **ESSENTIAL TIP** FOOTWEAR CAN MAKE OR BREAK A TRIP; HIGH-ALTITUDE MOUNTAINEERING BOOTS WORK WELL; LOCALS USE THICK-SOLED GUMBOOTS BOUGHT IN LEH

LIVING BUDDHIST

Buddhism is the foundation of life for the people of Zanskar. Almost every village has a monastery, and many Zanskaris spend time as nuns and monks – some undertake extended periods of isolated contemplation. Zanskar monasteries represent the two prominent branches of Buddhism: the Drukpa Kagyu and Gelugpa or Yellow Hat sect. Some monasteries here are ancient, and house precious religious murals and artworks. On the Chadar trek, you may be able to see the beautiful *gompa* (monastery)at Lingshed, and the nunnery at Zangla. If you come to Zanskar in summer, don't miss the magnificent 10th-century Karsha Gompa, near Zanskar's capital, Padum.

ALL CHANGE IN ZANSKAR

Zanskar has been isolated for centuries, but as the outside world encroaches, Zanskari culture is on the brink of change. A new road is being built that will soon connect Padum to Leh in Ladakh. Some of this road is being constructed in the Chadar River gorge itself. Along the road will come Western goods and values that conflict with the simple, spiritual Zanskari way of life. Tourism, presently moderate in summer and minimal through winter, will most likely increase. Locals see it both as a blessing and a curse, and know they will have to defend their unique language and culture closely if it is to survive.

THE ADVENTURE UNFOLDS

Setting off from the aptly named Ladahki village of Chilling, your first steps on the ice of the Chadar River are hesitant. It takes a while to get used to the thought of the river moving beneath the ice and to trust that mere frozen water will hold your weight. Where the ice is broken, precarious scrambles are necessary across the rocky walls of the gorge. When you leave the river and walk into the valleys of Zanskar, there may be thigh-deep snow to slog through, or perhaps a well-trodden snowy path. Either way, stay close to your guides.

Watch your feet, but don't forget to look up. The river cuts through narrow, rocky gorges from which high cliffs soar. Frozen waterfalls cling here, hanging in translucent cascades like giant torrents of candle wax. All around is the arid alpine landscape – painted in hues of tan, orange and burnished gold. You emerge from a bend in the river and glimpse snow-shrouded peaks gleaming in the distance against an azure sky, then you're into the shadows of a gorge again, where your breath hangs freezing in the air. Keep your eyes open for wildlife: snow leopards slink across the high alpine meadows, hunting bharal (Himalayan blue sheep); and marmots, ibex, wolves and bears are often seen around the Chadar. Lammergeiers soar on the mountain thermals above.

Most walkers come to the Chadar as part of an organised group, with cooks to provide food, camp staff to set up tents, and porters to carry it all. This style of expedition probably means starting the day with a cup of hot coffee and eating three-course meals in a heated tent at night. Some expeditions arrange homestay accommodation with villagers in Hanumil, Pidmo and Zangla.

Spending time in Zanskar villages, and interacting with Zanskaris as you walk, is a wonderful immersion in their ancient culture.

MAKING IT HAPPEN

Tour companies in Leh and in the West organise treks on the Chadar. Project Himalaya organises small groups, which reduces environmental impact. Good gear is essential; take a sleeping bag graded to -30°C, thick-soled waterproof boots that grip the ice, and sturdy walking poles.

AN ALTERNATIVE CHALLENGE

If you're a hardy walker, avoid the tour company crowds and savour the most authentic experience of all: an ice trek with Zanskaris. Enquire in Leh about groups of villagers returning to Zanskar, and arrange to walk the Chadar with them. You'll carry your own food and gear, and sleep as Zanskaris do in riverside caves. Your group may be able to set up homestays in villages once you reach Zanskar. Learn some words of Zanskari before you leave and revel in their culture.

OPENING SPREAD Walking the Zanskar gorge between Nerak and Hanumil. **ABOVE (L)** Novice monks play a game at Phuktal Monastery in Zanskar. **ABOVE (R)** Zanskaris travel the frozen river every year but tour operators now offer guided treks. **LEFT** Looking towards the Zanskar range from Leh.

ARMCHAIR

* ***Zanskar: The Hidden Kingdom*** (Michel Peissel) About travelling in Zanskar in the 1970s, when it was untouched by the outside world.

* ***Where Heaven and Mountains Meet: Zanskar and the Himalayas*** (Olivier Föllmi) A compendium of thoughts and images from the author's visits to Zanskar over 20 years.

* ***Journey from Zanskar: A Monk's Vow to Children*** (2011) A touching film illustrating how seriously Zanskaris are taking the fight

to preserve their culture in the face of change.

* ***Ancient Futures: Lessons from Ladakh for a Globalising World*** (Helena Norberg-Hodge) Tracks changes in Ladakh since it opened up to Western goods and tourism: food for thought for any visitor.

* ***Chadar: The Ice Trail*** (2009) This riveting documentary follows a caravan of Zanskaris hauling timber along the Chadar and chaperoning a group of young children to school in Leh.

DOG-SLED THE YUKON

SLED BEHIND A HARD-WORKING TEAM OF ALASKAN HUSKIES, GLIDING THROUGH EPIC SNOW-BLANKETED LANDSCAPES AND OVER FROZEN LAKES IN THE FAR NORTH CANADIAN TERRITORY ON THE FRINGE OF THE ARCTIC, WHERE DOG-SLEDDING IS ALMOST A RELIGION.

194

It's possible to dog-sled in most Arctic countries and regions, but there's something special about working a team of dogs in Canada's Yukon territory. This is true canine country, where even the capital city, Whitehorse, offers doggie massage and physiotherapy services.

Most notably, however, the Yukon is home to the Yukon Quest, a 1600km dog-sled race that's as much a matter of survival as speed, racing through mountainous terrain in temperatures that can plunge below -50°C. Even the best sledders take more than nine days to complete the race – little wonder it's billed as the toughest dog-sled race on the planet, and sometimes even the toughest race of any kind in the world.

To experience dog-sledding in the Yukon, you don't necessarily need to endure such extreme hardship. Dog-sledding adventures can be as brief as a one-day trip, or you can stay for weeks on end, perfecting your dog handling skills, polishing your sled control and refining your dog care. You can radiate out from a home base each day, or spend nights camped out in the spruce and poplar forests, testing not just your mushing skills as you rocket over the land behind a team of excited dogs, but also your ability to cope with subzero nights sleeping on the snow.

Learning the basics of sledding will only take a day or two, and developing an affinity with the barking bits of fur will come even easier. Mushing skills include helping the dog team when climbing slopes, braking, leaning and, most complex of all, steering.

Anticipate a few face plants in the snow as you discover the very fine art of weight distribution and leg position when moving at speed, all while trying to remember the golden rule: never, ever let go of the sled... even when your face is three inches under the snow.

ESSENTIAL EXPERIENCES

* **Guiding a dog team along trails through deep spruce forest.**

* Bedding down on the snow, with a team of snuffling dogs outside.

* **Watching for the aurora borealis – the Northern Lights – as darkness slips over the Yukon.**

* Hanging around to watch how the pros do it in the Yukon Quest.

* **Checking out the world's longest fish ladder (266m) at Whitehorse.**

LOCATION YUKON TERRITORY, CANADA I **IDEAL TIME COMMITMENT** THREE DAYS TO THREE WEEKS I **BEST TIME OF YEAR** DECEMBER TO MARCH I **ESSENTIAL TIP** PACK WARM; GOOSE DOWN IS IDEAL FOR JACKETS AND SLEEPING BAGS

YUKON QUEST

The 'toughest dog-sled race on the planet' traces its origins to a saloon in Fairbanks, Alaska, in 1983, when four mushers pondered the idea of an international sledding epic, racing along historic routes through the Yukon territory and Alaska. A year later, the Yukon Quest was born, following the route along the Yukon River used by prospectors in the late 19th century to reach the Klondike gold fields. That year, 26 teams set out from Fairbanks, bound for Whitehorse. The inaugural winner was Sonny Lindner, who completed the 1600km in 12 days. In 2010 Hans Gatt set the fastest time of nine days and 26 minutes.

THE SOURTOE CLUB

The Yukon is a frontier kind of place, filled with tough people and rough experiences, such as the membership ritual for the Sourtoe Club at Dawson City's Downtown Hotel. To become a member of this club, you must down a shot of whisky containing a rather unusual item: an amputated toe. The toe, which looks a little like an old prune with a toenail, must touch your lips. It's a tradition that dates back to the 1970s when a riverboat captain found a toe in his cabin, brought it to town and one thing led to another – a bet that nobody would pop the toe in their drink. In the years since, tens of thousands of people have done just that.

■ THE ADVENTURE UNFOLDS

When you wake, it is -22°C outside the tent, a temperature at which the cold feels more like an ache than a sensation. But if you want consolation, there are eight of them just outside: your dogs, curled up contentedly on the bare snow.

You are camped at the edge of a lake, frozen into the land, the spruce trees around it painted white with snow. Before your breakfast, you must first serve the dogs their food – they worked all day for you yesterday, and this morning you must work for them.

A couple of hours later you are away, curling through the forest. The temperature has warmed to about -10°C, and you've stripped down to a T-shirt...who would have thought -10°C could feel almost balmy?

Eight dogs charge ahead of you. Yesterday they spent much of their running time staring over their shoulders, eyeballing you, unsure about your ability. Today, however, they are intent on the track ahead. You have been accepted.

Your trail weaves in and out of the forest, gliding over frozen lakes as if atop clouds. Across one there are moose tracks, but the moose is nowhere to be seen – what animal is going to show itself to a team of volatile dogs? You come to the slopes above the kennels, from where the track snakes down to the shores of Lake Laberge. There's a corner here you know well – you have crashed the sled into a tree here every day so far. Will today be different?

Gently, you glide up to the tree, then release the brake. It's a hard-left corner, so you throw your weight onto your left leg while dragging your right leg out wide in the snow as a brace. The sled turns and bumps against the tree but you hold your position. You are through the corner. You are truly mushing now.

■ MAKING IT HAPPEN

Unless you happen to have packed half a dozen dogs into your suitcase, you'll need to join an organised dog-sledding trip. They are plentiful in the Yukon. One of the most experienced is Cathers Wilderness Adventures on the shores of Lake Laberge near Whitehorse – trips can include a section of the Yukon Quest. Air North flies between Vancouver and Whitehorse.

■ DETOUR

If epic tales of sledding have gripped you, head north to the Alaskan town of Wasilla. Though better known these days for its connection to Sarah Palin, who was once the city mayor, it's also home to the headquarters of the Iditarod, the famed dog-sled race through Alaska. On-site is a museum with photos, displays, Iditarod trophies and race footage. It also organises dog-sled day trips on a section of the Iditarod.

OPENING SPREAD Sledders in the 715km Iditarod race cross the frozen Yukon River. **ABOVE (L) AND (R)** Dog tired: the dogs do the hard work but the human racers feel the pace. Each team has 12 to 16 dogs with six running at a time. **LEFT** The aurora borealis ripples above the Yukon's spruce trees.

ARMCHAIR

* *Yukon Quest: The Story of the World's Toughest Sled Dog Race* (Lew Freedman) See how the tougher half live on the trail in this history of the 1600km sled race.

* *The Songs of a Sourdough* (Robert W Service) Get the feel of the land with this famed collection of poems from the man known as the Bard of the Yukon.

* *The Call of the Wild* (Jack London) The classic dogs-in-the-Yukon tale – a mutt named Buck and the Klondike gold rush.

* *Mush! A Beginner's Manual of Sled Dog Training* (Charlene LaBelle) A guide to all things sledding, including riding, racing and training.

SNOWSHOE BULGARIA'S RILA MOUNTAINS

IN A WINTERY LAND – WHERE CRISP AIR AND FLUFFY POWDER FRAME JAGGED PEAKS, FROZEN WATERFALLS AND ICY ALPINE LAKES – EXPLORE A POCKET OF PRIME EUROPEAN MOUNTAINOUS WILDERNESS ON FOOT AND VISIT A FAMOUS MONASTERY: A WALLED FORTRESS SURROUNDED BY DENSE FOREST.

People have been exploring southwestern Bulgaria's Rila Mountains for millennia, from the Romans to the Byzantines, but only recently has winter become a time to journey into the solitude of this dense range of steep peaks, glacial lakes, and beech and spruce forests. Adventurers are drawn to this stunning, frozen natural world for pure recreation, and they stay for days.

With the creation of the Rila National Park in 1992, visitors were given the opportunity to explore the park using a chain of *hizhas*, or mountain huts, even in the winter. The basic accommodation makes it possible to strap on snowshoes for multiday adventures that, at the end of each day, land you in warm huts with hot meals shared by boisterous mountain lovers.

The name Rila means 'lots of water' – fitting for a place that sources some of the major rivers on the Balkan Peninsula and boasts 120 lakes. On a snowshoe trip, you'll trek around the most popular string of lakes, the glacier-carved Seven Lakes, which freeze in October and melt in June. While most visitors see these lakes during the packed summer months, in winter you'll have them to yourself – a chance to commune with the sounds of silence as you take in long views that include these frozen pockets of water cradled in barren rock.

Because the area has been protected for decades, wildlife thrives here, which means you may spot roe deer, wild goats and footprints from bears, foxes, wolves or wild boars during your daily jaunts.

While snowshoeing in the Rila Mountains doesn't require the kind of skills that, say, off-piste powder skiing or ice climbing do, the daily treks will get your heart pumping and your legs working for hours at a time, especially as you ascend ridges well above the tree line, then run (or walk) down powdery slopes. That combo makes for deep sleep, hearty appetites and total relaxation.

ESSENTIAL EXPERIENCES

❋ **Glimpsing the jagged peak of Mt Musala, the Balkans' highest peak and known as the 'Bulgarian Matterhorn'.**

❋ Relaxing at the end of a day of walking with a glass of wine in one of the park's cosy mountain huts.

❋ **Entering the walled fortress of the Rila Monastery, where magnificent murals are plastered on graceful arches and columns.**

❋ Running your hands over some of the 80m of ice that makes up the frozen Skakavitsa Waterfall.

❋ **Silently strolling through the Parangalitsa Reserve, which holds some of Europe's oldest spruce forests.**

DISTANCE THREE TO FIVE HOURS OF WALKING PER DAY | **ELEVATION** 800M TO 2900M | **LOCATION** SOUTHWEST BULGARIA | **IDEAL TIME COMMITMENT** FIVE TO EIGHT DAYS | **BEST TIME OF YEAR** JANUARY TO MARCH | **ESSENTIAL TIP** BRING YOUR BEST WINTER BOOTS TO KEEP YOUR FEET WARM AND DRY

Every August, members of an international religious movement called the White Brotherhood meet in the Rila Mountains to perform rituals for its new year. Thousands of practitioners, dressed in white, perform dance rituals and sing near the Seven Lakes. The religion is based on the teachings of Bulgarian Petur Dunov (1864–1944), a priest who taught a combination of Christianity and mysticism based on brotherly love, healthy living and meditating in the outdoors.

■ THE ADVENTURE UNFOLDS

The wind is blowing outside your cosy mountain hut, which is surrounded by metres of fluffy snow, but all you need to do is drink tea, eat pancakes and strap on some snowshoes that will allow you to float across the powder as you traverse the flanks of Bulgaria's highest mountain range.

Like most travellers you're with a guide and a small group. (Independent adventures here can be logistically challenging, with hut, hotel and guesthouse reservations, not to mention route picking.) But you'll find plenty of opportunities for solitude: a picnic lunch in the trees or a solitary pause to take in the jagged tip of Mt Musala, at 2925m the country's highest peak.

Because you're spending multiple days inside the park, your walking will take you to some of the region's most impressive sights, including the 80m Skakavitsa Waterfall. In winter, the water turns to ice, creating a bulky coating for boulders that draws ice climbers from around the continent.

Many tours include a stop at the Rila Monastery, a Unesco World Heritage Site that was founded in the 10th century by the hermit Ivan Rilski. Because the monastery has been rebuilt twice (first by the Russian Church after Ottoman raids, then following a fire in 1833), vivid frescoes and intact relics make this monastery one of Bulgaria's most beloved attractions.

But it's the wilderness that will stay with you, the challenging climbs leading to views of the surrounding mountain ranges, and the walks through the quiet forests of Macedonian pines that have been thriving for hundreds of years.

■ MAKING IT HAPPEN

Most visitors start from Sofia, 100km north, but the region is accessible from smaller towns closer to the mountains, including Rila Village, Govedartsi and the ski resorts of Borovets and Malyovitsa. Bring good winter gear: a waterproof outer shell and trekking pants, long underwear, winter boots and sunglasses. Most outfitters provide technical gear, but check. Sofia-based Zig Zag Holidays and Odyssia-In provide reliable trips.

■ DETOUR

Nearby, in the Pirin Mountains, the Bankso ski resort draws budget skiers and Euro partiers. Expect all manner of lodgings, from mountainside posh to simple private rooms, fine dining and pumping nightlife. Recent improvements and additions have included faster lifts and a modern gondola. The resort has hosted a few World Cup races, a testament to the groomed runs and snow-making systems that allow skiers to hit slopes as early as December, with or without nature's help.

OPENING SPREAD Autumn reaches the Rila mountains. **ABOVE (L)** Rila's monastery is the oldest in the Slav world and an architectural gem. Founded as a response to society's moral decline, its murals depict the suffering of sinners. **ABOVE (R)** The White Brotherhood is an outdoors-loving religious sect.

ARMCHAIR

❊ *The Mountains of Bulgaria: A Walker's Companion* (Julian Perry) Provides detailed information about hiking in the Rila Mountains.

❊ *Sweet Dreams: Bulgarian Folk Tales* (Ivona Hecht) The perfect title to have in your hand before dozing off to sleep in a mountain hut, it tells some of the country's most magical tales.

❊ *The Way Back* (2010) Part of this film by Peter Weir was shot in the Rila Mountains.

❊ *The Gerak Family* (Elin Pelin) Published in 1911, tells the story of a traditional rural community in transition to modern life – a common situation in the towns and farms surrounding the national park. The book has twice been made into a film.

❊ *The Balkans in World History* (Andrew Baruch Wachtel) A good summary of this rich cultural region shaped by the Ottomans, Roman Catholics, and ancient Greeks and Romans.

ANIMALS

GREAT ADVENTURES

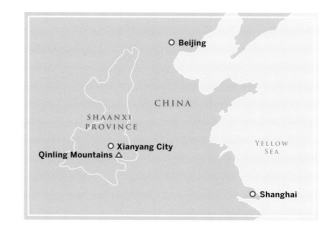

SEE PANDAS IN CHINA

WE'RE GOING ON A BEAR HUNT: CLAMBERING UP THE MOUNTAIN, SNEAKING THROUGH THE BAMBOO, TRACKING ACROSS THE FOREST, TRAMPING ACROSS THE SNOW… FOLLOWING THE TRAIL OF CHINA'S MOST ICONIC AND ENIGMATIC BUT LEAST COLOURFUL ANIMAL: THE GIANT PANDA.

202

The giant panda is one of nature's most beautiful mistakes: a vegetarian carnivore. Perhaps because of its rotund physique and perpetual, rather foolish-looking grin, China's endangered icon is usually portrayed as bumbling and permanently hungry. The latter isn't far off the truth – with a digestive system poorly adapted to its 99% bamboo diet, the giant panda spends some 14 hours every day eating 10kg or more of the fibrous vegetation – but as anyone who's tried to catch a glimpse of a wild panda will aver, it's stealthy enough to give most wildlife-watchers the run-around.

In fact, despite whispers and ancient legends, the *da xiong mao* ('great bear cat', as it's known in local parlance) was so elusive as to be virtually unknown until, in 1869, Catholic missionary and naturalist Père Armand David obtained a skin; there was a further wait of another half-century till a live specimen was seen by a Westerner. Now pandas only survive in the high forests of Sichuan, Gansu and the Qinling Mountains of Shaanxi Province.

Pandas were rare even before hunting and habitat destruction decimated the population, but numbers are rising, thanks to the establishment of a string of over 60 nature reserves and the introduction of protective measures such as logging bans. A recent survey estimated the population at around 1600.

Neighbouring reserves in Shaanxi's Qinling Mountains – notably Changqing and Foping, southwest of Xi'an – offer the best chances of a sighting. Panda population densities are relatively high – up to one panda per 1.5 sq km in Foping – and experienced trackers are on hand to lead panda-spotters up into the forests. Even so, this is no walk in the park: bank on long days tackling steep gradients, pushing through dense thickets, often in subzero temperatures, and pray for a healthy dash of luck. You'll need it – and so does the panda.

ESSENTIAL EXPERIENCES

* **Learning to spot the telltale signs of a nearby panda before catching a rare glimpse of a wild bear amid the bamboo stands and pine trees.**

* Soaking up authentic rural village life on a stroll through the sleepy streets of Huayang old town, stopping to admire roosting crested ibis.

* **Tucking into local Shaanxi cuisine – wide noodles, pickled garlic and dumplings, livened up with a dash of thick, oily chilli sauce.**

* Exploring the valleys and hills of Foping Nature Reserve amid lush forests and past crumbling temples and farmhouses.

* **Watching for takin and golden pheasant in the misty peaks of Changqing Nature Reserve.**

ELEVATION 3767M | **LOCATION** QINLING MOUNTAINS, SHAANXI PROVINCE, CHINA | **IDEAL TIME COMMITMENT** ONE WEEK TO 10 DAYS | **BEST TIME OF YEAR** MARCH | **ESSENTIAL TIP** BRING WARM, STURDY BOOTS – HIKING UP STEEP SLOPES THROUGH SNOW CAN QUICKLY CHILL FEET

WHY PANDAS HAVE BLACK EYES

Science isn't sure: possibly for camouflage, for identification by mates or to intimidate rivals. Legend, however, has a different take. This is one version of a Tibetan folk tale. Long ago, a brave shepherdess was killed by a leopard while defending a panda, whose fur was ivory white. Other pandas gathered to mourn, black ash bands on their arms. Hugging each other, their paws and shoulders became blackened; wiping tears away and holding paws to their heads to muffle their sobs, their eyes and ears were also smeared with ash. So now pandas have black eyes, ears, arms and shoulders.

THE ADVENTURE UNFOLDS

You've been awake since dawn, your search fuelled by bowls of gloopy *congee* (rice porridge) and green tea. Venturing into a verdant side valley in Foping, your local tracker scans the low-lying foliage for clumps of ramsons. Snatching a handful, he munches the fragrant leaves, leaving in his wake a pungent vapour trail. Pandas have a highly developed sense of smell and this plant's nickname is 'bear garlic'.

Unconventional breath freshener aside, you're thankful to be following this veteran scout. A former hunter, he knows every wrinkle and hidey-hole that might harbour a coy panda. He's also surprisingly lithe, leaping up vertiginous slopes, between mossy rocks and through dense bamboo thickets, waiting for you to catch up with head cocked, listening above your hoarse breathing for any sounds of bamboo being split or munched. Scrambling higher, he gathers evidence of recent panda 'activity', which consists largely of two things: eating and pooping. He crumbles a vivid green dropping the shape of a sweet potato in his hands. 'Moist, fresh,' he grunts. 'Last night, or maybe this morning.'

Minutes turn into hours, morning turns into afternoon, and sweat turns into an uncomfortable damp patch on your back. Then, between the vertical slats of a bamboo screen, you see what he sees, and your heart skips. Lounging back, legs akimbo and surrounded by torn bamboo leaves, is a giant panda methodically crunching a short, sweet stem. She looks the most contented creature on earth – though you're not far behind.

MAKING IT HAPPEN

Changqing has several tracks, so covering ground is easier than in Foping. The latter, though, offers a wilder experience and, reportedly, more pandas. The small town of Huayang, gateway to Changqing, has a comfortable hotel; visitors to Foping usually stay in the reserve's Expert Building's basic lodging. Arrange transport, accommodation and trackers in advance.

DETOUR

If you don't spot a wild giant panda, consider dropping into one of the breeding centres in Sichuan Province, southwest of Shaanxi. The breeding station at Wolong Nature Reserve, long a flagship centre for panda conservation, was badly damaged in a 2008 earthquake, so it's best to head to Chengdu and its Research Base of Giant Panda Breeding. The base is home to scores of giant pandas, bred here from an initial population of six animals taken from the wild in 1987, as well as red pandas and golden snub-nosed monkeys.

OPENING SPREAD Laidback lunch: pandas eat up to 15kg of bamboo shoots daily but derive little energy from their diet. **ABOVE (L)** A *takin* (goat-antelope) takes a peek in the Qinling Mountains. **ABOVE (R)** Wolong Nature Reserve in Sichuan. **LEFT** Pandas feeding in the Qionglai Mountains.

ARMCHAIR

* ***Panda: Back from the Brink*** (Zhou Mengqi) Eye-catching images of pandas in their environment.

* ***Wild China*** (2008) A lavish, photo-rich book accompanying the six-part BBC natural-history series on DVD – beautiful and evocative.

* ***The Way of the Panda*** (Henry Nicholls) How a bear can be more than just a bear: a fascinating overview of China's monochrome icon, this is as much cultural history as natural history.

* ***Chinese Wildlife*** (Martin Walters) Good general introduction to the country's species and habitats, with illustrations and plenty of helpful practical information.

* ***The Last Panda*** (George B Schaller) One of the greats of modern conservation shares his experiences from four years spent in Sichuan's panda reserves, and his take on the challenges facing this endangered species.

205

WALK WITH WOLVES IN YELLOWSTONE

UNKNOWN TO THE MAJORITY OF ITS THREE MILLION ANNUAL VISITORS, YELLOWSTONE NATIONAL PARK HIDES SOME OF THE WILDEST CORNERS OF THE AMERICAN WEST. BED DOWN WITH GRIZZLIES, ELK AND WOLVES ON THIS TREK THROUGH THE MOST REMOTE WILDERNESS IN THE LOWER 48 STATES.

Yellowstone National Park boasts true marvels: exploding geysers, thundering waterfalls and some of the largest herds of bison and elk on the continent. It's also one of America's most popular parks, visited by over 30,000 people per day in the peak months of July and August. But hike a mile away from a road, and you'll lose 99% of the tourists. Trek into the park's remote southeastern corner, known as the Thorofare, and you'll lose pretty much everybody.

The spectacular valley is bordered to the north by huge Yellowstone Lake, to the east by the brooding, volcanic Absaroka Mountains, and to the south by the Bridger-Teton Wilderness. Apart from the odd ranger's cabin, the land is home only to populations of grizzly bears, wolves and elk.

Trappers, hunters and Native Americans have long used the broad valley, following game trails and the migration routes of the local wapiti elk herds. The Hayden Survey visited in 1871 and their reports led to the creation of the world's first national park the following year.

A trek into the Thorofare is a physical and logistical challenge, involving at least a weeklong trek into the heart of nowhere, so you need to have excellent wilderness skills, including experience of fording rivers and camping safely in grizzly country. There are no easy escape routes if you run into trouble.

You can make life easier by employing a local outfitter to arrange a horse trek through the region. Or you could use a boat shuttle to deposit you and a kayak or canoe at the southwestern branch of the lake, using the many backcountry lakeshore sites to explore the region around Trail Creek trail before being picked up again a few days later.

Whichever way you do it, for sheer primeval wildness and immersion in the natural world, with the right preparation and back up, there's not an adventure for a thousand miles that can beat it.

ESSENTIAL EXPERIENCES

* **Watching the sun set crimson and gold over the silvery waters of Yellowstone Lake.**

* Staying awake through the night as you imagine all the bloodthirsty animals that could be the source of that tiny scratching at the corner of your tent.

* **Feeling the hair stand up at the back of your neck as you spot your first wolf in the wild.**

* Listening to the silence and the solitude, knowing that you are as far away from a road as you can get in the lower 48 states.

* **Gulping your first burger or cold beer after a week dining on ramen noodles and marshmallows.**

DISTANCE 112.5KM | **LOCATION** YELLOWSTONE NATIONAL PARK, WYOMING, USA | **IDEAL TIME COMMITMENT** ONE WEEK | **BEST TIME OF YEAR** AUGUST TO SEPTEMBER | **ESSENTIAL TIP** BRING MOSQUITO REPELLENT, BINOCULARS AND AN EMERGENCY BEACON

SUPERVOLCANO!

Few campers in Yellowstone realise that they have decided to pitch their tent atop one of the world's largest supervolcanoes. Much of the park is in fact floating above a giant 200km-deep hot spot of magma, which provides the fuel for the world's most dense collection of geysers and hot springs. Scientists estimate that the last major eruption was 600,000 years ago, when Yellowstone's mountains were blown away and superheated ash blocked out the sun, creating a global volcanic winter. The next eruption? Well, that's due any time in the next 10,000 years or so...

■ THE ADVENTURE UNFOLDS

The weeklong trek starts with a two-day walk down the eastern shore of Yellowstone Lake, North America's largest mountain lake, whose outline traces the caldera of the Yellowstone supervolcano. Camp sites offer fine dusk views of the lake and the chance to spot pelicans, otters and ospreys.

By the end of the second day you reach the wide, flat open valley of the meandering Upper Yellowstone River, its creeks thick with cutthroat trout (and merciless clouds of mosquitoes in early summer – bring repellent). All around lie burned and fallen trees from the huge wildfires of 1988.

The valley is a great place to spot moose, elk and grizzlies as well as summer wildflower blooms. For the next day or two, listen for the howling of the Delta wolf pack, the most remote and least studied of Yellowstone's wolf populations. Packs constantly shift numbers, strength and territory, so check the latest locations with rangers. In this primeval land of grizzlies and wolves, it comes as quite a shock to realise that you are now firmly part of the local food chain, so bring some bear spray for some peace of mind.

As you continue south, the Thorofare Trail follows the Upper Yellowstone River (the longest undammed river in the US) to reach the Thorofare Patrol Cabin at the park's southernmost extent. Just across the border by the headwaters of the Yellowstone lies a geographical curiosity. Here, high on Two Ocean Plateau, a creek of the same name branches into two streams; one is headed east for the Atlantic Ocean, the other west to reach the Pacific – truly a continental divide.

At this furthest point you are perhaps 50km from the nearest road, about as far from the modern world as you can get. There are a couple

ARMCHAIR

* ***Hawk's Rest*** (Gary Ferguson) Lyrical account of a season spent at the Hawk's Rest ranger's cabin deep in the Thorofare.

* ***Lost in My Own Backyard*** (Tim Cahill) Witty and engaging series of Yellowstone-related essays from the American travel writer.

* ***Decade of the Wolf*** (Douglas W Smith & Gary Ferguson) Chronicles the politics and science behind the reintroduction of wolves to Yellowstone.

* ***Back of Beyond*** (CJ Box) Murder mystery set among outfitters in the park's remotest corner, from the Wyoming-based author.

* ***Yellowstone*** Imax big-screen film that shows daily in West Yellowstone.

* ***The Yellowstone Story*** (Aubrey L Haines) The definitive account of the founding of America's first national park by a former park ranger.

of choices back to civilisation. Head straight east via the South Boundary Trail all the way to the South Entrance, or branch northwest following the Continental Divide Trail to lovely Heart Lake, a worthy destination in its own right.

▨ MAKING IT HAPPEN

Backcountry camp sites need to be booked well in advance, especially in August, and you need to pick up permits in person. Bridge Bay Marina offers boat shuttles to the northern point of the lake's Southeast Arm. Outfitters can arrange horse trips into the Thorofare, mostly from the Bridger-Teton Wilderness to the south, and companies like Wildland Trekking offer guided trips.

▨ AN ALTERNATIVE CHALLENGE

If you don't have time for a long backpacking trip into the backcountry, consider a guided wolf-watching trip. The highly regarded Yellowstone Association Institute offers three-day wolf-watching courses and hikes that take you to the best locations and teach you about wolf behaviour, communication and restoration efforts. Other courses range from backpacking trips to photography and bird-watching seminars.

MARK NEWMAN | LONELY PLANET IMAGES

OPENING SPREAD Firehole River and Lower Geyser Basin. **ABOVE** About 100 wolves in ten packs roamed Yellowstone National Park in 2011. **BELOW** Yellowstone's wolves occasionally hunt bison. Adult male bison weigh up to 800kg; the wolves prey on the ill and injured.

YELLOWSTONE'S WOLVES

In 1995, wolves were released back into Yellowstone for the first time in 70 years. Since then, the animals have thrived, with numbers peaking at around 175 individuals in 2003. Not everyone is happy to see them back in the region, however. Wolves have trimmed the numbers of elk, upsetting local hunters, and the attacks on sheep and cattle in neighbouring communities have angered ranchers. Still, the reintroduction of the wolf has undoubtedly restored a tangible wildness to the park. Few things quicken the pulse like the sound of a wolf howl echoing across Yellowstone's scenic valleys.

DEMOCRATIC
REPUBLIC
OF CONGO   UGANDA
                                   KENYA
       Kampala O
          O Entebbe

          O Bwindi Impenetrable National Park

RWANDA
            TANZANIA
  BURUNDI

TRACK MOUNTAIN GORILLAS IN UGANDA

THERE IS NOTHING – ABSOLUTELY NOTHING – LIKE A CLOSE ENCOUNTER WITH AFRICA'S GREATEST APES. HIKE THROUGH DENSE FOREST AND MASTER STEEP SLOPES TO SIT DOWN FOR AN HOUR'S CONTEMPLATION WITH ONE OF MANKIND'S CLOSEST RELATIVES: AN ALMIGHTY SILVERBACK.

There are estimated to be 700 mountain gorillas remaining in the world. Just 700. You could fit them all aboard one Airbus A380. You wouldn't, of course – these great apes prefer to roam a jungly patch of central Africa, the lush and thicketed highlands where Uganda, Rwanda and the Democratic Republic of Congo merge. Unfortunately, they're in direct competition with a crowded and growing human population. Habitat destruction, disease transfer, bushmeat-hungry poachers and war mean the gorillas' lot is not an easy one.

Enter ecotourism. Convincing local people a gorilla is worth more alive than dead is helping to safeguard the species. And it means that travellers (those who obtain a pricey permit) get to sit within metres of these formidable, yet curiously familiar creatures. Both Rwanda and Uganda have a well-developed gorilla-tracking infrastructure; you can end your day's hike in a luxury bathtub overlooking the rainforest if your budget will stretch. Renowned primatologist Dian Fossey worked in Rwanda, one reason most tourists head there. Uganda, however, offers equally good sightings, plus other distractions such as rafting the Nile, cruising Lake Mburo and hiking the Rwenzoris.

There are eight habituated gorilla groups in Uganda's Bwindi Impenetrable National Park, each numbering between five and 20 primates. You'll join a guide and no more than six hikers to track a specific group: some stay closer to park HQ, others lollop way over international borders. But these are wild animals; you might stumble upon them after 20 minutes or see nothing after many sweaty hours. It's a semi-strenuous adventure; the weather can be challenging, the terrain steep, the distance very variable. Gorilla tracking is also governed by strict rules: no children under 15 are allowed, no loud noises, flash photography or pointing; forget it if you're suffering from diarrhoea or a cold. When it happens, however, it's the wildlife encounter of a lifetime.

ESSENTIAL EXPERIENCES

* **Raising your binoculars as you hike through the forest to spot some of the 350-odd resident bird species.**

* Discovering a recently made nest and a mound of gorilla dung, which is still warm to the touch – you're getting close...

* **Realising that the huge black shape just behind the next bush is not a rock, but an enormous silverback.**

* Spending an enchanting, emotional, if-only-it-could-last-longer hour in the company of a whole gorilla group as they eat and play.

* **Taking more time to walk in the jungle with a local guide, looking out for chimpanzees, colobus monkeys, elephants and bush pigs.**

DISTANCE 2KM TO 20KM | **LOCATION** BWINDI IMPENETRABLE FOREST, SOUTHWEST UGANDA | **IDEAL TIME COMMITMENT** TWO DAYS | **BEST TIME OF YEAR** YEAR-ROUND | **ESSENTIAL TIP** NEVER STARE DIRECTLY AT A GORILLA

GORILLA GUIDE

There are two different species of gorilla (eastern and western), each with two subspecies. Those in Uganda and Rwanda are eastern mountain gorillas (*Gorilla beringei beringei*). The eastern lowland gorilla (*Gorilla beringei graueri*) is the largest subspecies, with the biggest recorded silverback measuring 1.94m; there are around 5000 in the Democratic Republic of Congo. The western subspecies are the western lowland gorilla (*Gorilla gorilla gorilla*) and the Cross River gorilla (*Gorilla gorilla diehli*). The former is the most widespread and abundant (around 200,000) but tricky to see; Gabon is the best bet. The Cross River type live in Nigeria and Cameroon; only 300 remain.

GORILLAS IN THE MIST

American zoologist Dian Fossey first visited Africa in 1963, and returned in 1966 to study mountain gorillas. She established the Karisoke Research Center in Rwanda, and spent countless hours studying the animals, earning their trust by imitating their behaviour. Locals called her Nyiramachabelli – 'the woman who lives alone on the mountain'. She greatly furthered understanding of gorillas and publicised their plight; after her favourite gorilla, Digit, was killed by poachers in 1977, she founded a fund in his name. Fossey was murdered in 1985, but not before her book, *Gorillas in the Mist*, relayed her story to the world.

THE ADVENTURE UNFOLDS

Impenetrable? There's a clue in the name. You've been hiking for two hours now through the aptly named Bwindi Impenetrable National Park and your legs are wobbly from clambering up vertical slopes and from negotiating the toupee of unstable vegetation underfoot. You're hot and bothered, and only half-looking for colourful birds in the canopy. Then your guide stops, and motions you to do the same. In the anticipatory silence you hear your heart thrum and – yes – the crunch of something moving up ahead. Gorillas.

You peer into the distance to try to discern any black specks. Then a huge rock moves, revealing itself to be not stone, but the biggest, most powerful animal you've ever seen. It's so close! You know you're not supposed to get nearer than 7m, but is this imperious silverback aware of the rules? You kneel, so as to appear less of a threat, though you can hardly imagine this big daddy being scared of anything. Suddenly two tiny gorillas come tumbling over, bowling into the silverback and bouncing right off; he doesn't even flinch.

There are 20 gorillas in all – mums with babies, juveniles fighting, adults grooming or just flopped out amid the bushes. They are so impressive, so expressive, so unflustered by your presence. You take a few photos but then put your camera away – you have only one hour with these great apes, and don't want to waste it looking through a lens. Instead, you sit in silence and just watch, the effort of the journey forgotten, the moments spent in the gorillas' company worth every step.

MAKING IT HAPPEN

Southwest Uganda has two gorilla parks: Bwindi Impenetrable Forest and Mgahinga National Park. Bwindi is more biodiverse and lower, offering easier hiking. Gorilla-tracking permits are compulsory, expensive and oversubscribed; book well in advance via the Uganda Wildlife Authority or a tour operator. Ideally, allocate two days to almost guarantee a sighting.

AN ALTERNATIVE CHALLENGE

The Rwenzori Mountains (Mountains of the Moon), home to Africa's third-highest peak – Mt Stanley, 5109m – stretch 110km along the Uganda-Congo border. They're draped in jungle and inhabited by a wealth of wildlife, yet hardly anyone hikes here. It's tough going, with high humidity and rainfall, and squelchy terrain, but Bakonzo porters will lighten your load and huts provide scenic shelter. Try the Loop Trail, a 48km, six- or seven-day circuit taking in Kitandra Lakes, the Bigos Bogs and views over the Congo Basin.

OPENING SPREAD A mountain gorilla feeds by stripping stems. **ABOVE (L)** Trekkers and guides in search of mountain gorillas in Bwindi Impenetrable Forest. **ABOVE (R)** King of the jungle: a silverback mountain gorilla. **LEFT** Meet the relatives: our evolutionary paths split about 10 million years ago.

213

ARMCHAIR

* *Gorillas in the Mist* (Dian Fossey) Memoir of the conservationist who lived (and died) among Rwanda's gorillas; made into a movie in 1988.

* *In the Kingdom of Gorillas* (Bill Weber & Amy Vedder) The authors' experiences of studying with Fossey and their founding of an ecotourism project (against her wishes) to help save the gorillas.

* *World Atlas of Great Apes and Their Conservation* (edited by Julian Caldecott & Lera Miles) An encyclopaedic guide to the planet's six great ape species.

* *Primates of the World* (Ian Redmond & Jane Goodall) Beautifully illustrated guide to almost 300 primate species, from mountain gorillas to mouse lemurs.

WASH ELEPHANTS IN THAILAND

AN UP-CLOSE ENCOUNTER WITH THE WORLD'S LARGEST LAND MAMMAL IS AS SOULFUL AS IT IS AWE-INSPIRING. DUST OFF YOUR CHILDHOOD DREAM OF BEING A WILDLIFE BIOLOGIST AND SPEND TIME AT AN ELEPHANT SANCTUARY, WHERE YOU'LL CONTRIBUTE TO THE WELFARE AND PRESERVATION OF AN ENDANGERED SPECIES.

214

Elephants have always played an integral role in Thai life. With a centuries-long tradition of domestication, these magnificent creatures have been employed for warfare, transportation and as hard-going labourers in a once-thriving logging industry. But the 1989 Thai ban on logging effectively rendered 70% of these elephants 'unemployed', creating a precarious economic position for both the mahouts (elephant handlers) and their charges, whose daily dietary needs alone weigh in at close to 200kg. Many owners turned to tourism, taking elephants street-begging in urban areas, having them paint pictures and perform tricks or offering rides. With little legal protection for their welfare, captive elephants have suffered a range of ill effects. Depleted in population, the Asian elephant has been placed on the IUCN Red List of endangered species.

Enter elephant sanctuaries, where rescued, injured or retired pachyderms are given a reprieve from their working life and a certain amount of freedom. A young Thai woman, Sangduen Chailert, first garnered widespread publicity for rescuing injured and traumatised elephants, opening the Elephant Nature Park (ENP) in 1995, 60km north of Chiang Mai in northern Thailand. In 2007 Katherine Connor and her family established the intimate Boon Lott Elephant Sanctuary (BLES), an 80-hectare reserve one hour's drive from Sukhothai, which provides rescued elephants with medical attention and rehabilitation.

Such projects have become part of a slow-moving wave of consciousness around the wellbeing and protection of elephants, as well as the economic challenges of mahouts, who are employed at sanctuaries and elephant education and conservation centres. Sanctuaries offer travellers the opportunity to spend time among the elephants in their natural habitat, and a chance to learn firsthand about mahouts and local village culture.

ESSENTIAL EXPERIENCES

* **Having your days punctuated by the not-so-distant sound of happy elephants trumpeting.**

* Cooling off in the natural swimming pool at the Tad Duan waterfall in Si Satchanalai National Park.

* **Imagining you're a zoologist as you quietly follow and observe elephant behaviour in the animals' natural habitat.**

* Sampling the amazing array of locally grown, just-picked tropical fruit (longkong, langsat, mangosteen) at the local market.

* **Trying some of your newly learned Thai words with a pachyderm – and seeing if she understands you!**

* Feeling an elephant's gentle nudge as you stroke her surprisingly smooth, freckled skin.

LOCATION NORTHERN THAILAND | **IDEAL TIME COMMITMENT** ONE WEEK | **BEST TIME OF YEAR** NOVEMBER TO MARCH
ESSENTIAL TIP BE PREPARED TO GET WET AND DIRTY – IT'S PART OF THE FUN!

THE MAHOUT

It's believed that the unique role of the Asian mahout began as many as 5000 years ago. Once a revered occupation, achieved through years of training from father to son, professional mahouts have gradually been losing status: domestic elephant use for transportation and work in Asia has decreased, third-party ownership has become common and traditional training methods are now regarded as abusive. With a healthy elephant's lifespan closely equating that of a human, the bond between a mahout and his charge remains the longest possible between man and animal.

EXPLORE KRUGER'S WILDERNESS TRAILS

GETTING DEEP INTO AFRICA DOESN'T MEAN SPOTTING THE BIG FIVE FROM THE COMFORT OF A SAFARI JEEP. IT'S GETTING OUT, ON FOOT, INTO QUIET WILDERNESS ISOLATION, SEEING THE DETAILS THAT MAKE THE WHOLE, AND FEELING THE HEART OF AFRICA BEATING STRONG.

218

The Kruger National Park is a vast swathe of bushland on South Africa's eastern border with Mozambique. Covering nearly 20,000 sq km, it's one of the largest national parks in Africa, a natural world little altered since the indigenous San people first lived here 20,000 years ago. Game spotters have been coming here since 1898, when the park was founded, but most visitors still see the park from behind the windscreens of their vehicles – only disembarking in the safety of the rest camps.

Since the 1970s, in a back-to-nature drive, the park has been developing foot trails for visitors. There are now seven trails, each with its own unique characteristics, and each based out of an isolated, rustic camp away from the visited parts of the park. Out here it's only you and seven fellow-walkers, ultraknowledgeable guides and incredible wildlife to view. You won't see any other people and you won't be separated from nature by metal and glass. Just you – on foot – deep in the African bush.

The Kruger Wilderness Trails aren't for everyone. First – no children under 12; you have to be able to work with the group in possibly dangerous situations, as there's always the threat of being charged by animals like rhinos, elephants or buffaloes. You'll trek on dusty, steep and rocky terrain, often off track, and for up to 20km a day. You may walk in the baking heat or the dawn chill, through thorn trees that tear your clothes; there may be snakes, and there will be plenty of insects, malaria-carrying mosquitoes included.

With all those caveats, walking in the wilderness of the Kruger National Park is nothing short of an adventure of a lifetime. This is a magnificent journey on which you can feel like the first human that trod the Earth. You'll travel through a glorious African Garden of Eden, and shed the burdens of modern life. These days in the wilds could change you forever.

ESSENTIAL EXPERIENCES

* **Immersing yourself in African nature: no barriers or fences, just you and the bush.**

* Revelling in a silence so profound, you can hear your own heartbeat – or is that the heartbeat of Africa?

* **Thrilling at the real, though carefully managed, danger of meeting animals face-to-face in the wild.**

* Spotting a rarely seen bird like the gorgeous, elusive Narina trogon – and finding that just as exciting as sighting one of the Big Five game.

* **Seeing the ancient, mystical rock art of this area's earliest inhabitants.**

* Falling asleep to the night-time sounds of the bush.

DISTANCE UP TO 50KM | **LOCATION** KRUGER NATIONAL PARK, SOUTH AFRICA | **IDEAL TIME COMMITMENT** SEVEN DAYS | **BEST TIME OF YEAR** YEAR-ROUND | **ESSENTIAL TIP** OBEY YOUR GUIDE UNQUESTIONINGLY – YOUR SAFETY DEPENDS ON IT

FACING THE DANGER

Being eaten alive: it's our most primeval fear. Yet one of the greatest things about walking in the territory of wild and potentially dangerous animals is that frisson of excitement that comes from considering one's vulnerability. Is it dangerous to walk the Wilderness Trails of the Kruger? Well, potentially: but with an expert guide, armed with a high-calibre rifle, who knows the territory and understands animal behaviour, the risk is minimal...perhaps less than the danger of actually getting here. No walker has ever been attacked on a Kruger Wilderness Trail: the biggest danger you'll face is that of getting blisters.

THE ADVENTURE UNFOLDS

The Kruger's walking trails are a sensual experience: a chance to feel, hear and smell the bush, with no artificial barriers. Even if you don't tick the boxes for spotting all the big game, you'll learn a lot about the bush – and yourself.

You'll start your three-night, four-day Kruger Wilderness Trail by travelling to an untouched reach of the park, with no roads, no electricity, no sounds except for those of nature. Accommodation is in standing tents or A-frame huts, most with shared reed-walled facilities open to the stars. The communal area is a shady *lapa* where meals are served from the basic bush kitchen and stories are recounted around the campfire.

The next three days begin at 5.30am, in the predawn chill. Most game activity happens at this time. Leaving camp you might see hyenas or jackals, or a family of warthogs trundling through the bush, tails held high.

Your guide points out the minuscule as well as the large scale: you'll see the incredible tree-spanning webs of golden orb spiders, watch dung beetles at work and learn the workings of termite mounds. Your guide will identify animal spoor (footprints) and scat (dung)...and then he may just put his finger to his lips and whisper, 'Lion!', 'Elephant!' or 'Cheetah!' The (armed) guides are extraordinary trackers who can read the ground like a book; if there's big game around, they'll take you to it.

An encounter on foot with a white rhino, a herd of elegant giraffes, even a lounging leopard if you're lucky, is unforgettable. In many parts of the park there are also San rock paintings.

MAKING IT HAPPEN

These wilderness trails are stratospherically popular: book up to a year ahead through South African National Parks. From Johannesburg, most rest camps in the park from which trips depart can be reached in a six-hour drive. Bring khaki-coloured clothes (preferably cotton), sturdy footwear, insect repellent, hat and sunscreen, malaria prophylactics and a torch.

AN ALTERNATIVE CHALLENGE

If you find it impossible to get onto a Kruger Wilderness Trail, you can still get out on foot. Kruger's main rest camps run small group walks (eight people) that depart early morning and offer a few hours of full immersion in nature, guided by a knowledgeable armed ranger. Mountain-biking game-spotting trips are also on offer and, if you want something really tough, the Oliphants River Trail is a guided 42km backpacking route along the wildlife-rich banks of the Oliphants River Valley. You sleep in your own tent...and you carry everything.

PETER JOHNSON | CORBIS

PETER JOHNSON | CORBIS

221

OPENING SPREAD Raiding the larder: a young leopard with an antelope killed by its mother. Leopards store food in trees, out of lions' reach. **ABOVE (L)** Cape buffalo are among Africa's most dangerous animals. **ABOVE (R)** An elephant herd. **LEFT** Male giraffes use their necks to fight for dominance.

ARMCHAIR

* *Signs of the Wild* (Clive Walker) A classic for budding game trackers; essential on your wilderness trail.

* *A Field Guide to the Mammals of Southern Africa* (Chris & Mathilde Stuart) This beautiful photographic reference will soon have you au fait with a diversity of game.

* *Illustrated Guide to the Birds of Southern Africa* (Ian Sinclair et al) The gold standard of birding guides in this part of the world.

* *Where to Watch Game in the Kruger National Park* (Nigel Dennis) An essential guide for your pre- or postwilderness-trail DIY game spotting.

* *The Kruger National Park: A Social and Political History* (Jane Carruthers) Fascinating background reading on how, and why, the Kruger came to be.

RIDE WITH THE KHAMPAS

JOIN KHAMPA COWBOYS ON A HORSE TREK THROUGH THE WILD VALLEYS AND PASSES OF WESTERN SICHUAN, LINKING THREE OF THE REGION'S MOST IMPORTANT MONASTERIES WITH SOME SPECTACULAR MOUNTAIN SCENERY FOR A TANTALISING GLIMPSE OF A LOST TIBET.

222

Savvy travellers know that real Tibet isn't limited by the arbitrary borders of the Tibetan Autonomous Region (TAR); rather, it spills off the plateau into the neighbouring provinces of Qinghai, Yunnan and Sichuan. The eastern region, Kham, is renowned for its deep, forested gorges, remote alpine valleys and the bravado of its resident Khampas. The entire region offers a taste of traditional Tibetan culture that is getting harder to find in Tibet proper these days. And, since it's way off China's mainstream tourist radar, it is largely devoid of the pesky permit regulations that hamstring independent travel in central Tibet.

This trip, a mix of the spiritual and the physical, links three rarely visited medieval monasteries with some challenging day hikes and wilderness rides, so you can soak up pristine mountain scenery during the day and then explore butter-lamp-lit prayer halls and the warrenlike medieval chapels of the monasteries. A highlight will doubtless be discussing Buddhist dialectics with maroon-robed monks or chatting with wild-haired nomads in the high valleys. Time your trip well and you'll catch one of the region's spectacular summer horse festivals, held at nearby Litang and Jyekundo (Yushu).

The Khampas of Western Sichuan infuse the region with colour and charm. Recognisable by red or black braids in their long hair, they're the affable rogues of eastern Tibet, sporting cowboy hats and brown *chubas* (robes), and flashing grins. The women wear ornate coral and turquoise jewellery and tease their hair into 108 separate braids. Khampas have long had a reputation for banditry, and formed the core of the armed resistance to the Chinese after the 1959 invasion. Western Sichuan is still a politically tense region and is often hit by riots or demonstrations. The Chinese authorities occasionally close monasteries or cancel festivals, so check the political situation before setting off.

ESSENTIAL EXPERIENCES

❋ **Joining maroon-robed monks for a prayer ceremony, surrounded by lines of chanting novices and golden Buddha statues.**

❋ Admiring the carved wooden blocks of the nearby Derge Monastery, one of Tibet's most important traditional printing presses.

❋ **Spinning prayer wheels as you join pilgrims on a clockwise walk around stupas, shrines and stones carved with sacred Tibetan mantras.**

❋ Joining nomadic herders in their yak-hair tents for a cup of salty yak-butter tea and a bowl of *tsampa* (ground barley meal).

❋ **Joining your horsemen in hanging prayer flags or throwing printed prayers into the sky at the sublime and sacred lake of Yilhun La-tso.**

ELEVATION 3800M TO 4600M | **LOCATION** WESTERN SICHUAN, CHINA | **IDEAL TIME COMMITMENT** TWO WEEKS | **BEST TIME OF YEAR** JUNE TO SEPTEMBER | **ESSENTIAL TIP** WATCH OUT FOR FIERCE GUARD DOGS IN REMOTE HERDERS' CAMPS – IT HELPS TO CARRY A STICK OR TREKKING POLE; CONSIDER GETTING A RABIES INOCULATION BEFORE TRAVELLING

TIBET OUTSIDE TIBET

The Chinese and Tibetans have very different definitions of Tibet. For the Chinese authorities, Tibet is the Tibetan Autonomous Region, a province-sized region that covers central and western Tibet 'proper', centred on the capital, Lhasa. Tibetans, however, consider it to be the whole of the Tibetan plateau, which continues northeast to the high grasslands of Amdo (Qinghai Province) and eastwards through the deep-forested gorges and high ranges of Kham (parts of Sichuan and Yunnan Provinces). The Tibetan regions outside of 'Tibet' have traditionally enjoyed closer contact with the Chinese lowlands but are still very much culturally Tibetan.

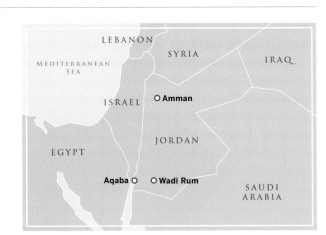

CAMEL TREK IN WADI RUM

A PARCHED DESERT LANDSCAPE OF TOWERING CLIFFS AND SAND-FILLED VALLEYS. EERIE FORMATIONS OF EONS-OLD RUST-RED ROCK, WHISPERING OTHERWORLDLY ECHOES. THE SOFT PADDING OF YOUR CAMEL – AND IN THE DISTANCE, YOUR CAMP FOR THE NIGHT, DEEP IN THE DESERT WITH THE BEDOUIN.

226

Ever since the 1962 film *Lawrence of Arabia* brought the spectacular deserts of Jordan into Western consciousness, Wadi Rum has fired the imaginations of adventurers. A series of valleys carved through soaring granite and sandstone formations in the far south of Jordan, Wadi Rum has a vast, natural beauty that is spellbinding. Add to that the romance of the nomadic Bedouin way of life here, and you have the makings of a singularly attractive adventure.

The wadi (Arabic for valley) has long lured visitors to its harsh terrain. Climbers come here to test themselves on cliff faces; trekkers climb its rocky mountains and natural arches; off-road drivers zoom around in 4WDs. But to really feel the heart of this place, you need to spend time here, to camp under its clear skies, wonder at its fiery sunsets and meet its inhabitants. And the best way to travel is as the local Bedouins do – on the undulating back of a camel.

Camel trekking Wadi Rum is high adventure, allowing you to reach deeply remote places, but you don't need to be particularly physically adventurous. A trek here might be a few hours' amble on camelback – or it might be an ambitious multiday expedition. Either way, you'll be taken care of by hospitable guides, and with all the logistics arranged, all you'll have to do is ride your ship of the desert through this natural splendour.

And then there's the cultural dimension to travelling Wadi Rum. Come here with the Bedouins: only they really know the wadi. They'll show you the most magnificent reaches of their territory, and they'll treat you with wonderful generosity. This is a culture in which hospitality is aligned with honour. You'll be invited into tented camps, offered genuinely warm greetings and abundant smiles. You'll drink sweet, spicy tea, eat a Bedouin feast and hear stories of desert life on carpets round the campfire, before sleeping in a traditional goats' hair tent beneath a sky brilliant with stars.

ESSENTIAL EXPERIENCES

✳ **Absorbing yourself in the vastness and silence of Wadi Rum, and hearing its towering cliffs echo back the slightest whisper.**

✳ Meeting the Bedouin, possibly the most hospitable people in the world.

✳ **Getting to know your camel, and learning about what makes these sensitive, emotional beasts tick.**

✳ Scrambling to some of Rum's summits or rock arches for a sublime bird's-eye view over the desert.

✳ **Camping out at night in Wadi Rum, falling asleep under a firmament spangled with a billion stars.**

DISTANCE 30KM TO 40KM PER DAY | **LOCATION** WADI RUM, SOUTHERN JORDAN | **IDEAL TIME COMMITMENT** ONE WEEK | **BEST TIME OF YEAR** YEAR-ROUND | **ESSENTIAL TIP** BRING A FOAM SADDLE PAD TO STAY COMFORTABLE ON MULTIDAY CAMEL TREKS

BEHIND THE VEIL IN WADI RUM

The desert seems so much like men's territory: men proudly mounted on their camels, men at the wheels of their 4WDs, men guiding and negotiating with tourists. As a visitor, you may encounter few Bedouin women – but there is a way to learn about women's lives in the Wadi Rum desert: if you're a woman. Family-run Wadi Rum Tours connects small groups of female visitors with the ladies in their family. Women shop together in the Rum village market, then go out to the desert to cook a meal, drink tea and spend time. In female company, the ladies shed their veils and chat freely about their lives – and they'll be curious about yours. It's a unique insight into a normally hidden part of desert life.

THE ADVENTURE UNFOLDS

Meet your camel. He's a tall fellow. The dromedaries used in Wadi Rum can be up to 27 hands tall at the hump – almost the height of two average horses. A camel's gait produces a strange, rocking motion that can be unnerving for the uninitiated, but the trick is to stay relaxed and confident; camels are intuitive animals and they are deft at sensing the emotional state of their rider.

For multiday treks, you'll always be accompanied by a mounted guide. The format for most treks is to meet with your guides at Rum village, where the road into Wadi Rum ends. Here your gear will be packed into a 4WD support vehicle, and you'll be introduced to your camel. Then, mounted on your steed, you'll make an exhilarating departure into the expansive, noiseless desert.

Padding along, you'll get used to your camel's noises (his hissing doesn't mean to sound unfriendly), movements (he moves both legs on one side at once) and smells (he may be pungent), while learning the commands to make him stop, go and lie down. Riding a camel is much less technical than riding a horse: your guide will probably hand you the reins within half an hour.

Make sure your wadi trek lasts at least five days, long enough to explore important sites – the colossal Seven Pillars of Wisdom, Lawrence's Spring, the soaring Burdah rock bridge and the petroglyphs of Alameleh – and to see Khazali Canyon with its rock art and the precipitous cliffs of Barragh Canyon. You need this long simply to breathe and feel the desert, to spend time with the people, and to let it all get under your skin.

MAKING IT HAPPEN

Wadi Rum is three and a half hours' drive from Jordan's capital, Amman, and 40 minutes from the Red Sea resort town of Aqaba. There's now a visitors centre at the entrance to Wadi Rum where tours, including camel trekking, can be arranged. Many Wadi Rum Bedouin families have a web presence, offering their services as guides. Bedouins of Wadi Rum and Jordan Tracks are two frequently praised family operations, who'll take you trekking for an hour, or a week, or more.

AN ALTERNATIVE CHALLENGE

If you don't fancy a camel trek you can still reach Wadi Rum, camp with the Bedouin and immerse yourself in the desert. There are many variations of 4WD tours – from hour-long to multiday expeditions. Short trips can be booked on the spot at the Wadi Rum visitors centre. With mechanised transport, you also have the chance to get further out into the desert in a shorter time – and spend more time in the less visited parts of the valley.

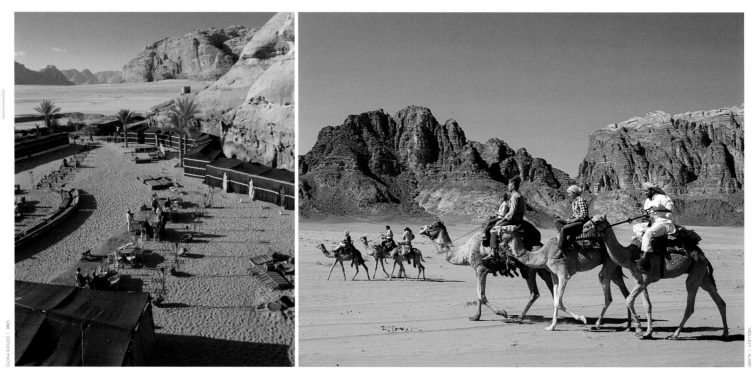

OPENING SPREAD Red planet: Wadi Rum has represented the landscape of Mars in movies. **ABOVE (L) AND (R)** Tented Bedouin camps are the bases for excursions into the desert on camels. The Bedouin prefer 4WD vehicles to travel Wadi Rum today.

ARMCHAIR

❋ **Treks and Climbs in Wadi Rum, Jordan** (Di Taylor & Tony Howard) A handy adventure guide for side trips when you need a rest from the camel's back.

❋ **Lawrence of Arabia** (1962) Much of this classic movie was filmed on location in Wadi Rum: the backdrops are awe-inspiring.

❋ **Red Planet** (2002) Parts of Wadi Rum were used as a stand-in for the surface of Mars in this sci-fi flick.

❋ **Seven Pillars of Wisdom** (TE Lawrence) Lawrence's account of his involvement in the 1916–18 Arab Revolt, in which he describes Wadi Rum as 'vast, echoing and God-like'.

❋ **Camel** (Robert Irwin) A fascinating, highly illustrated account of the role of camels in history and their place in present-day societies throughout the world.

WATER

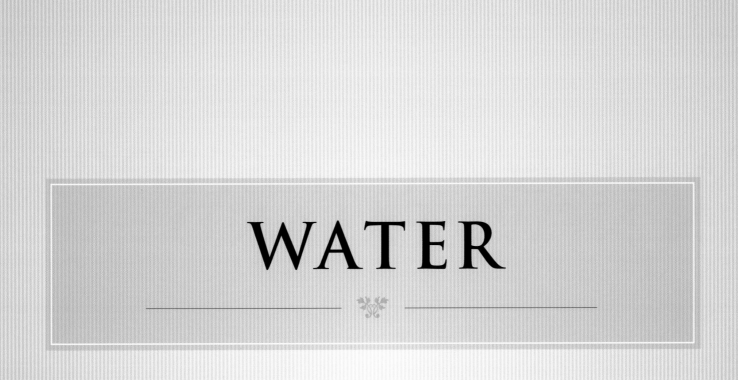

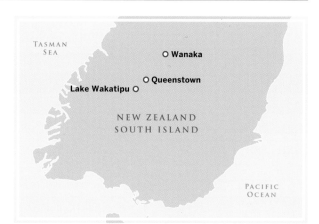

WHITE-WATER SLEDGE IN NEW ZEALAND

RAFTING TOO TAME FOR YOU? HOW ABOUT DISPENSING WITH THE BOAT AND TAKING ON NEW ZEALAND'S ICY WATERS FOR A MORE UP-CLOSE-AND-PERSONAL WHITE-WATER ADVENTURE, LURCHING AND SPLASHING THROUGH WILD RAPIDS BEHIND A GLORIFIED BOOGIE BOARD.

230

If white-water rafting has you yearning for something more individual, white-water sledging might be just the ticket. Known variously as hydrospeeding, river surfing, riverboarding or white-water sledging, it's rafting for one, clinging to the grips of a sledge as the river tries to have its wicked way with you.

Sledging traces its origins back to the 1970s, when a group of Frenchmen stuffed a sack full of life jackets and polystyrene, and used it to float down a river. During the 1980s, this ad hoc equipment morphed into river sledges, resembling ocean boogie boards. Today, riverboarding is a competition sport and features in adventure races – in fact, it's said that around one-third of all white-water activity in Europe is on sledges. Commercial sledging trips operate in countries including the USA, Slovenia and Norway, and one adventurer has even piloted a white-water sledge over a 22m-high waterfall in Costa Rica.

Adrenalin-thirsty New Zealand was one of the first countries to adopt white-water sledging as an adventure activity, introducing it in the late 1980s, and today there are operators in Wanaka, Queenstown and Rotorua. Sledgers are fitted out with boards, helmets and flippers, with guides in the water pointing out the best river lines.

The classic white-water sledging river in New Zealand is the Kawarau (also the site of the world's first commercial bungee jump), which flows midway between Queenstown and Wanaka after draining out of Lake Wakatipu. This river pitches sledgers through grade III rapids with inviting names such as Man-eater, Rollercoaster and Roaring Meg, the latter named for a prostitute who once worked the nearby gold fields. In Rotorua, things can get really manic on the Wairoa River, where you'll be tossed and turned by grade V rapids – this is said to be the biggest sledging run in the world.

ESSENTIAL EXPERIENCES

* **Kicking into position to surf a standing wave.**

* Breathing in a mouthful of water as a rapid drags you underwater – at least be prepared for it.

* **Popping out the other side of the Man-eater rapids for a flat finish to a wild ride.**

* Relieving sore muscles with a hot-spring soak in Rotorua after sledging the Wairoa River.

* **Kicking back in a lounge chair as you catch a postsledging movie at Wanaka's Cinema Paradiso.**

DISTANCE UP TO 12KM | **LOCATION** QUEENSTOWN, WANAKA AND ROTORUA, NEW ZEALAND | **IDEAL TIME COMMITMENT** HALF A DAY | **BEST TIME OF YEAR** DECEMBER TO MARCH | **ESSENTIAL TIP** THE THICKER THE WETSUIT, THE BETTER

GLACIAL FLOUR

If you're sledging the rivers of the South Island, you'll immediately notice the unusual grey colouring of the waterways. This is caused by so-called glacial flour, or rock flour, fine particles of rock that have been ground down by the grating of glaciers against rock. These silty particles are carried away in streams and rivers, turning the water almost milky in appearance. When the rock particles later settle in glacial lakes, an alchemy of sorts occurs, with the glacial flour so light, it stays suspended in the water. The refraction of light from the flour turns the lakes a brilliant turquoise blue, most famously seen at Lake Tekapo and Lake Pukaki.

■ THE ADVENTURE UNFOLDS

The Kawarau River is foaming like a saucepan of boiling water, though the water temperature is no more than about 9°C – not so long ago it was snow. Thank goodness for this wetsuit and the surging warmth of your adrenalin. You kick out from the rocky riverbank and the current begins to tow you downstream, slowly at first then at speed. Your fate is now something that's between you and the river alone.

You churn into the first rapid and you're immediately seized by a whirlpool that sucks you underwater into a damp black hole, spinning you and then spitting you out like the husk of a seed. You surface to see that others in the group have drifted from the middle of the river into the vortex of an eddy, where they swirl about like leaves.

The river speeds you past standing waves, until at last you feel the confidence to take on one of these monsters. Approaching the next rapid, you turn the board, reversing into the wave. As you hit it, you kick like an Olympic swimmer and suddenly you're atop the wave, surfing it, even if only for a couple of seconds.

You hit the final rapids, the furious Man-eater, and then the waves break and you become momentarily airborne before slapping back into the river. The water churns violently, and whirlpools slew your board, stopping you quicker than brakes. Your legs flap about like ribbons as you take your river punishment, circling the watery twister once more. This time you know better than to fight the whirlpool and it releases you back into the current.

The river flattens and you're through, exhausted, relieved and energised, your emotions as turbulent as the river. You may never raft again after this.

ARMCHAIR

* **New Zealand Adventure Guide** (Bette Flagler) Broaden your adventure scope with this guide to all things challenging by a native Kiwi.

* **The Penguin History of New Zealand** (Michael King) Popular history of the nation.

* **New Zealand's South Island Rivers: A Guide for Canoeists, Kayakers and Rafters** (Graham Egarr) If you want to be truly prepared before you take the plunge.

* **New Zealand Whitewater** (Graham Charles) Aimed at kayakers, this book will also help sledgers, with plenty of useful info about 125 runs throughout the country.

* **The Lord of the Rings: The Fellowship of the Ring** (2001) In the first of Peter Jackson's trilogy, the Kawarau River was the site of the Argonath statues.

RIVER GRADES

Like most outdoor adventures, rapids present degrees of difficulty and, as with rock climbing, the level of difficulty is quantifiable. Rapids are classed according to an International Scale of River Difficulty, which begins at grade I and climbs to grade VI. Grade I rapids contain small regular waves with easy passage, while grade V rapids are very difficult and considered the extreme end of things for commercial trips. Grade VI rapids were once described as unrunnable, though successful runs by kayakers have seen that softened to unraftable. Newcomers to white water will probably find they're comfortable at about grade II or grade III.

▣ MAKING IT HAPPEN

There are white-water sledging companies based in Wanaka, Queenstown and Rotorua. In Wanaka, Frogz Have More Fun is one of the country's original operators, and leads trips on the grade III Kawarau River. Kaitiaki Adventures in Rotorua runs trips on the Kaituna River and the grade V Wairoa River.

▣ AN ALTERNATIVE CHALLENGE

White-water rafting offers a similar experience to sledging, but with the added comfort that you're sharing the craft with a few other people, including at least one person who knows exactly what they are doing when things start to get a bit bumpy and chaotic.

Unsurprisingly, for a destination that has a well-earned reputation as an adventurer's Utopia, New Zealand has almost as many rafting opportunities as there are rivers in the country. The Rangitata River is considered one of the best, while other popular rafting waterways include the Kawarau and Shotover Rivers on the South Island, and the Rangitaiki and Kaituna Rivers on the North Island – Kaituna River trips include a very dramatic drop down the 7m-high Okere Falls.

OPENING SPREAD Meet Roaring Meg, a tumultuous stretch of the Kawarau river in Otago. **ABOVE** Dropping in: rafters on Kaituna river, which flows from Lake Rotorua in the North Island. **BELOW** Lake Pukaki near Mt Cook: it is fed by Lake Tekapo and the Tasman river.

WINDSURF THE COLUMBIA RIVER GORGE

HOIST YOUR SAIL FOR A MAGIC CARPET RIDE ON STEROIDS. DANCE OVER THE CHOP AS YOU BLAZE A TRAIL PAST A PARADISE OF PRISTINE FORESTS AND MOUNTAIN VISTAS, FIZZING SO FAST YOU'LL NEED A DE-ADRENALIN SHOT TO BRING YOU BACK DOWN.

234

Launching a windsurf or kiteboard in your own private wind tunnel is a secret fantasy of sailboarders worldwide. Fortunately, turning this dream into reality is as simple as making your way to the Columbia River Gorge in the Pacific Northwest. Extending more than 100km, this enormous canyon is the only navigable route through the mountain range known locally as the Cascades. And therein lies its attraction, because differences in wind pressure at opposite ends of the Cascades, coupled with the mountainous terrain, have combined to create a jet stream that effectively blasts its way through the gorge. The result is the ultimate wind-ride for experienced boarders who come from every part of the planet to savour the rush.

With dozens of designated launch sites, the gorge provides epic conditions at any time of year. But when the westerlies kick in, 60km/h wind gusts are not uncommon, which is why it is regarded as a true windsurf and kiteboarding mecca, not to mention a preferred contest location for the pros.

In the warmer summer months, winds average a moderate 20km/h to 25km/h, with the added bonus of sheltered spots for anyone looking to learn. Take advantage of this before heading out into the more treacherous zones, and whatever you do, don't attempt to cross the river unless you're a seasoned veteran. Not only is the gorge still a busy shipping route, as it has been for 200 years, there's also plenty of flotsam, not to mention extremely strong currents.

But the Columbia River has more to offer than just wind-borne recreation pursuits. It's also one of the few places where you can snowboard in the morning and pull in for a kite session in the afternoon.

Oh, and did we mention it's also a pristine wilderness boasting a bewildering concentration of waterfalls, including the 190m Multnomah Falls, the tallest falls in Oregon?

ESSENTIAL EXPERIENCES

* **Looking back up at the misty heights of the Cascades as you set off on dawn patrol.**
* Having your sail punched by the fist of Thor.
* **Feeling your arms ripping from your shoulders as you do everything you can to keep your ride under control.**
* Getting lifted higher, further, longer than you've ever been before.
* **Chilling postsession with your homies, ready to do it all again tomorrow.**

LENGTH 130KM | **LOCATION** HOOD RIVER, OREGON, USA | **IDEAL TIME COMMITMENT** HALF A DAY | **BEST TIME OF YEAR** JUNE TO SEPTEMBER | **ESSENTIAL TIP** PACK YOUR SMALLEST KITE/SAIL TO HANDLE THE 50KM/H+ WINDS

KEEP CLEAR

Oregon isn't quite Deliverance territory but it still pays to observe the local laws while you're riding the river. Sailboarders can be fined up to US$5000 for obstructing shipping laneways, and if you spot a sheriff's boat, steer clear as you're not allowed within 500m. The tankers are particularly hazardous, as their size causes large 'wind shadows' – if you do get too close, you might find there is literally no power to blow you out of harm's way. It's the kind of situation that could have you squealin' like a pig...

UNDERGROUND THREAT

The fate of the Columbia River lies in the success or failure of one of the most extensive environmental cleanup operations in the world. Until their decommission at the end of the Cold War, nine nuclear reactors along the banks of the river discharged plutonium into the water course. While unpleasant, the real danger comes from a million gallons of radioactive waste that has leached into underground aquifers and is slowly moving towards the Columbia River. Experts predict that if the cleanup stalls or fails, the poisoned water from the aquifers could pollute the river within 10 years.

THE ADVENTURE UNFOLDS

Cruising the historic Columbia River Highway (Highway 100) is the perfect precursor to riding the Columbia River Gorge. Completed in the 1920s, Highway 100 was purposefully designed to showcase the mountains, canyons, cliffs and spectacular waterfalls for which the gorge is renowned. It also means you can check out the lay of the land and river before you set sail.

The real action starts at your launch site on the banks of the Columbia River. You've picked your spot after consulting the weather charts and knowledgeable locals back in Fort Hood, knowing that along the gorge even a few kilometres can mean drastically different water and atmospheric conditions. You pull on your wetsuit, rig up your smallest kite and prepare for launch. The water is freezing, like the locals said it would be. Above the far shore, clouds skitter above a sheet of conifers that cloak the hills, a small gust catches your kite and you're off, skidding across the water like a new-age Messiah.

Lurching forward, you notice the changing hues of the river, signifying shifts in the current. Like an enormous mass of living liquid, it's constantly on the move. Ahead, an overladen barge slugs its way along the well-plied shipping lane. You angle your arms and shift your weight as another gust approaches, and like a hand from the heavens it plucks you from the water and throws you up towards the mountains.

Shredding your aerial manoeuvre, you land majestically as another gust shunts you forward, like your kite is caught in the doors of a freight train. Then you either hang on for the ride of your life, or get dragged into a world of pain.

MAKING IT HAPPEN

Head to Hood River, the nearest town, about 60km from the gorge. Be warned that this place fills up fast whenever races are on or the wind is nuking. An easier and cheaper accommodation option is to camp at sites within the Columbia River Gorge National Scenic Area, which spans the entire length of the gorge. Renting a car will give you the flexibility to choose your launch site depending on the wind, the atmospheric conditions and the river's strong currents.

AN ALTERNATIVE CHALLENGE

Still working on your pro credentials? No worries, try the Sandspit at Hood River where you'll find moderate, consistent conditions along with some of the planet's most experienced sailboarders and kitesurfers to help hone your skills before you take on the gorge. Alternatively, you can always hike the nearby hills and get a bird's-eye view of the action. Even on a calm day you can watch and learn from dozens of shredders. Wear proper boots though – the area is notorious for rattlesnakes.

237

OPENING SPREAD Columbia River Gorge in winter. **ABOVE (L)** The new breed: kiteboarders come out to play. **ABOVE (R)** Windsurfing the Columbia river. **LEFT** At 190m Multnomah Falls in the Columbia River Gorge National Scenic Area is the second highest year-round waterfall in the US.

ARMCHAIR

* **Pokin' Round the Gorge** (Scott Cook) A lover's guide to the Columbia River region, featuring saucy images and secret spots ideal for intimacy!

* **The World Kite and Windsurfing Guide** (Udo Hoelker) Once you've shredded Columbia River, plan your next trip with this formidable resource showcasing over 1200 of the best windsurf locations worldwide.

* **Wild Beauty: Photography of the Columbia River Gorge, 1867–1957** (Terry Toedtemeier & John Laursen) A coffee-table book revealing the magnificence of this area and how it changed following dam construction that began in the late 19th century.

* **The Windsurfing Movie** (2007) Directed by Johnny DeCesare, this film shot at locations around the world is considered the definitive movie about windsurfing.

THREE MEN IN A BOAT

The success of *Three Men in a Boat* was extraordinary. Not only did it make Jerome Klapka Jerome into a household name, the book sold over a million copies in its first 20 years – extraordinary for the late 19th and early 20th century. It also inspired a new generation of leisure boaters who flocked to the Thames to emulate Jerome's adventure. Like all great successes, it spawned a sequel. In *Three Men on the Bummel*, Jerome brought back the characters of his real-life friends who travelled with him on the boat, except this time they were cycling through Germany. Critically well received, it failed to do for the Bummel what *Boat* did for the Thames.

■ THE ADVENTURE UNFOLDS

This trip is all about experiencing complete freedom in the midst of the urban sprawl. Whether you take three days or 15, row 3km or 30km, camp in the skiff or book into a B&B, it's your call. However, operating many of the river's 45 locks that are on your route is the only thing you don't get to opt in or out of.

If you're inclined to fish for your supper, head for a tributary, such as the River Bourne in Chertsey, where you angle for freshwater trout, pike and flounder. Surprisingly, the Thames is also home to colonies of seahorses and invasive crustaceans like the Chinese mitten crab and crayfish. As you pass through the locks and weirs, you may notice fish ladders erected to help salmon (reintroduced to the Thames in 2007) fight their way upstream. Feeding on the marine life are kingfishers, cormorants and numerous geese, ducks and gulls, not to mention majestic swans with their 'ugly ducklings' in tow.

Three Men in a Boat enthusiasts can almost perfectly re-create Jerome's original journey. Not only did the author provide wonderfully rich descriptions, but the route of the Thames has hardly altered and most of the inns and pubs Jerome and his companions visited are still open for business.

After passing through Goring Gap, the narrowest stretch of the Thames Valley flowing snugly between verdant hills stretching westwards to the Berkshire Downs and the Chilterns woodlands in the east, you arrive at Whitchurch, Jerome's last stop. Pull up at the wharf and make your way for a meal at the 18th-century Swan Inn, where a beleaguered Jerome and friends declared 'sod this for a game of soldiers' and trotted off home.

■ MAKING IT HAPPEN

You can hire a skiff online and even arrange for the boat to be transported to where you want to start your journey. At around 24km from central London, Walton-on-Thames is a perfect launching point for first timers not sticking to Jerome's journey. Once you're on your way, it's easy to moor the skiff just about anywhere, although tying up near a pub that overlooks the Thames is an ideal way to combine security with pleasure.

■ AN ALTERNATIVE CHALLENGE

Instead of being on the Thames, why not cycle beside it? London is infamous for its maddening traffic, but the city boasts some great cycling tracks that extend along both banks of the river. You can ride virtually traffic free from the riverbank at Richmond all the way to picturesque, increasingly posh Putney. The route passes the Dove, England's oldest surviving riverside pub, which claims to have the smallest bar-counter in the world. A favourite of novelist Graham Greene, it has a beautiful balcony overlooking the Thames.

OPENING SPREAD Pick your skiff: rent a boat at Richmond-upon-Thames. **ABOVE (L)** Three men in a boat in Shillingford, Oxfordshire. **ABOVE (R)** The Thames passes grand riverside properties on its way to London. **LEFT** The green and pleasant land of Lechlade, Gloucestershire, near the river's source.

ARMCHAIR

* **The Wind in the Willows** (Kenneth Grahame) The anthropomorphic 1908 classic takes place in the middle to upper reaches of the Thames, and even has Toad and friends 'messing about in boats'.

* **The Thames: A Cultural History** (Mick Sinclair) Recounts interesting anecdotes about the river, from its legendary lock keepers to its tunnels and bridges.

* **'London Calling'** (The Clash) The music video for the anthem by the iconic punk rockers was shot at Battersea Park's Festival Pier, looking onto a dramatic, storm-blasted Thames in the winter of 1979.

* **The Water Music** (Handel) Handel's chillaxing masterpiece was premiered on the royal barge of George I in 1717 after the king decided to hold a concert while sailing up and down the Thames.

KAYAK AND CRUISE ANTARCTICA

A WORLD OF GLISTENING WHITE, WHERE ICEBERGS CALVE, WHALES BREACH AND PENGUINS MINGLE IN THEIR MILLIONS... TO VISIT ANTARCTICA – BY EXPEDITIONARY VESSEL AND SEA KAYAK – IS TO LEAVE THE WORLD OF MAN AND SUBMIT ENTIRELY TO THE WONDER OF NATURE.

242

A continent that no one owns, with no permanent human population and no capital – Antarctica (cliché alert) is the planet's last true wilderness. In this frozen zone at the bottom of our world, Mother Nature is still totally in charge. She seems to be venting her fury here though: Antarctica is the coldest, windiest and driest continent. Arable land? 0%. Ice cover: 98%; the other 2% is barren rock. In short, 14 million sq km of freezing, hostile nothing. So why is it so beautiful? The existence of this gargantuan land was not known until the 19th century. Maoris, whalers and Captain Cook had previously nibbled at the region's edges, spying sub-Antarctic isles. But it wasn't until 1820 that the main landmass was first glimpsed, then confirmed as a continent in 1840. There followed a flurry of expeditions, keen as Boy Scouts to tick off firsts in this unwelcoming but irresistible new world.

Getting to Antarctica is less perilous these days. Tourist cruises began in the 1960s, and boomed from the '80s. Today, during the November to February austral summer, fleets of vessels carrying around 34,000 passengers set sail for the Antarctic Peninsula, surrounding southern isles and, most intrepid of all, the Ross Sea. Antarctica is busier than it was. You'll spot other visitors: the birds, seals, penguins and whales that breed and feed amid the floes.

Cruising is a physical doddle. There are no Shackleton-type exertions; you just need to be able to get in and out of a Zodiac, the rigid-hulled inflatables that whisk explorers from big ship to shore. But there are ways to up the adrenalin levels: many vessels carry kayaks, so you can sidle into coves for extreme ice close-ups. There may also be opportunities for tougher hikes or even (shudder) ice diving. But even if your most strenuous task is lifting your binoculars to focus on a blue whale flicking its tail, this is still the adventure of a lifetime.

ESSENTIAL EXPERIENCES

* **Mingling among the noisy, stinky, enormous king penguin colonies on South Georgia.**

* Zipping past the face of a skyscraper-high iceberg in Paradise Harbour, aboard a tiny Zodiac.

* **Squeezing through the mile-wide Lemaire Channel, flanked by mountains.**

* Viewing the bergs, seals and penguins from sea-level, on a kayak expedition.

* **Sharing a beach on the South Shetland Isles with Adélie, chinstrap and gentoo penguins, and elephant and crabeater seals.**

* Raising a dram to Shackleton – the explorer is buried in the whalers' cemetery at Grytviken, South Georgia.

DISTANCE FROM 2000 NAUTICAL MILES | **LOCATION** ANTARCTIC PENINSULA | **IDEAL TIME COMMITMENT** TWO TO THREE WEEKS | **BEST TIME OF YEAR** NOVEMBER TO FEBRUARY | **ESSENTIAL TIP** TAKE GINGER TO COMBAT SEASICKNESS

A PLACE OF PEACE

On 23 June 1961, a dozen countries signed the Antarctic Treaty, a landmark agreement to demilitarise and preserve the White Continent. Today, 46 countries (comprising 80% of the world's population) are members. The treaty's aims are clear: to ensure Antarctica is used only for peaceful purposes, and that it's not exploited for nuclear testing or waste disposal; to guarantee the freedom of scientific research; and to remove the potential for sovereignty disputes over its territories. Each year, members meet to discuss pressing issues, such as environmental pressures and the impact of tourism, in the hope of safeguarding this wilderness for the future.

A PLACE OF PENGUINS

Seven species of penguin are found on Antarctica and the sub-Antarctic islands. Adélies, named after the wife of French explorer Dumont d'Urville, are small black-and-white birds with white eye rings. Chinstraps have a black line across their throats; they're the second most numerous species. Macaronis are the first — there are 12 million breeding pairs of these orange-tufted creatures. Rockhoppers, the smallest species, also have head tassels. Emperors are the largest, growing up to 1m; kings are 20cm shorter and breed in vast numbers on South Georgia. Small gentoos flock here too, identifiable by their orange bills and white eye flashes.

THE ADVENTURE UNFOLDS

You've found your sea legs. Crossing the dreaded Drake Passage to get from Ushuaia to the South Shetland Islands was a rocky ride. Dramatic though, watching waves crash on deck, feeling the full force of Poseidon in a strop. But then – calm. The tidal torrents became mirror-smooth. The last ripple you saw turned out to be a humpback flexing its fluke.

You haven't decided what you like best yet. The elegant Arctic terns are a contender, as are the elephant seals, guarding the beaches with cantankerous grunts, and the orcas, the albatrosses, the minkes and the penguins, who don't care for rules and peck at your boots when you're trying to keep your distance.

Then there's the land itself. How can there be so many shades of white? Icebergs glitter and glow blue or emerald green; some are carved into elegant shapes, while others loom like mountains. It's gorgeously terrifying. Yesterday, as you passed an ice wall, a chunk the size of a caravan plunged into the water with a mighty boom. Your favourite moment, though, has been your small piece of peace. There are only 100 passengers on your ship – more intimate than the vast vessels carrying thousands, and you can get ashore more frequently. But still, that's 100 people, plus naturalists, guides and other crew.

So you join a kayak excursion. The land felt vast before, now it feels infinite; from kayak-level you feel like a microscopic krill. You paddle to a quiet cove. A crabeater seal bobs up, keeping its beady eyes on your progress. You paddle on, under an ice arch, past a berg of dazzling blue. And, for a moment, you lose sight of the others – it's just you, that crabeater and the world's wildest place.

MAKING IT HAPPEN

Most Antarctic cruises disembark from Ushuaia, south Argentina, where they can be booked, often at discounted rates. But advance booking is advised. Itineraries range from one to three weeks. Shorter trips go to the Antarctic Peninsula; longer routes also visit South Georgia and the Falklands. Choose your ship based on its itinerary, facilities and size (bigger boats are more stable, smaller vessels enable more shore landings).

AN ALTERNATIVE CHALLENGE

Today, reaching the South Pole is more about hard cash than hard graft. With US$40,000, it's possible to fly there aboard a ski-plane – covering in hours the wilderness that took early explorers many months to cross. Fly from Punta Arenas in Chile to Union Glacier Camp, to acclimatise to life on Antarctica; from there it's a four- to five-hour flight to the Geographic South Pole, to walk round the globe in a few footsteps, visit the Amundsen–Scott Station and, of course, buy souvenirs. For details, contact Adventure Network International.

OPENING SPREAD Dodging icebergs: Antarctica's largest iceberg was B15-A at 2500 sq km. **ABOVE (L)** Kayaking Lemaire Channel off Graham Land, the area of Antarctica closest to South America. **ABOVE (R)** Young Weddell seals at Lutzow-Holm Bay. **LEFT** Adélie penguins raising chicks on Paulet Island.

ARMCHAIR

* **Antarctica** (Lonely Planet) Handy guidebook to the continent, including booking advice and maps.

* **The Worst Journey in the World** (Apsley Cherry-Garrard) The Antarctic classic; tells the tale of Captain Scott's ill-fated polar expedition.

* **Frozen Planet** (2011) The BBC's breathtaking TV series shows the poles in all seasons, bursting with life and battered by katabatic winds – essential viewing.

* **Scott of the Antarctic** (1948) Black-and-white movie retelling of Scott's journey, filmed largely in Norway. Ralph Vaughan Williams' rousing score was later reworked into his Sinfonia Antarctica.

* **Terra Incognita: Travels in Antarctica** (Sara Wheeler) The travel writer joined the USA's Antarctic Artists' and Writers Program, and then the British Antarctic Survey; the results are a thoughtful meditation on the White Continent.

RAFT THE AMAZON

FEW ADVENTURES ARE MORE INDIANA JONES IN FEEL THAN EXPLORING THE
BACK AND BEYOND OF THE AMAZON. ADD TO THAT THE THRILLS AND SPILLS
OF WHITE-WATER RAFTING, AND YOU'RE ONTO AN ADVENTURE WORTHY OF
THE FEDORA'D MAN HIMSELF.

246

Every river has to start somewhere and the mighty Amazon, the longest
waterway on the planet, starts right here on the Río Apurímac, home to some
fantastic white-water rafting. While many Peruvian adventures are easily
accessible by weekend warriors and armchair adventurers, this one takes the
level of commitment several notches higher.

Located deep within the mountains close to the home of Peru's Incan
heritage, the Río Apurímac cuts a deep swathe into the earth, forming a
canyon that's twice the depth of the Grand Canyon. Starting close to Cusco,
it starts as a trickle and eventually grows to a torrent. In total, the river
stretches over 1000km before it meets the Amazon, which continues for
another 6500km before meeting the Atlantic Ocean. Safe to say, you won't be
rafting the whole thing.

The majority of trips are around three days long, taking in the river's most
thrilling sections. The more intrepid can easily spend 11 days or more on
the river, however, finding adventure after adventure. The really wild-eyed
explorers among you can attempt to travel its full length to where it meets the
Amazon – good luck with that, because if you do it, you'll be the third group
ever to have safely completed the trip.

No matter how long you spend on the river, you'll be rewarded with
spectacular scenery and the chance to spot some iconic Peruvian wildlife,
perhaps including pumas, which have been glimpsed on the riverbanks.
The canyon walls grow to a staggering height of 3000m – claustrophobic,
committing and jaw-dropping awesome all at once. Peru is a land of
extraordinary experiences and this trip, just steps from one of the planet's
adventure capitals, takes you to an untouched world.

ESSENTIAL EXPERIENCES

* **Feeling the rush of rafting one of the top 10
  rivers in the world.**

* Taking in the solitude of the river and the canyon –
  so close to civilisation but true wilderness.

* **Learning about the fascinating Incan history
  that surrounds the area: walking the Inca
  Trail, exploring the Pisac ruins and, of course,
  visiting Machu Picchu.**

* Tasting some of the unique and underappreciated
  Peruvian cuisine available throughout the
  region: *monoya* (mint) tea to help with altitude
  acclimatisation and *cuy* (guinea pig) if you're
  feeling adventurous.

DISTANCE THREE TO 11 DAYS ON THE RIVER | **LOCATION** SOUTHEASTERN PERU | **IDEAL TIME COMMITMENT** THREE DAYS | **BEST
TIME OF YEAR** MAY TO NOVEMBER | **ESSENTIAL TIP** BE SURE TO FACTOR IN SOME EXTRA ACCLIMATISING TIME FOR WHEN YOU FIRST
ARRIVE IN CUSCO - THE 3300M ALTITUDE WILL SLOW YOU DOWN!

THE INCA TRAIL – IS IT WORTH IT?

The Inca Trail is one of those hikes that gets written about in travel lit, adventure magazines and all over the web as *the* thing to do. Well, in a sea of 'it' things to do, is it really worth all the hype? In a word – yes. It's easy to get to the start of the Inca Trail and feel fairly jaded about the whole production. Sure, it's busy and there's a mountain of hype higher than the highest pass on the trail, but that hype is well earned. Stunning vistas, some great history and walking right to Machu Picchu – yep, it's worth it.

■ THE ADVENTURE UNFOLDS

Departing from Cusco, it's a scenic and historic drive upriver to the Apurímac canyon and the start of the rafting. This trip has been named as one of the top 10 rafting experiences in the world and that will come as no surprise once you behold the river. Over a millennia the relentless flow of water has carved a canyon that runs 3000m deep. At its bottom the Río Apurímac snakes its way through the mountains and past historic Incan ruins; the river is a feast for the eyes and the soul.

Once you hit the water, the action is on. In Quechua, the native language of Peru, Apurímac means 'the Great Speaker' – Incan priests would consult the river for advice, and it would speak back. It's fair to say that once the rapids start crashing over your raft, and you are among the river's froth and fury, you'll be having a chat with it too.

With a steady stream of class IV and V rapids to keep things interesting, both new rafters and well-bloodied experts will be entertained. The white-water isn't ultra continuous; there are plenty of gaps in the action to collect your thoughts and perhaps your swimming companions. All of the tricky bits are easily scouted before you run them, and despite the sheer steepness and claustrophobic nature of the canyon, rapids that look a bit too much can easily be skipped.

Whether you choose to make this a short, three-day expedition or really stretch it out, seeing the sun rise above the skyscraper canyon walls is a sight you'll never forget, and this alone is perhaps worth the trip itself.

■ MAKING IT HAPPEN

Cusco is home base for much of the action in Peru. While many visitors arrive here as the base of operations for tackling the Inca Trail and onward to Machu Picchu, organising a rafting trip from here is a piece of cake. There are numerous accommodation options in this historic city and plenty of other things to do while you are there. Activities Peru, River Explorers and Eric Adventures all run safe and fun rafting trips.

■ AN ALTERNATIVE CHALLENGE

So water isn't your thing? No worries – jump on a bike. The steep hillsides aren't just good for rafting, they're also a prime location for mountain biking. There are several riding options available, from introductory to hard-core. Cycling the Sacred Valley is a huge highlight, which will see you leaving from Cusco and gliding through the valley, passing several small villages along the way. Finish in Pisac – one of the best-preserved Incan sites in Peru – and be sure to save some time to explore.

OPENING SPREAD Amazon tributaries snake across Tambopata-Candamo National Reserve. **ABOVE (L)** A village chief of the indigenous Shipibo-Conibo people of the Peruvian Amazon. **ABOVE (R)** The Río Apurímac cuts a way through the Andes. **LEFT** Machu Picchu was built by Incas in the 15th century.

ARMCHAIR

* **The Milk of Sorrow** (2009) Critically acclaimed and Academy Award–nominated, the film tells the story of one woman's journey to raise enough money to bury her recently deceased mother in the village in which she was born.

* **The Conquest of the Incas** (John Hemming) Regarded by many as the definitive history of the end of the Incan Empire and the Spanish invasion that created the Peru we know today.

* **Fitzcarraldo** (1982) This classic film by Werner Herzog tells the story of an ingenious but insane dreamer who travels upriver in search of rubber trees. The only thing standing in his way is a stretch of land he needs to portage his 300-tonne boat over! Production of the film was so tense that a Peruvian chief cast in the film offered to murder the leading man, Klaus Kinski, as a favour to the director.

COASTEERING IN PEMBROKESHIRE

WHAT YOUR PARENTS STOPPED YOU DOING AT THE BEACH AS A CHILD: THIS IS HOW COASTEERERS DESCRIBE TRAVERSING THE SEAWARD SIDE OF BRITAIN'S COASTLINE BY JUMPING, SWIMMING AND SCRAMBLING. RELIVE THE WETTER, WILDER, FUNNIER VERSION OF YOUR CHILDHOOD.

250

This adventure is new compared to most adrenalin rushes, but not that new. Everyone from seabird egg-gatherers to those who simply wanted to access that next cove along, and weren't daunted by the sea being in their way, has done this seaside scramble-cum-swim in some form. But it wasn't until the 1970s that the term 'coasteering' was first used. Twenty years later, adventure companies started offering thrill-seekers the chance to indulge.

It's a simple concept. Leave the beaches and calm waters behind as you scale stretches of dramatic, seemingly inaccessible, coastline at sea level: preferably when there's a swell. No surprises, then, that Britain is world coasteering capital, and that Pembrokeshire, with its spectacular, relentlessly rocky coasts and ideal swell conditions for such capers, is the hub. Forget cliff-top paths, boats or ropes: we're talking about clinging to wave-drenched rocks, jumping off 12m cliffs and floating into rarely seen caves to make your way along the shore. Unlikely and ungainly as it seems (you'll outdo those kings of cliff-side comedy, the puffins, in your blundering runs and jumps), coasteering will probably be the most fun you have had on the other side of the high-tide line.

Why? This is pure, childish pleasure; fun anyone can have. You don't need to be a certified diver or to have the skill of a surfer. Throwing yourself into churning Welsh seawater sounds daft but once you're in, you feel revitalised. Lying on your back in surprisingly Caribbean-coloured water, looking up at the sea-bashed walls of a cave concealed from the world above, in a spot that was previously the sole domain of waves, you'll get it. And you'll wonder why a pastime that anyone of reasonable fitness over the age of eight can try, and that unfolds a stone's plop from one of Britain's best-loved coastal paths, has taken so long to get going.

ESSENTIAL EXPERIENCES

* **Launching yourself off-cliff into the sea for the first time.**

* Battling 2m swells to cling to slimy cliffs until the inevitable tumble back into the sea.

* **Floating into creeks and glimpsing unique views of Wales' diverse cliff life, from seabirds to seaweed.**

* Spotting Atlantic grey seals.

* **Strolling through the magical medieval mini city of St Davids.**

DISTANCE 300M TO 600M | **LOCATION** NORTH PEMBROKESHIRE, WALES | **IDEAL TIME COMMITMENT** FOUR HOURS | **BEST TIME OF YEAR** SEPTEMBER TO OCTOBER | **ESSENTIAL TIP** DON'T COASTEER WITHOUT A GUIDE – COASTGUARDS REGULARLY RESCUE WOULD-BE ADVENTURERS TRYING TO GO SOLO

SAIL CROATIA'S DALMATIAN COAST

WEIGH ANCHOR, HOIST THE MAINSAIL, AND WITH THE ISLANDS OF DALMATIA
BEFORE YOU, SAIL BETWEEN THE HISTORIC AND NATURAL JEWELS OF CROATIA'S
ADRIATIC COASTLINE. WHEN A LITTLE LANDLUBBING APPEALS, COME ASHORE
TO FORESTED COVES, FISHING VILLAGES AND ANCIENT FORTIFIED TOWNS.

254

The Dalmatian coast of Croatia is 360km long, stretching from the town of
Zadar in the north to the Bay of Kotor on the border with Montenegro to the
south. It takes in the dramatic and historic cities of Split and Dubrovnik, over a
thousand islands, countless beautiful beaches, jewel-like coves and quiet bays.

Local legend has it that Marco Polo was born on the Dalmatian island of
Korčula, but you don't need to be a world-changing adventurer to discover
Croatia's Adriatic shores. With reliable wind, abundant uncrowded anchorages
and near-endless summer sun, the Dalmatian coast is one of the world's
best and most easily navigated sailing destinations. Add to that the region's
eventful 2000-year history and strong cultural identity, and you have the
makings of the perfect maritime adventure.

Island-hopping off Dalmatia is as much about the stopping as the time at
sea. Cruise your yacht among the 147 (mostly uninhabited) Kornati Islands,
where impossibly clear waters fringe sculpted cliffs and caves. Or try Mljet
Island, which supports the eponymous densely pine-forested national park.
Then check out magnificent Diocletian's Palace in Split, started in AD 295, and
the Unesco World Heritage city of Dubrovnik, founded in the 7th century.

The heartbreakingly gorgeous island of Hvar, with its olive groves, lemon
trees and perfect medieval villages, has been well and truly 'discovered', so if
you want to see perhaps the most beautiful island in Dalmatia, you'll have to
put up with the crowds. To get away from it all, try the islands of Pasman and
Ugljan in the north of Dalmatia, or remote Palagruza way out in the Adriatic.
Sail to golden Zlatni Rat on the island of Braco to sunbathe on Dalmatia's
best beach, or simply see where the wind takes you; there are countless other,
nameless stretches of sand and secret coves that only a sailor can get to.

ESSENTIAL EXPERIENCES

* **Arriving in a deserted cove, dropping anchor into the azure depths, and plunging in.**

* Wandering in awe through ancient World Heritage–listed towns and peaceful, historic fishing villages.

* **Smelling the scent of sun-warmed pine wafting over your boat as you pass forested islands.**

* Catching fish as you sail and barbecuing them over the coals on a remote beach.

* **Feeling the salt spray fresh on your face as the *maestral* breeze fills your sails and you cruise to the next gorgeous anchorage.**

* Savouring fabulous seafood alfresco at the tiniest harbourside restaurant, and sipping Croatian wine as you laugh with the locals.

DISTANCE 360KM | **LOCATION** DALMATIA, CROATIA | **IDEAL TIME COMMITMENT** TWO TO THREE WEEKS | **BEST TIME OF YEAR** MAY TO MID-JULY, MID-AUGUST TO SEPTEMBER | **ESSENTIAL TIP** BEWARE OF STRONG TIDAL CURRENTS IN NARROW PASSES BETWEEN ISLANDS

TASTING DALMATIA

Whether you catch your own, buy it in the markets or order it in restaurants for every meal, you can eat your fill of wonderful seafood in Dalmatia. Crab, white fish, lobster, oysters, *lignje* (squid) and the delicious *jirice* – tiny deep-fried whitebait – are all on the menu. Dalmatian *brodet* (mixed fish stew) with polenta is another regional treat. You'll also sample local cheeses like the delicious *livanjksi sir* made on Hvar from ewes' milk; and *paški sir*, a sharp, salty cheese from the island of Pag. Fantastic Dalmatian prosciutto – known as *pršut* – is often served for grazing, tapas style, with cheese and local olives.

DALMATIA BY SEA KAYAK

There's a way to travel the Dalmatian islands even closer to the water. This is a place that's deeply appealing to sea kayakers. With many unpopulated islands and isolated spots in national parks for overnight camps, sea kayaking here is a way to really get off the beaten track. It can also be very challenging, especially when the wild *bora* blows. It pays to go with a local guide who understands the strong tidal currents around the islands, and who can always find a landing spot in case of an emergency. Outfitters right along the coast offer trips from a few hours to a couple of weeks on the water; take one, and it's sure to be unforgettable.

THE ADVENTURE UNFOLDS

Cruising outfitters along the coast can set you up with a bareboat, which – if you know the ropes – you can sail yourself. With no roads to follow and no one to tell you where to go, cruising this way is a sublime kind of freedom. If you're not comfortable skippering, there are plenty of crewed sailing trips on offer.

Dalmatia's waterways are stunningly transparent. Cast off and you may soon have dolphins surfing your bow wave. As you sail, dangle a line; sea bream, mackerel and tuna are plentiful. Squid is a much-prized catch from boats at anchor. While at rest, you can snorkel and spearfish to stock the ship's pantry.

You'll need to learn about the winds here. In summer, the northwest maestral wind blows most afternoons. For cruisers, this means lazy mornings on the boat, swimming, fishing, discovering seaside villages or lazing on the beach. Later you might weigh anchor and, in a few hours of exciting sailing, reach your next port or anchorage. Though it's rarer in summer, you might also experience the bora, capricious northeast winds that rage down from the mountains and then stop as suddenly as they started. There's also the light southerly scirocco that wafts in from the Sahara – which may have you motoring, not sailing, if you're heading south.

Spend your evenings strolling the narrow streets of the incredible medieval village you've chanced upon, drinking excellent wines, dining alfresco and getting to know the friendly locals. The food is fabulously Mediterranean, and deliciously big. So draw up a chair, cradle a fine Croatian red (a wine so full-bodied, Croatians call it *crno* – black), and watch your vessel bob on the bay.

MAKING IT HAPPEN

Over a hundred companies right along the coast here offer yacht and bareboat charters: most allow one-way hires, and you can travel in either direction. May/June and September/October are preferred by experienced sailors: though winds may be more challenging, there's more solitude to be had. June to August, winds are most consistent and predictable, but you won't be alone on the water. For a bareboat charter, bring your skipper's International Certificate of Competence and VHF operator's certificate.

AN ALTERNATIVE CHALLENGE

Even if you're a nonsailor, having a maritime adventure in Dalmatia is still possible. Ferries link the larger islands with the Croatian mainland (as well as with several ports in Italy) and, though you will give up the solitude and freedom of being master of your own vessel, you can still get to many of this region's beauty spots. Water taxies also take passengers between smaller islands – letting you get off the beaten track a little more.

OPENING SPREAD The medieval sea-fort of Dubrovnik, Croatia, is nicknamed the Pearl of the Adriatic. **ABOVE (L)** Sea-kayaking around Vis Island. **ABOVE (R)** Moored in Dubovica Bay on Hvar Island: the Dalmatian archipelago offers sheltered sailing and kayaking. **LEFT** Bathing at Brač Island.

ARMCHAIR

* ***Fast Track to Sailing: Learn to Sail in Three Days*** (Steve Colgate & Doris Colgate) This beginner's sailing manual is mandatory reading before your Dalmatian cruising adventure.

* ***Travels into Dalmatia*** (Alberto Fortis) This book (translated from Latin and republished in 2007) was produced in 1778 by a travelling Italian abbot, and includes accounts of travels through Dalmatia's islands.

* ***Croatia Cruising Companion*** (Jane Cody & John Nash) This is *the* handbook to cruising Croatia's coast, with navigation guides and essential info on ports and anchorages.

* ***A taste of Croatia*** (Karen Evenden) As much travel memoir as recipe book, this book is full of delicious Croatian inspiration.

* ***Dabbling in Dalmatia*** (Michael Fawcett) Thinking of giving it all up and retiring here? Read this first.

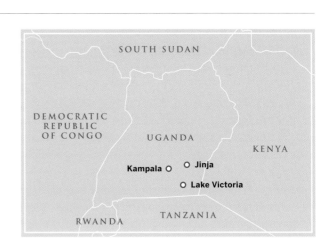

RAFT THE SOURCE OF THE NILE

THE NILE: IT'S EXOTIC, HISTORIC AND, YES, SOMEWHAT DAUNTING. BUT FORGET ABOUT THOSE EGYPTIAN CRUISE SHIPS LAZING THEIR WAY ALONG THE RIVER – IF YOU'RE LOOKING FOR A REAL NILE ADVENTURE, HEAD TO ITS SOURCE IN SOUTHWESTERN UGANDA AND GET IN A RAFT.

The Nile stretches an astonishing 6680km, rising in the fertile greenery of Uganda, winding through the parched desert of Sudan and finally entering the historic sands of Egypt. Along the way, it transforms from a raging, rapid-choked thrill ride to a lazy, wide expanse navigated by riverboats overflowing with tourists.

Near its source, in the heart of Uganda, the Nile is anything but calm. As the riverbank walls close in, the river drops in altitude, exploding into a froth of liquid adventure – the perfect formula for white-water rafting.

The beauty of a guided rafting trip is that you don't have to be an expert to jump right in at the deep and frothy end. With an expert guide to help steer your raft through the rampaging rapids, all you need to do is follow instructions and hang on tight. Although it isn't a requirement to be a strong swimmer, being comfortable in the water is essential, as there is a very good chance you are going to go for a swim at some point – and of course, that's half the fun.

The rapids here are graded class V – and since there's only one class above that, VI, you get the picture that this won't be a placid float down the river. You can expect big standing waves, rocks, drops, foaming hydraulics and plenty of white water. It's nothing that the raft, your guide and, hopefully, you can't handle.

Rafting in Uganda started in 1996 when some intrepid expat New Zealanders (typical) thought that rafting the Nile would be an excellent laugh. Since then, its popularity has steadily grown and the number of travellers who've tested themselves against the river is now well into the thousands. Safety standards are high, and the thrills-and-spills count is off the charts.

ESSENTIAL EXPERIENCES

* **Feeling the rush of some of the best class V white-water rafting on the planet.**

* Glimpsing the untouched jungle and wild surroundings of the river.

* **Witnessing mountain gorillas in their natural habitat in the far southwest of Uganda.**

* Revelling in the wonder that you are standing at the source of the Nile – the longest river on the planet.

* **Speeding through the jungle on a mountain bike – just another activity to experience in the adrenalin capital of Africa.**

* Looking for crocodiles in the Nile – hopefully not when you are swimming in it!

LOCATION SOUTHWESTERN UGANDA | **IDEAL TIME COMMITMENT** ONE TO TWO DAYS | **BEST TIME OF YEAR** YEAR-ROUND
ESSENTIAL TIP IF YOU WEAR CONTACT LENSES, BRING ALONG AN EXTRA PAIR AS RAFTING TRIPS ARE NOTORIOUS FOR WASHING CONTACTS AWAY

258

FACTS ABOUT THE NILE

The Nile is the longest river in the world, covering an area of at least 3,349,000 sq km. Stretching a staggering 6680km, it passes through Kenya, Eritrea, Congo, Burundi, Uganda, Tanzania, Rwanda, Egypt, Sudan and Ethiopia. The river has two tributaries – the Blue Nile and the White Nile. The White Nile originates in Lake Victoria in Uganda, while the Blue Nile starts in Ethiopia, in Lake Tana, before joining the White Nile in Khartoum, Sudan. Thanks to a 1929 treaty, Egypt has the option to veto any project on the Nile that could adversely affect downriver water flow.

THE NILE CROCODILE

Two things spring to mind when you mention the Nile: the fact that it flows through Egypt, and that Nile crocodiles sun themselves along its banks. What distinguishes the Nile croc from its freshwater cousins is that they like the taste of travellers. The Nile crocodile can grow to a length of 5.5m and can weigh 700kg – not the sort of animal you want to tangle with. Unlike most croc species, they are comfortable hunting both in and out of the water. In the Nile it will hunt fish, and when it ventures onto land it's been known to take down giraffes and juvenile elephants.

■ THE ADVENTURE UNFOLDS

You can raft the Nile as a full-day trip or just dip your toes in for a half-day adventure. On the full-day trip, you start early with a pick-up in either Jinja or Kampala. At the rafting base, you'll be kitted out in your gear: a life jacket, helmet and paddle. No bulky wetsuits are required – the water of the Nile is refreshing when you go for a planned or not-so-planned swim in the river.

After suiting up, it's back in the van for a quick 15km trip downriver to the start of the adventure. The guides slip the rafts into a tranquil pool and give you some last-minute pointers before jumping on board. After a bit of practice on the flat water, it's time to get into it. There's no gentle lead-up for the beginner, though – your introduction to rafting on the Nile is a 4m drop through a washing machine of white water!

The Ugandan Nile isn't a continuous canyon of rapids; mercifully, between each section of thrill and spill is a calm stretch of water. These calm sections are perfect for catching your breath, going for a swim or just steeling yourself for the next challenge – and believe me, there are plenty of challenges to come!

With eight rapids of grade IV or higher, and several smaller runs to negotiate, you aren't short of excitement on this trip. Your guide will help you get through the tougher sections, with all the tricky rapids scouted and planned before you start your run. Safety is looked after by the crew too – a safety boat accompanies you as you charge through the white water to pick up the pieces if you spill into the drink. And speaking of safety – there aren't any hippos in this section of the Nile and crocodiles steer clear of this section too – phew.

■ MAKING IT HAPPEN

The night before your trip, plan to sleep in either Jinja or Kampala, or even more conveniently in Bujagali Falls – just a few steps from the start of the rafting trip. There are plenty of companies on the ground that can take you rafting, but safety standards range widely between them. Three recommended operations are Adrift, Nile River Explorers and Nalubale Rafting.

■ AN ALTERNATIVE CHALLENGE

If this rafting adventure sounds too hardcore, or if you're made of tougher stuff and want a bigger challenge, there are several alternative options available. You can go for a half-day rafting trip if you'd prefer to get a bit less wet, or conversely, you can go for a two-day rafting trip if you can't get enough.

Rafting not your thing? Go for a cruise on a riverboat, learn to white-water kayak, strap yourself into a jet boat for a thrill ride or ditch the raft altogether and try the same section of river on a riverboard.

261

OPENING SPREAD The Nile rushes through a 7m-wide gorge at Murchison Falls, which lends its name to a surrounding national park. ABOVE Rafting Bujagali Falls, Uganda. LEFT Beware the toothy grin: in 2010 a Nile crocodile ate Hendrik Coetzee, the first man to kayak the Nile from source to sea.

ARMCHAIR

* **Dark Star Safari** (Paul Theroux) This African travel classic tells the story of travelling from Cairo to Cape Town via rail. Theroux is a master of the travel anthology and this is one of his best.

* **Sowing the Mustard Seed** (Yoweri Museveni) The current President of Uganda tells his own story of the overthrow of former dictator Idi Amin and his rise to power.

* **The Last King of Scotland** (2006) Forest Whitaker's portrayal of the charming but murderous Idi Amin is magnetic – essential viewing before coming to Uganda.

* **The African Queen** (1951) Classic Hollywood film starring Humphrey Bogart and Katharine Hepburn shot on location in Uganda.

FLORIDA

GULF OF
MEXICO

Everglades City O
Everglades National Park O　O Miami

CANOE FLORIDA'S WILDERNESS WATERWAY

MARVEL AT THE SPLENDOUR OF ONE OF THE WORLD'S LARGEST AND MOST
VIBRANT SMALL-CRAFT WATERWAYS: A NETWORK OF INTERCONNECTED
MARSHLANDS, MANGROVES, RIVERS AND STREAMS TEEMING WITH WILDLIFE.
THE ROAD LESS TRAVELLED IS OFTEN BEST WHEN IT ISN'T A ROAD AT ALL.

The Wilderness Waterway is to paddlers what the Appalachian Trail is to hikers: 159km (a minimum seven days of hard paddling) that snakes through one of America's most beautiful and least understood national parks, offering unparalleled wildlife close-ups and stunning scenery every bit of the way. The journey is a bit like paddling back in time through a part of American history – most of Florida used to look like this before the invention of bulldozers and backhoes enabled the destruction of swampland on an epic scale.

As recently as the early 20th century, a thin sheet of water covered as much as 28,500 sq km, creating one of the country's most unique habitats and harbouring unique animals and plants. Bromeliads, orchids, palms and even hardwood forests thrived, providing habitats for all sorts of animals that nowadays are on the brink of extinction, such as the American crocodile and Florida panthers, which currently number only around one hundred. The now-ubiquitous alligator has a commanding reign over this amazing 'River of Grass'.

The area was first written about by Hugh L Willoughby in 1898, after he made a west–east crossing of the vast sawgrass prairies in 1897. Save for the chickees (raised wooden platforms for camping), the Wilderness Waterway looks much as it did then. The communities of 'Gladesmen' and indigenous tribes may have gone, but wildlife still rules and the only form of transport in this roadless expanse remains watercraft: boat, skiff, kayak or canoe.

The Everglades National Park was established in 1947 to protect this serene and wild ecosystem. Interestingly, the park's creation was due in large part to the efforts of a developer, Ernest F Coe. He envisioned an expanse of 2,000,000 acres and was so adamant about these boundaries (which even included Key Largo!) that the creation of the park was almost scuttled completely. Even so, it remains the largest protected area east of the Mississippi River.

ESSENTIAL EXPERIENCES

✳ **Marvelling at unbroken vistas of sawgrass prairie as you glide through mangrove channels, lakes and lagoons.**

✳ Encountering close up a host of birds and animals that many people never see.

✳ **Enjoying the utter stillness that comes from being as far away from motorised vehicle traffic as one can be.**

✳ Paddling around Florida's Ten Thousand Islands, all but a handful uninhabited.

✳ **Camping on chickee stilt platforms at nightfall beneath a canopy of glittering stars.**

✳ Travelling one of America's most epic waterways that – thankfully – has been pristinely preserved, affording a look at what most of Florida looked like for millennia.

DISTANCE 159KM | **LOCATION** EVERGLADES NATIONAL PARK, FLORIDA, USA | **IDEAL TIME COMMITMENT** ONE WEEK | **BEST TIME OF YEAR** JANUARY | **ESSENTIAL TIP** WATCH OUT FOR ALLIGATORS

HUGH L WILLOUGHBY

While Native Americans lived in and around the area for centuries, the Everglades, America's largest freshwater swamp, was not written about in any depth until Hugh L Willoughby of the University of Pennsylvania traversed the region in 1897. His journal entries became the still available title *Across the Everglades* and while the writing is dry (pun intended), the voyage was not: portages across the mud and shallows were common, and dry places to sleep were few and far between. His experiences and flora and fauna finds provide a fascinating glimpse back at the history of this 'River of Grass'.

THE FLORIDA PANTHER

Sadly, most people's only glimpse of these animals in the wild is on the side of the road: impacts by vehicles are the number one threat to the wild populations. While habitat loss (male Florida panthers require approximately 520 sq km of territory per cat) is the prime reason they're on the endangered species list, the few animals left need all the help they can get. Protect them (and yourself!) by minimising the chances of an accident. Observe posted road signs and be alert – especially during the dawn, dusk and night-time hours – for anything crossing the road.

■ THE ADVENTURE UNFOLDS

The put-in for a west–east journey starts at the Gulf Coast Visitors Center in Everglades City. Clearly marked signs then guide paddlers across the waterways, lagoons, inlets and sawgrass prairies, with camping on beaches or chickees.

The journey goes through almost all the ecosystems the park has to offer, starting with miles of mangroves and tannin-stained water. Little blue herons and snowy egrets erupt with squawks from the shallows as your vessel slips by, the verdant mangroves subduing the sounds of paddling. The mangroves slowly melt into coastal estuary, where salt and brackish water mix, and manatee and sea turtle sightings are common. Here one can look out across Florida Bay at the Ten Thousand Islands. All but a handful of these islands are uninhabited. While many are open to campers, it's vital to obtain park permission prior to embarking on your trip and to stick to designated areas.

Gradually you'll trade the bay for sawgrass prairie: seemingly never-ending stretches of waist- to head-high grass like the prairies out west, except here they grow out of a paddy that's only dry in certain areas and at certain times of the year. At the highest points you'll find tropical hardwood 'hammocks' (stands of trees) which support larger mammals – look for deer, feral pigs, raccoons and (for the very lucky) a glimpse of the endangered Florida panther.

During the last days of the journey, camping is on chickees, which require some careful manoeuvring and preparation for tide, wind and current so as to not damage the canoes. Capable and experienced paddlers will find the seven to eight days as rewarding as a canoe trip can be.

■ MAKING IT HAPPEN

Bring gear as for any canoe trip, plus ample drinking water – factoring in delays due to inclement weather, navigational mistakes or accidents. Though mosquitoes and no-see-ums aren't as bad in winter, they're present year-round, and it's worth remembering that most of those submerged 'logs' are alligators. GPS, appropriate nautical charts and night-time navigation skills are vital. Everglades Adventures offers a variety of packages and full or partial guided tours.

■ DETOUR

A worthwhile side trip is to Big Cypress National Monument, which borders part of Everglades National Park. One quick peek and you'll see why there's a line between the two: massive cypress trees blanketed with Spanish moss (a kind of lichen) create a totally different ecosystem from the sawgrass prairies and low-lying keys, yet this too is primarily swampland. Canoe any of the five NPS Big Cypress day trips or ask at the ranger station if you plan a longer stay.

265

OPENING SPREAD The marshy mosaic of the Florida Everglades. **ABOVE** Kayakers exploring the Everglades National Park can camp beside the water. **LEFT** The Florida panther is no longer the Everglades' top predator. Illegally released giant Burmese pythons, which grow up to 5m, plague the region.

ARMCHAIR

* **A Field Guide to the Birds of North America** (Roger Tory Peterson) An invaluable asset to identifying the numerous waterfowl.

* **Paddler's Guide to Everglades National Park** (Johnny Molloy) Useful insights for first-timers as well as Glades veterans.

* **Across the Everglades** (Hugh L Willoughby) Details his 1897 trip along the waterway.

* **Double Whammy and Tourist Season** (Carl Hiaasen) Hiaasen's riotously funny works of fiction (which blend mystery, adventure and comedy as only Hiaasen can) centre on Florida, and should be required reading.

* **The Orchid Thief** (Susan Orlean) An evocative, literary look at the area, which became the movie Adaptation starring Nicolas Cage.

RAFT TASMANIA'S FRANKLIN RIVER

RUN THE RIVER THAT CHANGED A NATION. AFTER A FEW DAYS IN THIS PRIMEVAL WILDERNESS, SO NEAR AND YET SO FAR FROM CIVILISATION, YOU'LL UNDERSTAND WHY EFFORTS TO STOP THE FRANKLIN FROM BEING DAMMED FORGED A DEEP ENVIRONMENTAL CONSCIOUSNESS ACROSS AUSTRALIA.

266

Few journeys have such potential to change lives as a rafting adventure on Tasmania's pristine Franklin River. From the moment you launch your raft beside the Lyell Highway, right until you pop out into the Gordon River more than a week later, you won't have seen a house, a field or almost any other human mark on the landscape. You may not even have seen any other people on the river. And yet the Tasmanian capital city of Hobart is, at times, less than 150km away.

Named after Tasmanian governor and ill-fated North West Passage explorer Sir John Franklin, the river was first run by John Hawkins and John Dean in 1958, in collapsible canoes, seven years after their first attempt. It would be another 12 years before the river was rafted. Among the early pioneers was a Tasmanian GP named Bob Brown, who named many of its natural features and would go on to become leader of the Australian Greens political party.

By the late 1960s, the Franklin River was also being eyed off as a potential dam location, leading to Australia's most famous and furious environmental battle as protestors blockaded the remote site. It was a fight that eventually helped sway a Federal election, when the Labor Party promised in 1983 to prevent the dam's construction. Spearheading the battle was a moody photo of Rock Island Bend by Peter Dombrovskis that would become perhaps the most famous landscape photo in the country.

It wasn't long before commercial rafting trips began operating on the river, with floats fluctuating from barely moving flat water to unraftable rapids through the Great Ravine. This may be the ultimate accessible wilderness experience in Australia.

ESSENTIAL EXPERIENCES

* **Drifting through the silent world of the 100m-deep Irenabyss.**

* Scrambling high above the river and rapids as you portage through the violent water world of the Great Ravine.

* **Paying photographic homage to Rock Island Bend as you drop over Gaylard Rapids.**

* Sleeping beneath rock overhangs beside the roar of the river's longest rapids at Newland Cascades.

* **Viewing Aboriginal artefacts inside Kutikina Cave, one of the sites that led to Tasmania's Southwest being granted cultural status on the Unesco World Heritage list.**

DISTANCE 125KM | **LOCATION** FRANKLIN-GORDON WILD RIVERS NATIONAL PARK, TASMANIA, AUSTRALIA | **IDEAL TIME COMMITMENT** SEVEN TO 10 DAYS | **BEST TIME OF YEAR** DECEMBER TO MARCH | **ESSENTIAL TIP** BUILD EXTRA DAYS INTO YOUR ITINERARY, AS RISING WATER LEVELS CAN STRAND RAFTERS FOR A FEW DAYS

PLAYING IT SAFE

If you have ambitions to raft the Franklin independently, extreme caution is required. Southwest Tasmania is remote country, and the pitfalls on the river are myriad. Water levels can rise and fall like tides following rain, and white-water dangers such as stoppers and strainers are all too common, as are submerged logs and boulders. Be certain to read the Parks & Wildlife Service's rafting notes.

THE ADVENTURE UNFOLDS

James Calder, the man who named the Franklin River in 1840, described the Great Ravine as a 'hideous defile'. The rapids are as furious as Tasmanian devils, their white noise reverberating off the canyon walls. It's difficult to think with this roar, but think you must, for you're now at the trickiest section of the river. It's taken four days to get here, and it will take one gymnastic day to battle your way through its 5km passage. You climb out of the raft and watch as the guides throw it over the lip of a rapid, diving in after it as you scramble across a narrow ledge of rock on the cliff face. And so it goes on, brutally named rapid after brutally named rapid – the Churn, Thunderush, the Cauldron – until the Great Ravine finally spits you out into a calmer world, a place of pandani grass trees and gentle waterfalls.

You lurch through Propsting Gorge, shuddering downstream on rapids that are more open and forgiving than the constricted mess of the Great Ravine. In the afternoon you arrive at Gaylard Rapids. Beyond this fall – a drop as high as the rafts are long – is the distinctive wedge of rock that forms Rock Island Bend. As you tip over the lip, however, you're so intent on missing the eddy to the left that you barely even notice this most famous of Tasmanian scenes. Within moments you're rippling through the bumps of Newland Cascades, making camp on a rock ledge above the rapids.

Water levels are low, making it possible to walk back along the rock platforms to Rock Island Bend. Here, you sit and watch as the famous photo becomes a motion picture.

MAKING IT HAPPEN

Rafting the Franklin independently is a serious business, in the reach of only the most experienced white-water warriors. Most rafters will choose a guided trip, putting in on the Collingwood River and finishing at Sir John Falls on the Gordon River. A small number of companies, including World Expeditions, offer guided rafting trips.

DETOUR

From the camp site at the end of the Irenabyss, take a day out to climb to the summit of one of Australia's most striking mountains. Frenchmans Cap is like an anvil of white quartzite rising above all other peaks around it, its south and east faces carved into vertical cliffs up to 400m high. To reach it, most hikers have to walk in for two or three days from the other side, squelching through the infamous 'Sodden Loddon' valley – a soup of mud – but rafters can reach the summit on a day hike from the Franklin River.

OPENING SPREAD Portaging past Log Jam rapid on the Franklin river. **ABOVE** Small packrafts are able to take on moderate rapids. **LEFT** The natural splendour at Rock Island Bend is paddlers' reward. Access to the Franklin is the result of a determined battle by Australians against a dam project.

ARMCHAIR

* ***Tasmania's Wilderness Battles: A History*** (Greg Buckman)
  Historical account of various environmental fights in Tasmania, including the Franklin River blockade.

* ***The South West Book*** (edited by Helen Gee and Janet Fenton)
  Multi-themed book on the natural environment and pioneers of the Southwest Tasmania wilderness, including a good chapter on the Franklin River.

* ***Shooting the Franklin: Early Canoeing on Tasmania's Wild Rivers***
  (John Dean) Accounts of early Franklin expeditions from one of the first men to canoe it.

* ***Death of a River Guide*** (Richard Flanagan) Fictional account of a Franklin trip, from a Tasmanian author with vast experience on the river.

PADDLE WITH ORCAS IN BRITISH COLUMBIA

WITNESS ONE OF NATURE'S GREAT SPECTACLES AS YOU SIT ON THE ROLLING OCEAN IN A KAYAK, OBSERVING ORCAS SWIM THROUGH JOHNSTONE STRAIT IN PURSUIT OF SALMON RETURNING TO THEIR BIRTHPLACE TO SPAWN. THESE AWESOME PREDATORS ARE BIGGER THAN YOUR BOAT, AND THEY'RE SO CLOSE…

270

Welcome to the food chain as a spectator sport. Each summer, masses of salmon funnel through narrow Johnstone Strait, between Vancouver Island and the British Columbia mainland, on their way to spawning grounds in the Fraser River near Vancouver. This is said to be the world's most prolific salmon-spawning river, with up to 50 million fish returning here each year. And in their wake come a host of predators, none more spectacular than orcas. More killer whales are said to pass through here than through any other waters on Earth.

Inside Passage cruise liners travel through the strait, but the most intimate way to witness the orcas is from a kayak. Whether you're kayaking across the strait, which narrows to less than 3km at points, or simply following the kelp lines along the shores of Vancouver Island, orca sightings are almost certain. There are thought to be around 250 whales in the strait during summer, and you'll probably also get to see the likes of bald eagles, Steller sea lions, Dall's porpoises and perhaps even a minke whale.

Trips here usually involve camping behind the rocky beaches that line the strait, where the orcas' sounds by night are almost as impressive as the sight of them by day. Days are spent poking along the coast of Vancouver Island, which is smothered in tall forest, or heading across the strait, where the topography is like that of an underwater canyon, plunging to 500m on islands such as West Cracroft and Sophia.

It's also just as likely that you'll observe orcas from the shore; salmon commonly swim near to the nutrient-rich kelp lines with pods of orcas inevitably in tow, sometimes bringing them to within just a few metres of the Vancouver Island coastline.

ESSENTIAL EXPERIENCES

* **Dodging salmon as they leap from the waters around your kayak.**

* Watching as a pod of orcas rises from the waters off the nose of your kayak.

* **Taking a break from the water to hike among giant cedars on West Cracroft Island.**

* Falling asleep in your tent to the sound of passing orcas.

* **Paddling the shores of Vancouver Island in sight of bald eagles, Steller sea lions and Dall's porpoises.**

LOCATION JOHNSTONE STRAIT, BRITISH COLUMBIA, CANADA | **IDEAL TIME COMMITMENT** THREE TO SIX DAYS | **BEST TIME OF YEAR** JUNE TO SEPTEMBER | **ESSENTIAL TIP** REMEMBER THAT KAYAKERS ARE NOT PERMITTED TO PADDLE INSIDE THE ROBSON BIGHT (MICHAEL BIGG) ECOLOGICAL RESERVE; THE AREA IS HEAVILY PATROLLED

ORCAS

Orcas have long been given a bum rap. In the oldest known description, written during the days of the Roman Empire, the so-called killer whales were portrayed as 'an enormous mass of flesh armed with menacing teeth'. In the 1970s, US Navy diving manuals warned that orcas will 'attack human beings at every opportunity'. And yet there has never been a recorded attack on humans in the wild. Orcas, which can grow to 9m in length and are the largest member of the dolphin family, are generally classified into two major types: transient, which hunt marine mammals; and resident, which feed almost exclusively on fish. The orcas in Johnstone Strait are resident whales, which means you need only be nervous if you're a salmon.

ROBSON BIGHT

Most kayaking companies concentrate their trips around the fringes of Robson Bight, a small bay about 15km southeast of Telegraph Cove. They do so with good reason. Robson Bight is noted for its 'rubbing beaches', where orcas swim up to the shores to rub against the smooth pebbles – it's the only place in the world where they're known to do this. In 1982 the Robson Bight (Michael Bigg) Ecological Reserve was established as the world's only dedicated orca sanctuary. Boats and kayaks aren't allowed to enter the reserve, which is patrolled by wardens.

■ THE ADVENTURE UNFOLDS

The orcas have sounded again like an alarm clock. The sun has just risen and, from your tent, you can hear the rush of air as a pod surfaces just offshore. It's like having visitors from the deep knock at your front door. You breakfast on the beach, watching salmon pop from the strait like corn. The orcas have moved on – you saw their enormous fins heading into Robson Bight – and a Steller sea lion darts about the ocean surface in their place. It's enjoying its breakfast even more than you, tossing unlucky salmon about like a shot putter.

It's mid-morning by the time you ready the kayaks. You slide out from the smooth, rounded rocks of the beach, turning north, away from the bight, hugging the shores and hoping not to be brained by a leaping salmon – already one has clattered into your kayak. From the tops of the trees, a bald eagle watches you pass, while cruise liners parade past in the distance.

You've paddled only a few hundred metres when you hear the sound again – the blow of a whale. Ahead, fins appear, slicing through the water. You stop paddling and glide over to the kelp line, grabbing a strand to anchor you in position atop the water. Regulations prevent you from going within 100m of the whales, but nothing can stop the whales from coming closer to you. The fins disappear for a minute and then resurface, perhaps 50m from where you sit inside your cocoon of fibreglass. A male orca leads the pod, its 2m-high fin rising higher than you, leaning over with the weight of gravity. You feel no bigger than krill, so close to such a creature. The pod moves so gracefully it's tough to imagine that it's hunting right now.

■ MAKING IT HAPPEN

The remoteness of the area around Johnstone Strait and Robson Bight means that the vast majority of kayakers come on guided paddles. Port McNeill and Telegraph Cove are the usual starting points, with water taxi transfers to beach camp sites. Port McNeill and Telegraph Cove are near to Port Hardy, which has Pacific Coastal flights to and from Vancouver.

■ AN ALTERNATIVE CHALLENGE

If you want to mix and match your whale adventures in Canada, head for the northern town of Churchill (famous for its polar bear encounters), where it's possible to swim among some of the thousands of white beluga whales that gather in Hudson Bay each summer. On swim tours you'll be kitted out in a dry suit – you're approaching the Arctic Circle, after all – and a snorkel set before taking to the waters among the curious whales, which grow up to 5m in length. You'll probably also see polar bears on the trip, though thankfully not when you're swimming.

OPENING SPREAD A breaching orca requires an exit speed of 40km/h. **ABOVE** Rafted kayakers watch an orca in Johnstone Strait. The orcas of the Pacific northwest have been closely studied. **LEFT** Granite Bay on Quadra Island, one of a group of islands between north Vancouver Island and the mainland.

ARMCHAIR

* **_Listening to Whales: What the Orcas Have Taught Us_** (Alexandra Morton) Stories from the author's 20 years as an orca researcher, predominantly in the waters of British Columbia.

* **_Field Guide to the Orca_** (American Cetacean Society) Dedicated guide about viewing orcas, from techniques to facts about the animals.

* **_Free Willy_** (1993) Yes, that movie – get warm and fuzzy about orcas in this feel-good tug on the heart strings.

* **_Orca: Visions of the Killer Whale_** (Peter Knudtson) Portrait-rich book of orcas, with discussion on such issues as the creature's communications, history and environmental threats.

* **_Passage to Juneau: A Sea and its Meanings_** (Jonathan Raban) Campfire reading about the British travel writer's journey through the Inside Passage in a yacht.

RAFT THE COLORADO RIVER

TO FLOAT THROUGH THE GRANDEST CANYON OF THEM ALL IS TO TRAVEL ACROSS MILLENNIA. BUT AS WELL AS AWESOMELY ANCIENT ROCK WALLS, THERE ARE QUIET BEACHES, TUMBLING FALLS AND THE CHANCE TO PIT YOURSELF AGAINST SOME OF THE WILDEST WATER IN THE WORLD.

274

That the first person to successfully navigate the length of the Colorado River had only one arm says more about the man than the undertaking. Civil War veteran John Wesley Powell's 10-strong team set off on their mission to chart the then-uncharted river in June 1869, in four heavy (and quite unfit for purpose) oak rowing boats. It was a fearful voyage, haunted by the prospect that the next meander might plunge them over an unknown waterfall. But on 29 August, Powell emerged from the Grand Canyon – his crew bedraggled and depleted – as an American hero.

Powell put-in at Green River Station, Wyoming, and floated some 1400km to Arizona's Grand Wash Cliffs. Today's rafters don't travel so far. The official launch point is Lees Ferry (Mile 0), at the northeast edge of Grand Canyon National Park; the Colorado empties into Lake Mead 443km later (Mile 277).

It's still an epic ride, however. There are 160-plus rapids to negotiate, ranging from mere ripples to rip-roaring rides. There are side canyons to hike into and rock pools to swim in. And then there's the geology: the red-orange-yellow-black walls that flank your progress are up to two billion years old.

A full run, Lees Ferry to Pearce Ferry (on Lake Mead), can take just under three weeks in an oar-powered boat. Those with less time can do sections: an Upper Canyon expedition, from Lees to Phantom Ranch (Mile 87), takes around four days, ending in a hike up to the rim – there's no road out from the bottom. A Lower Canyon stretch, say from Phantom to Diamond Creek (Mile 226), starts with a trek down, and takes five or six days. Every inch of the ride is fascinating. The Upper realms allow a gentler introduction, but have more white water overall – and highlights such as Vasey's Paradise, a fecund garden at Mile 31. The Lower run has the biggest rapids, and access to the narrow and falls-filled Olo and Matkatamiba slot canyons. Undecided? Do the lot.

ESSENTIAL EXPERIENCES

* **Camping out on a sandbar by the riverside, and waking to watch the sun gradually seep down the canyon walls.**

* Tackling some gnarly white water, such as boulder-strewn Hance Rapid and the big waves of Hermit.

* **Mooring up for a trek into a side canyon, to find swimming pools, cascades and ancient petroglyphs.**

* Relishing the quiet bits, where you glide in calm waters just shooting the breeze.

* **Getting into geology, studying two-billion-year-old rock striations as you float by.**

* Hitting iconic canyon hikes (perhaps Bright Angel Trail or the walk to Tapeats Creek) early, before the sun gets too fierce.

DISTANCE 443KM | **LOCATION** ARIZONA, USA | **IDEAL TIME COMMITMENT** FIVE TO 18 DAYS | **BEST TIME OF YEAR** MAY TO OCTOBER | **ESSENTIAL TIP** PREPARE FOR VERY HOT AND VERY COLD WEATHER, YEAR-ROUND

RATING THE RAPIDS

Rivers worldwide are graded I to VI, I being scarcely rippled, VI being suicidal. According to this classification, the Colorado is a IV (intermediate), encompassing numerous I–III rapids, plus some Vs. However, the Colorado has a unique 1–10 ranking system, a 10 here equalling a regular V. Two undisputed 10s are Crystal Rapid (Mile 98) and Lava Falls (Mile 179). Crystal was formed in 1966, when a flash flood created the treacherous 'rock garden'. Lava's so big that Powell portaged around it; today, guides perform rituals at Vulcan's Anvil – a volcanic plug, sacred to the Hualapai, just upstream – to ensure safe passage.

■ THE ADVENTURE UNFOLDS

As you float along the green-tinged Colorado – which is currently taking a breather between contractions of white-water fury – you gaze at the canyon wall: layer upon layer of geological history stacked like a club sandwich. The smooth black stuff at the bottom – Vishnu schist, so your guide says – is older than the dinosaurs; above that sit strata of blood-orange, purple, ochre and gold.

Uh oh, something's afoot. The walls narrow, the water picks up pace... there's a rapid upcoming. You and your boat-mates adopt the ready position, paddles raised to row like billy-o, and prepare to be tumbled like a sock in a washing machine. Your guide hollers instructions you can barely hear as the inflatable pitches amid majestic chaos. Then all is still. Another torrent conquered.

Life's rhythm on the river is sublime. Days are spent gliding serenely or being bucked ferociously (dependent on the Colorado's whim). But you also take breaks. The beauty of being at the canyon bottom is the exclusive access to sandy beaches and hidden caverns, to side streams with sun-warmed swimming holes and to ancient Puebloan sites hidden amid the cliffs.

Each evening you haul up at a shore-side camp, to toss a Frisbee, cook over a campfire and watch as the light is sucked out of your awesome abyss – but not before it sets all that red rock on fire. Then the stars are spectacular.

Amenities are basic: bush toilets lurk amid the tamarisk trees, 'showers' are dips in the side canyons' pools (the river itself is way too chilly). But that's half the pleasure – adjusting yourself to Colorado living, just you, your boat and millions of years of Mother Nature in very top form.

■ MAKING IT HAPPEN

On commercial trips, an accredited operator will arrange all the guiding and logistics; options range from day-long to three-week floats, on either motorised or oar-powered boats. Noncommercial private trips are for very experienced rafters who want to organise their own river-run; rafters must apply for permits via the 'weighted lottery' system, which is massively oversubscribed (there's a waiting list of several years).

■ AN ALTERNATIVE CHALLENGE

There is fine hiking around the Grand Canyon, but short walks here are made punishing by extreme temperatures, thin air and steep climbs. An excellent multiday option is to combine the South and North Kaibab trails; this 33km route from Yaqui Point (South Rim), down to the canyon floor, then up to the North Rim, takes three days (with stops at Bright Angel camp and Cottonwood camp or Phantom Ranch). You need a Backcountry Permit, which you can apply for up to four months in advance from the National Parks Service.

OPENING SPREAD Human life dates back 12,000 years in the Grand Canyon. Descendants of Puebloans still inhabit Havasu Gorge. **ABOVE (L)** Rafting Arizona. **ABOVE (R)** The river wild: taking on Hermit Rapid. **LEFT** Navajo Bridge, a popular bungee jump site, overlooks Lee's Ferry on the Colorado.

ARMCHAIR

✻ ***The Exploration of the Colorado River and its Canyons*** (John Wesley Powell) True tale of adventure in the unmapped southwest in 1869 – an American classic.

✻ ***Over the Edge: Death in Grand Canyon*** (Michael P Ghiglieri & Thomas M Myers) Accounts of the 550 unfortunates to have died hereabouts, from Powell's expedition up to the book's publication in 2001; includes safety tips too.

✻ ***Arizona, New Mexico & the Grand Canyon Trips*** (Lonely Planet) Inspirational guide, containing 58 themed itineraries.

✻ ***Lasting Light: 125 Years of Grand Canyon Photography*** (Stephen Trimble) A compilation of the best historic shots and the stories behind them.

✻ ***The River Wild*** (1995) Meryl Streep is the plucky rafter in this formulaic thriller that's full of white-water action.

Vanuatu ○

VANUATU   Yasawa Island ○   FIJI
                              ○ Viti Levu

NEW
CALEDONIA   PACIFIC OCEAN
      ○ Noumea

KAYAK THE YASAWA ISLANDS

SEA KAYAKING ISN'T SUPPOSED TO BE A LIFE-AND-DEATH STRUGGLE WITH MASSIVE WAVES, FREEZING SEA SPRAY AND FUN IN SHORT SUPPLY. SEA KAYAKING SHOULD BE PADDLING THE PLACID BLUER-THAN-BLUE WATERS OF THE YASAWA ISLANDS. NOTHING BUT SUN, SAND, BLUE SKY AND YOU.

278

The Yasawa Islands lie just northwest of Viti Levu, the largest in Fiji's collection of more than 300 islands. Comprising around 20 islands, the Yasawas are tailor-made for paddling exploration and are well suited for those who like camping.

Some islands will have welcoming locals who'll offer you a drink of kava or shout a friendly greeting of 'Bula!' as you pass by. Other islands you'll have all to yourself.

This South Pacific sea-kayaking adventure can be anything from a few days on the water to a couple of weeks. A moderate level of fitness is required, but much of the challenge of this trip is posed by the weather. If the wind gets up, and the waves grow bigger, the paddling can get pretty serious. It pays to be a decent swimmer too – not that there's much risk of going overboard (sea kayaks are very stable), it's more so you can enjoy the fantastic snorkelling along the way.

With trips like this, as long as the weather cooperates, there's plenty of time to explore the islands as you paddle, go for a swim, a snorkel or just lounge around on your own deserted island.

While it's easy to find kayaking day trips, getting hooked into a longer trip is a taller order. That's what sets this trip apart from other tropical sea-kayak adventures: the opportunity to get into the rhythm of camping on a different island every night.

If azure blue water, white-sand beaches and kayaking around the quiet backwaters of the South Pacific without another group in sight sounds like your sort of thing, then this is the trip for you.

ESSENTIAL EXPERIENCES

* **Hearing the gentle sounds of the South Pacific lapping against the shore of your own deserted desert island.**

* Marvelling at the seemingly millions of fish at play among the coral reef as you snorkel around.

* **Tasting that strange brew kava, and feeling the relaxing effects as it washes a day of hard kayaking from your muscles.**

* Feeling the soft sand squash between your toes as you set foot on yet another private island hidden from the rest of the world.

DISTANCE FOUR TO 11 DAYS | **LOCATION** FIJI | **IDEAL TIME COMMITMENT** TWO WEEKS | **BEST TIME OF YEAR** MAY TO OCTOBER
ESSENTIAL TIP SWIMMING IS A GREAT WAY TO GET READY FOR LONG-DISTANCE SEA-KAYAKING TRIPS – IT STRENGTHENS YOUR SHOULDERS AND PREPARES YOU FOR ALL THE SNORKELLING ACTION!

IT'S NOT JUST ABOUT THE BEACH

When most people think about Fiji, they think the ocean and the beach. What they are missing is the heart and soul of this nation – the interior. On the larger islands, especially Viti Levu, when you travel to the interior you experience an entirely different Fiji. In many ways, the locals live as they have for centuries, in small villages. The interior is also a great place to go to escape the heat – the cool rainforested landscape teeming with waterfalls is a great alternative to the often stifling coast.

■ THE ADVENTURE UNFOLDS

Snorkelling and paddling in sheltered seas, camping on deserted islands – turning this dream kayaking trip into a reality is fairly straightforward, with operators available to handle all of the planning for you. All you need to do is turn up and they'll do the rest. The trip is graded as easy to moderate – so as long as you have a reasonable level of fitness, you're going to be heading home relaxed and recharged, not battered and sore.

The trip starts with a ferry from the main island in Fiji, Viti Levu, to the smaller island of Tavewa. This is home to the famed Blue Lagoon, where the movie of the same name was filmed. After getting your gear sorted, it's time to start paddling.

With each day of the trip consisting of about four hours on the water, it's too physically demanding. Many of the stops for the night are in small villages where you have the chance to stay with local families and experience this largely unchanged island culture firsthand. Accommodation is usually in a *bure*, a traditional Fijian hut of wood and straw, so connecting with the past is as easy as stretching out and drifting off.

As the trip continues, and you become more in tune with the sea and the rhythm of paddling, snorkelling, beachcombing and basking in the sun, the days begin to blend into one. Your technique improves: don't pull with your arms, pivot around your hips. With their lapping waves and the crackle of a campfire as the sun dips below the horizon, the camp sites begin to feel more like home than the bed you've left behind. And as the expedition finally draws to a close, it's tempting to just turn around and do it all over again – surely the sign of any worthy adventure.

ARMCHAIR

❋ *South Sea Tales* (Jack London) The ultimate adventure writer visited Fiji a century ago and wrote the short story 'The Whale Tooth', which is included in this collection of his work.

❋ *Cast Away* (2000) Tom Hanks redefined trapped-on-a-desert-island films with this solo tour de force. You'll never look at a volleyball the same way again, and the scenery of Monuriki Island, in the neighbouring Mamanuca Islands, is stunning.

❋ *Anacondas: The Hunt for the Blood Orchid* (2004) Fiji played the part of Borneo, big snakes were made by computers and the scenery looked nice.

❋ *The Blue Lagoon* (1980) Starred a young Brooke Shields and some hunk who frequents those 'where are they now' shows. The scenery is as pretty as the young stars.

MAKING IT HAPPEN

Without some local help, sea-kayak trips can be relentlessly difficult – if you think airports are a pain, try them with a sea kayak as part of your luggage! Luckily, this trip can be done with a minimal amount of gear to transport from overseas. If you're an experienced paddler you may want to bring your favourite life jacket or paddle – let your outfitter handle the rest. Southern Sea Ventures and World Expeditions both organise trips and have a good reputation for safety and fun.

AN ALTERNATIVE CHALLENGE

In 2010 the Fiji government changed the rules about who was allowed to surf where. Previously, resorts were able to restrict who surfed their breaks, limiting access to their hotel guests only – not any more. This has opened up a world of possibilities for surf trips around Fiji that won't necessarily break the bank. Fiji is known for some outstanding breaks – surf spots like Cloudbreak are legendary among the surfing fraternity. Be warned, though, the surfing in Fiji is generally for experienced surfers only. Nasty reef breaks mean that a wipe-out at the wrong time can turn you into fish food.

MARK DAFFY | LONELY PLANET IMAGES

OPENING SPREAD Enjoy a variety of watersports at Kuata Island in Fiji's Yasawas.
ABOVE Sea kayakers at Qaraiqe Bay, Nacula Island: protection from the sun is essential.
BELOW Privately-owned Nanuya Levu is where the 1980 film *The Blue Lagoon* was shot.

KAVA

It's not just the scenery that intoxicates: drinking kava is the quintessential Fijian experience. Made from the root of the same name, kava has been a part of South Pacific culture for centuries. The drink has a mild narcotic effect, leaving you relaxed and numb-tongued. Traditionally, drinking kava is a social experience. Everyone sits in a circle around a big community bowl, and takes a turn to drink out of a half coconut shell. It's the perfect way to sooth sore kayaking muscles.

ROW ACROSS SIBERIA'S LAKE BAIKAL

LAKE BAIKAL IS AN OCEAN OF FRESH WATER WITH ALL THE MOODS AND PERILS OF THE SEA. TO CROSS IT IN AN OPEN BOAT POWERED BY NOTHING BUT MUSCLE IS TO RELY ON PROVIDENCE AS MUCH AS PREPARATION – A DANCE WITH DEATH ON THE WORLD'S DEEPEST LAKE.

Lake Baikal forms part of Siberia's version of the African Rift Valley. It's here that the Asian continent is ever so gradually being torn apart. Though not the biggest lake in the world in terms of area (it ranks sixth), by water volume it is the undisputed champion. That's because it's also the deepest on Earth – achieving a maximum depth of 1632m, and averaging roughly 750m.

Looking on maps like a banana (a 636km-long banana), Baikal has the sort of shape that simply invites you to paddle from one side of it to the other. Depending on where you are along its length, it's a distance of between 40km and 70km. Standing at the lake's edge, peering at a fortresslike wall of emerald mountains that mark the far shore, the urge to make that journey just gets stronger. But it's also from this perspective that the mammoth scale of the place also begins to hit home. You first feel the summer chill that distinguishes Baikal from the otherwise sweltering region surrounding it. And what was a welcome invitation suddenly starts to seem more like a dare.

It's all about choosing the right window. In good weather you require only a modest level of fitness, and little more than a beginner's proficiency on the oars. By all means, take things rather leisurely; row as slow as you want, and as zigzag a course as desired. Just keep in mind that the longer you're out there, the more chance you have of getting caught in a legendary Baikal storm. And then no amount of skill and endurance will likely be enough to avoid disaster.

Thus, a row across Lake Baikal is not the average Siberian's idea of a day out. They'll think you unhinged for not packing at least an outboard motor. Understandable, since a typical fishing boat here looks more like something you'd find plying the brooding waters of the North Sea. But Baikal contains not a trace of salt – it is regarded as having some of the purest water on Earth.

ESSENTIAL EXPERIENCES

✳ **Exploring the maze of channels of the Selenga River delta.**

✳ Sighting a Baikal seal, one of 745 animal species endemic to the lake.

✳ **Fishing for omul, a very tasty member of the salmon family.**

✳ Meeting the Buryat, proud indigenous people of the Baikal region.

✳ **Climbing the Primorsky Range to get a bird's-eye view of the lake.**

DISTANCE 50KM | **LOCATION** SOUTHERN SIBERIA, RUSSIAN FEDERATION | **IDEAL TIME COMMITMENT** ONE WEEK | **BEST TIME OF YEAR** MID TO LATE SUMMER | **ESSENTIAL TIP** BAIKAL CREATES ITS OWN WEATHER, SO BE AWARE THAT CONDITIONS ON THE LAKE CAN DETERIORATE RAPIDLY

WHAT A LOT OF FRESH WATER!

Roughly 330 rivers, the largest of which is the Selenga, flow into Lake Baikal. But such is the massive overall volume of the lake (it holds 20% of the planet's fresh water) that a water molecule will reside in it for an average of 300 years before exiting via the Angara River. In fact, it is claimed that if all the world's rivers were to empty into Baikal for a year, they would still not quite fill it. And yet, its current capacity is a shadow of what it once was. For today there is a layer of sediment some 7km thick overlaying the floor of the rift, sediment deposited over millions of years by all those inflowing rivers such as the Selenga.

THE BURYAT PEOPLE

The Buryats are indigenous to the Lake Baikal region, and constitute the largest ethnic minority group in Siberia. They are both genetically and culturally closely related to Mongolians, being traditionally nomadic herders who live in gers. They have a history of rebellion against Communism and of being doggedly persistent in their aspirations to secede from Russia. As a result, they were heavily persecuted during Joseph Stalin's time as Soviet leader. The land of Buryatia is considered a cradle of shamanism, and even today shamans are highly respected figures in Buryat society. Among other things, they are responsible for maintaining a healthy spiritual connection between people and the sacred lake.

■ THE ADVENTURE UNFOLDS

Chances are that the sun will be beating down hard as you're disgorged into Lake Baikal from the mouth of the Selenga River. You choose one of the distant north-shore peaks, place it above the bow and keep it there. As the low-lying islands of the Selenga delta recede from view, and the vast homogenous expanse of Baikal swallows you, perception of speed disappears. Soon it's only the voice of common sense insisting that you are moving forward, and that 15 to 20 hours of rowing will get you to journey's end.

Within an hour you'll exchange shorts and T-shirts for winter clothing. And still the cold will slither up sleeves and trouser legs. The water is only a few degrees above freezing, and the surface heaves like the belly of a sleeping beast. As each oar stroke increases your distance from the southern shore, your sense of exposure steadily increases. It's not helpful to think about the 3m waves that could be whipped up if the wind blows with venom from the southwest, nor to dwell on how many minutes you could survive in that frigid water.

Night falls and the darkness seems to stir Baikal from its slumber. The breeze gradually intensifies, then gusts. Luckily it's from the north. You spend an hour virtually rowing on the spot, then start being pushed backwards over metre-high waves. Every second or third oar stroke levers through fresh air.

Yet, so long as the wind continues to blow on your nose, this will be about as tough as Lake Baikal can make things for you. And ultimately, copping this sort of battering is nothing less than bliss when compared with the mayhem likely to be handed out by a dreaded southwesterly!

■ MAKING IT HAPPEN

To cross via the Selenga River delta, put in at Selenginsk (60km from the river mouth and four hours by train from the city of Irkutsk, or an hour by train from Ulan-Ude). On the far shore, head southwest for 60km to reach Bolshoye Goloustnoye, and get a taxi to Irkutsk. Carry food for five days, plus camping gear, insect repellent, warm clothing and a waterproof shell. If you're not travelling with your own boat, it's feasible to purchase a reasonably cheap Russian-made poly or fold-up kayak at a fishing and hunting supplies store in Irkutsk or Ulan-Ude.

■ AN ALTERNATIVE CHALLENGE

Listvyanka (45 minutes by car southeast of Irkutsk) lies at the head of the Angara, the river flowing out of Lake Baikal. From here, you can row or paddle eastwards along the spectacular north shore of the lake. The lushly forested Primorsky Range dips sharply into the lake, producing cliffs, craggy headlands, and shingle beaches that are only accessible by boat.

OPENING SPREAD Olkhon Island on Lake Baikal measures 70km by 15km and is a popular party spot in the summer that can only be accessed by boat or seaplane. Most visitors camp but guesthouses are available. **ABOVE** Lake Baikal. **LEFT** A scene from the 2006 film *Serko*, the story of a Buryat girl.

ARMCHAIR

* **The Longest Row** (1985) Documentary about Peter Bird's 294-day world-first solo row across the Pacific Ocean, from San Francisco to the Great Barrier Reef. Surely, the ultimate rowboat adventure.

* **Dersu Uzala** (1975) By Akira Kurosawa, this film depicting the ingenuity and bravery of a Mongolian frontiersman is set in late-19th-century Siberia.

* **Sacred Sea: A Journey to Lake Baikal** (Peter Thomson) Homage to the geographical and ecological wonders of Baikal.

* **Birthplace of the Winds** (Jon Bowermaster) A chronicle of kayaking the Aleutian Archipelago of Alaska. The author and his companion experience acute levels of exposure to the elements.

KAYAK MOSQUITO BAY

NATURE CAN BE FANTASTICALLY WEIRD. AND PERHAPS NOWHERE MORE SO THAN IN PUERTO RICO. FOR HERE, IN A FEW SELECT BAYS – OF WHICH THERE ARE JUST A HANDFUL WORLDWIDE – YOU CAN KAYAK RIGHT THROUGH THE WORLD'S MOST WONDERFUL WATERY LIGHT SHOW.

286

Puerto Rico is a Latin–Yankee hybrid, geographically floating betwixt Caribbean Sea and Atlantic Ocean, culturally wafting between its island heritage and adopted Americanism. It is white-sand beaches and Afro-Carib beats; it is strip malls, drugstores and multilane highways. But there's one thing (or rather millions of tiny things) that are resolutely neither.

Pyrodinium bahamense are ancient species of dinoflagellate – or minuscule spheres of sea gunk, to you and me. These 446-billion-year-old organisms very much like the waters off Puerto Rico, at least in a few choice spots. They like the vitamins released by the roots of red mangrove trees, the relative lack of any pollution and the limited tidal exchange of their favoured bays. And because they like it here, they treat us to their unique pyro-tastic show.

Pyrodinium might be tiny, but they're tough. Each organism's simple insides are protected by armoured plates, studded with defensive pores called trichocysts. And when these pores are agitated – by a hand, say, or the sweep of a paddle – they respond by giving off light. One dinoflagellate does not a party make. But put lots together – say, 700,000 per gallon of water – and the result is a magical phosphorescence, the sea turned into a shimmering soup, lending anything it touches a radioactive halo of blue.

There are fewer than 10 places worldwide where this phenomenon occurs, and Puerto Rico is arguably the most spectacular. There are three bioluminescent bays on the archipelago: Phosphorescent Bay at La Parguera (though pollution has severely diluted its dinoflagellates); Laguna Grande at Fajarado; and – best of all – Mosquito Bay, on the small island of Vieques.

Here, you can head out after sundown in a kayak and watch as the world beneath you starts to glow. This is not a physical test of an adventure, but a chance to see nature at its most beautifully bizarre.

ESSENTIAL EXPERIENCES

❋ **Watching the sun set over the lapping Caribbean with a cool rum cocktail and a blast of *salsa romántica*.**

❋ Navigating around the mazelike mangrove trees, which become an otherworldly – and slightly creepy – realm in the darkness.

❋ **Tracing myriad fish gliding through the bioluminescence, leaving trails of glowing blue in their wakes.**

❋ Gazing up at a blanket of stars – and then down, to see those same celestial speckles perfectly reflected in the waters below; watch out for shooting stars.

❋ **Dipping your paddle into the bay to delight at the halo of light created around its gentle thrust.**

DISTANCE 6KM TO 10KM | **LOCATION** MOSQUITO BAY, VIEQUES, PUERTO RICO | **IDEAL TIME COMMITMENT** TWO TO FOUR HOURS |
BEST TIME OF YEAR AROUND THE NEW MOON, YEAR-ROUND | **ESSENTIAL TIP** DON'T WEAR DEET-BASED MOSQUITO REPELLENT

THE PULSE OF PUERTO RICO

Puerto Rico's got rhythm. And not just courtesy of local lass J-Lo. The island's musical heritage dates back to the wood instruments of the Taíno, the guitars of the colonising Spanish and the beats of the African slaves. The frenzied drumming of bomba and the sung stories of plena are popular folk genres. Salsa's king though. The local variation is *salsa romántica* – a softer version of the *salsa dura* created by New Yorker Puerto Ricans. Reggaeton – a mash-up of salsa, reggae and hip-hop – was brought by Jamaican labourers in the 1900s; lyrics tend to be racy.

■ THE ADVENTURE UNFOLDS

The short drive from Esperanza was rough – bouncing along a rutted track in an ancient 4WD. But now you're in your life jacket, waiting to climb into a kayak you can barely see since the sun's gone to sleep, and you're raring to go.

The paddle out through the mangroves is eerie in the extreme, like entering a Tolkienesque labyrinth where forces – good or bad – might lurk. You can't see much beyond your head-torch beam, which is a good thing. You did your research and have timed your trip with the new moon. The darkest nights provide the best bioluminescent displays, and trips don't even run when the moon is full, the ambient glow obliterating the awesome algal effect.

As you emerge from the mangroves into the bay, your guide pauses and explains a little about the special organisms you're now floating above: how old they are, how rare. He explains that you must not swim, and why anyone who has applied DEET-based insect repellent should not dip their hands in as the chemicals will kill the creatures. Then you paddle on – with a yelp. As you swoop your paddle through the calm seas, the churned water ignites. You row more forcefully and the blue-white blush intensifies, surrounding not just your oar but the whole outline of your kayak.

Something splashes to your right: you see a shoal of fish, each leaving luminous streaks in their wake. There's a bigger splash away in the darkness, perhaps one of the bay's sharks – tiger, nurse, reef and hammerhead types lurk here – out on its evening hunt... Another good reason to stay in the kayak, you think, and just enjoy the spectacle.

■ MAKING IT HAPPEN

Ferries leave Puerto Rico for Vieques daily, and take an hour. Night-time kayak and electric-motored boat tours of Mosquito Bay run from Esperanza; see Golden Heron Ecotours. Check a lunar calendar, as trips are best under a new or partial moon. Laguna Grande, at Fajarado, near Puerto Rico's airport, is a more accessible option. Don't take boats with nonelectric motors – they pollute and damage dinoflagellates. Don't swim.

■ AN ALTERNATIVE CHALLENGE

Puerto Rico offers fine diving, for all abilities. As a rule, head west to dive walls and caves, east for colourful reefs bursting with marine life. There are good, accessible sites off the south coast town of La Parguera, around Isla Desecheo (13km off Rincón), and around Culebra and Vieques. Isla Mona, 80km off the west coast, is the Holy Grail: this prehistoric-looking island is encircled by reefs and underwater formations, and frequented by sharks and humpbacks. Arrange a liveaboard trip from Rincón or Puerto Real.

OPENING SPREAD The island of Vieques: an area requisitioned by the US Army in WWII is now the Vieques National Wildlife Refuge, the largest in the Caribbean and home to three species of turtle. **ABOVE (L)** Glow in the dark: bioluminescent algae lights up the sea. **ABOVE (R)** Sit-on kayaks at Fajardo.

ARMCHAIR

* **When I was Puerto Rican** (Esmeralda Santiago) A moving memoir; the author conveys the tenderness and toughness of her childhood in Puerto Rico and her subsequent emigration to NYC.

* **Puerto Rico: Island in the Sun** (Roger LaBrucherie) World-class photobook full of enticing images.

* **Birds of Puerto Rico** (Herbert A Raffaele) A fine field guide, including illustrations of all the islands' avifauna, including the winter-visiting species.

* **West Side Story** (1961) The modernised Hollywood take on *Romeo and Juliet* sees the white working-class Jets at gang-war with the Puerto Rican Sharks on the streets of New York City.

* **Boricuas: Influential Puerto Rican Writings – An Anthology** (edited by Roberto Santiago) A wide collection of Puerto Rican literature, from colonial to modern times.

DRIVE

RACE A RICKSHAW

OPEN ROAD, OPEN SIDES, OPEN MIND – THRUMMING ACROSS THE SUBCONTINENT AT THE HELM OF A CLASSIC 145CC AUTORICKSHAW, DODGING HOLY COWS AND MECHANICAL CALAMITIES, GUARANTEES THRILLS, SPILLS AND A NEW RESPECT FOR THE WORKADAY PILOTS OF INDIA'S UBIQUITOUS THREE-WHEEL TAXIS.

290

To paraphrase the office sticker cliché: you don't have to be mad to drive here, but it helps. India's roads aren't for the faint of heart; whether you're on foot, pedalling a bike or jammed into a bus, the mayhem of packed city streets and truck-crammed highways is enough to bring on palpitations in anyone... except rickshaw drivers. Helming a canvas-topped, unstable three-wheeler with questionable brakes requires the kind of unshakable confidence and offensive driving tactics that would make a Manhattan cab driver kneel in awe.

The autorickshaw is such an icon of the Subcontinent, that it was only a matter of time before someone dreamed up the idea of a pan-Indian rickshaw odyssey. And so, in 2006, the first Rickshaw Challenge was born. The original event (the IndianARC rally) saw a cluster of customised rickshaws splutter from Chennai to Kanyakumari, covering some 1000km and taking in the beaches of Mamallapuram, the temples of Thanjavur and Madurai, cool hill stations in Tamil Nadu and a goodly proportion of South India's population of mechanics. Despite crashes, wrong turns and countless breakdowns – the two-stroke, 145.45cc engines, based on old Italian Piaggio scooter blueprints, are repeatedly patched up – the rally was a resounding triumph and repeats followed.

Currently, a handful of organisers arrange routes including Chennai–Mumbai, Trivandrum (Kerala) to Panjim (Goa), Panjim–Mumbai, Jaisalmer (Rajasthan) to Kochi (Kerala), Kochi to Shillong (Meghalaya) and Shillong–Jaisalmer, often with driving instruction, back-up mechanics and hotels provided. There's usually a charity fundraising element too. Fancy it? Prices for rickshaws vary depending on engine and body size, manufacturer and bartering skills, but you'll need around US$1000 for the rickshaw, plus a modicum of mechanical know-how, plenty of chutzpah – and a blemish-free karma.

ESSENTIAL EXPERIENCES

* **Dipping your toes into the Bay of Bengal at Mamallapuram after exploring the town's famous rock-hewn temples.**

* Sipping a cold beer in Puducherry at the end of your first day's rickshaw rallying.

* **Marvelling at the technicolour pilgrims thronging in and out of the yet-more-technicolour Sri Meenakshi temple in Madurai.**

* Watching pilgrims greeting the waves of the Indian Ocean as they crash against the swells of the Bay of Bengal at India's southern tip, Kanyakumari.

* **Making friends with mechanics – a new way of getting to know the locals as they perform engineering miracles on your truculent trike.**

DISTANCE 950KM (CHENNAI-TRIVANDRUM CLASSIC RUN) | **LOCATION** INDIA | **IDEAL TIME COMMITMENT** TWO WEEKS
BEST TIME OF YEAR LATE DECEMBER TO EARLY JANUARY | **ESSENTIAL TIP** BUY THE BEST TRAVEL INSURANCE YOU CAN AFFORD – ACCIDENTS WILL HAPPEN!

■ THE ADVENTURE UNFOLDS

You've pimped your ride – canvas roof and tin sides are freshly painted with team colours and gung-ho slogans – and crammed a crash course in driving and repairing an autorickshaw into a couple of days. You've scrutinised the maps and plotted your snaking route across Tamil Nadu and Kerala. You've even developed an affection for the aroma of fumes belched out with every throaty growl of your steed's engine.

Now you're itching to hit the road, but what you're not prepared for is how nearly everything on the road seems to want to hit you, as you gingerly wend through the crush of Chennai's traffic. Jamming on the brakes to avoid a collision with a cow moseying languidly across the road, your rickshaw threatens to lurch into a terminal forward roll. Your fingers are threatening to cramp, so tightly are you gripping the handlebars.

But as the city limits shrink in your rear-view mirror, and you creak towards your top speed of 55km/h, the tension eases and you start to recognise the real benefits of this foolhardy expedition. This is slow travel indeed. Following the back roads, you're able to take in the views over the Bay of Bengal, spotting small fishing villages and stopping to explore the rock-hewn temples as you reach the first night's stop at Mamallapuram.

Over refreshing mango lassis in a ramshackle restaurant, you share tales from the road, chuckling at accounts of close encounters with goats, wrestles with wrenches and unplanned dives into ditches caused by trucks or a moment's inattention. At times, it seems you'll never understand the bewildering psyche of India. But now, for a week or so, you're surrounded by throttle-happy lunatics just like you.

ARMCHAIR

❋ **No Full Stops in India** (Mark Tully) A long-time BBC correspondent describes his travels around the country, revealing subtle insights into the Indian psyche.

❋ **The Age of Kali** (William Dalrymple) Arguably the finest contemporary English-language travel writer in India investigates the joys and woes of the modern state.

❋ **The God of Small Things** (Arundhati Roy) This powerful, beautifully observed novel set partly in a small Keralan town gives a flavour of South Indian life.

❋ **Monsoon Wedding** (2001) Mira Nair's film delving into the intrigues and family dramas behind the big day is a hilarious, touching depiction of modern middle-class India.

❋ **On a Shoestring to Coorg** (Dervla Murphy) The grand dame of travel writing describes her budget odyssey south from Mumbai.

◼ MAKING IT HAPPEN

Access to the main starting points is easy, with international airports at Chennai, Mumbai, Kochi and Delhi, and domestic flights, trains and buses serving other endpoints. At the time of writing, two established companies – Chennai-based Rickshaw Challenge, which launched the first rally, and the Adventurists, a UK organisation – arranged rickshaw adventures across India. Avoid travelling in monsoon season – June to October across much of India.

◼ AN ALTERNATIVE CHALLENGE

Three wheels good, two wheels better? Many visitors to India choose to explore on another petrol-powered icon, the Enfield Bullet motorcycle, particularly when tackling the winding mountain roads in Himalayan regions such as Ladakh. But cycling is an alternative way of discovering rural India, offering more time for impromptu diversions and meeting locals. Pedalling between the big hitters and small villages of Rajasthan is a popular option; the other hot spot for beginners is Kerala, offering relaxing biking alongside its peaceful backwaters and between tea plantations and wildlife reserves. Count on covering about 50km per day.

TONY BURNS | LONELY PLANET IMAGES

OPENING SPREAD Rickshaws approach Charminar, the Mosque of the Four Minarets, in Hyderabad. **ABOVE** May the gods be with you: making an offering at Sri Meenakshi temple in Madurai. **BELOW** The two-stroke engine of an autorickshaw produces seven horsepower.

HUMAN FUEL

South India's mainly vegetarian, rice-heavy cuisine is one of the joys of travel around Kerala and Tamil Nadu. The big-value thali is the main event: a range of vegetable curries, dhal (soupy spiced lentils), rice and chapattis (flat, round bread) or puris (puffy fried bread) – usually refills come thick and fast till your stomach begs for mercy. Other treats include the masala dosa – a spiced lentil pancake filled with curried vegetables; vada – fried, spiced lentil doughnuts served with coconut chutney; bhajis and pakoras – fried vegetable patties; and samosas – pastry triangles filled with curried vegetables.

DRIVE THE WORLD'S DEADLIEST ROAD

KNOWN IN BOLIVIA AS EL CAMINO DE LA MUERTE ('THE ROAD OF DEATH'), THIS CRUDE STRETCH OF ROAD MARKS A SPECTACULAR DESCENT FROM THE BOLIVIAN ANDES TO THE FLOOR OF THE AMAZON BASIN. TREACHEROUSLY PLUNGING 3000M IN JUST 70KM, THIS IS ONE OF THE WORLD'S EPIC DRIVES.

294

The Camino de las Yungas (North Yungas Road) does not have an easy task: to find its way across the Bolivian Andes from La Paz, the highest administrative capital in the world, to the town of Coroico, over 3000m below, in less than 70km. Built by prisoners during the 1932–35 Chaco War between Bolivia and Paraguay, for 80 years this thin scar etched into the mountain flanks was the only way down into the northern Yungas region of Bolivia. Unfortunately, travelling along its length is as precarious as it is stunning.

Barely 3m in width, the rough, unsealed road zigzags erratically between countless hairpin turns, all the while sandwiched between a sheer mountain wall on one side and deadly 500m drops on the other. The road has its own rules: downhill drivers always have the right of way – forcing faster vehicles to slow and find a spot wide enough to allow trucks and buses to shimmy past. Barely a whisker stands between them and a plunge to the canyon floor. Vehicles pass on the left, rather than on the right like the rest of the country, so that drivers can better see when their outer wheel starts running out of road.

Add to this billows of dust, fog as thick as pea soup, seasonal mudslides and poorly maintained Bolivian vehicles, and you can imagine why the Inter-American Development Bank dubbed it 'the most dangerous road in the world' in 1995. Up to 25 vehicles a year were careering off the edge of the 'Death Road', with the BBC estimating that at one point between 200 and 300 people were losing their lives annually along this stretch of dirt.

In 2006, after 20 years of construction, a modern bypass road was finally opened, proudly boasting a pavement, dual lanes and guard rails. Most vehicles now travel along the new route, but sections of the old Camino de las Yungas remain open to those wishing to tango with the world's most dangerous road.

ESSENTIAL EXPERIENCES

* **Hurtling yourself down the deadliest road in the world, at ludicrous speeds, while on the back of a mountain bike.**

* Resettling the nerves after your hazardous descent in the sleepy town of Coroico, perched mid-hilltop and boasting wholesale views of cloud-draped valleys and Andean peaks.

* **Wandering La Paz's Mercado de Hechicería (Witches' Market) – filled with herbs, potions and the occasional llama foetus.**

* Learning about the fascinating historical journey of coca – from traditional herb to illicit drug – at La Paz's Coca Museum.

* **Macheteing your way through the depths of the Amazon jungle near the town of Rurrenabaque.**

DISTANCE 69KM | **ELEVATION** 4650M TO 1604M | **LOCATION** LA PAZ, BOLIVIA | **IDEAL TIME COMMITMENT** A FEW HARROWING HOURS OF YOUR LIFE | **BEST TIME OF YEAR** MAY TO OCTOBER | **ESSENTIAL TIP** BE SURE TO SIT ON THE LEFT OF YOUR VEHICLE FOR THE GORGEOUS/NERVE-RACKING VIEWS

LA PAZ, LAST STOP FOR GUINEA PIG

A common item to be found on La Paz menus is *cuy*, or guinea pig. Cuy have been part of the Andean culinary repertoire since pre-Inca times – long before their introduction into Europe as a must-have pet during the 16th century. They're ideal livestock: high in protein, fed on scraps, breeding profusely, and requiring less room and maintenance than other animals. Domesticated over 7000 years ago, they have adapted to survive South America's extreme environments: from Andean plains to barren coastal deserts. An integral part of Andean culture and folklore, *cuy* are often used by *curanderos* (traditional healers) in ceremonial rituals.

AMAZON ADVENTURE

Past the hilltop town of Coroico, the 'most dangerous road in the world' becomes merely 'ridiculously dangerous' as it snakes down to the Amazon Basin floor. Travellers brave enough to continue on for another 15 hours by road are rewarded by the sanguine town of Rurrenabaque. Straddling the Río Beni, this is a popular jumping-off point for riverboat adventures into surrounding rainforest. If you've ever wanted to live out your Indiana Jones fantasies, these week-long trips will have you catching live alligators, tracking panthers and man-eating boa constrictors, fishing for piranha and swimming with pink Amazonian freshwater dolphins.

◼ THE ADVENTURE UNFOLDS

At 3735m, La Paz is one of the highest cities in the world, but the first few kilometres of your journey involve climbing even higher to the windswept La Cumbre Pass (4650m). It feels like the public bus you're on is getting a better run-up before hurtling itself into the abyss. The vehicle is an ancient, creaking hulk, with 4WD wheels and axels raised to clear the mud heaps that coalesce during the wet season. Passengers pack the inside of the bus to the rafters, with bundles of goods and animals. At the highest point, the driver slows down to collect himself, refills his mouth with fresh coca leaves to fight off fatigue, throws a prayer towards earth goddess Pachamama and cranks up the pan-pipe music before hurtling down the mountain at unreasonable speeds.

Sitting on the left of the vehicle it's as if you're flying across the mountaintops. It's not until you crane your neck out the window and notice the outermost wheel skimming the road's very edge that you realise you are still earthbound. Just. Reminders of the precariousness of your situation line the roadside, which is punctuated by crosses mourning less fortunate former passengers. It's common to see a crumpled vehicle carcass lying in the valley bed below.

The three-hour journey down to Coroico is truly breathtaking – passing from cool Altiplano terrain to subtropical rainforest, through dense clouds and waterfall spray, all to a backdrop of grand Andean summits and canyons plunging deep into the earth. Whether the views justify the mediocre odds of completing the journey in one piece, however, is another matter altogether.

◼ MAKING IT HAPPEN

La Paz is reached by air via major South American airlines or bus from Peru and Chile. Public buses to Coroico and Rurrenabaque depart from Villa Fátima, but these now bypass the worst of the 'death road' by using the new highway. For the authentic death-defying experience, rent a car or arrange a downhill-biking trip with a reputable outfit such as Gravity Assisted Mountain Biking.

◼ AN ALTERNATIVE CHALLENGE

For those who guffaw in the face of danger, a popular way to tackle this journey is on two wheels. Mountain-biking thrill seekers have been putting themselves at the mercy of Bolivia's gravity since the 1990s, and numerous adventure outfits in La Paz organise downhill mountain-biking sojourns along the older sections of the North Yungas Road. The all-day descent involves a bone-shattering 50km downhill run at breakneck speeds, accompanied all the way by the smell of burning brake rubber. Make sure you bring a change of underwear.

OPENING SPREAD Drivers dodge danger at every turn. **ABOVE (L)** Bolivia's indigenous *cholita* style features an alpaca shawl and a *bombin* (bowler hat). **ABOVE (R)** Cycling down the road is a popular and similarly nerve-wracking alternative. **LEFT** Body language: a black caiman sends a warning.

ARMCHAIR

* *A Concise History of Bolivia* (Herbert Klein) Essential reading, with a meticulous account of Bolivia's past – from humans' first forays into the Andes to the revolutionary government of Evo Morales.
* *Inca-Kola: A Traveller's Tale of Peru* (Matthew Parris) A classic laugh-out-loud backpacker's tale of holiday misadventures through Peru and parts of Bolivia during the mid-1980s.
* *Top Gear: Bolivia Special* (BBC) Follow the madcap antics Jeremy

Clarkson and team as they take on Bolivia's roads, including the infamous Road of Death.

* *Alirina* A live recording by the Bolivian folk troupe Grupo Aymara, who first introduced traditional Andean flute and pan-pipe music to the West.
* *Quantum of Solace* (2008) James Bond fends off hackneyed bad guys out to stage a coup d'état for control of Bolivia's water supply.

RACE THE PLYMOUTH–BANJUL RALLY

A £100 BANGER, NO MECHANICAL KNOWLEDGE WHATSOEVER AND 6000KM OF DRIVING VIA TRAFFIC-CLOGGED CITIES, SNOWY MOUNTAINS, BENT BORDER GUARDS AND THE SAHARA DESERT – THIS IS, WITHOUT DOUBT, THE WORLD'S WACKIEST OF RACES.

298

'If you have a pile of excrement on your drive that needs scrapping, and the local car dump does not fill you with excitement, buy some cable ties and gaffer tape, some vodka and Pot Noodles, jump in and go south.'

These words from Dakar Challenge, organisers of the mad-cap jalopy jaunt from Plymouth to the Gambia, sum up the ethos of this adventure. Unlike the Paris–Dakar Rally, a 'leading sports competition' watched on TV by billions, the Plymouth–Banjul, which roughly follows the former's original route, is not a competition at all (and is watched mainly on the ground, by bemused West Africans). Indeed, racing is actively discouraged and the ability to laugh in the face of engine failure is deemed more important than being able to fix it.

Created in 2002 by 'crap car svengali' Julian Nowill, the idea is this: purchase an old banger for, ideally, no more than £100. Spend up to £15 on modifications (furry dice, flashing hubcaps...). Then drive said dud from south-coast England via France to Spain, push it onto a ferry for Morocco and keep on going until – with luck, bribes and WD-40 – you arrive in Banjul three weeks later.

There will be casualties en route; not all vehicles that start this journey – around 50 per departure – make the finish. Some putter out early in the Spanish mountains, others fail on Mauritania's Atlantic-lashed shores or in the sandy quagmires of Western Sahara. And there is no crack-mechanic support to help along the way. But the camaraderie (or tow ropes) of your fellow rallyers should see you through. This is about team spirit and thinking on your feet.

In the Gambia's capital Banjul, you and car part company. The trusty/ knackered wreck that's got you this far will be auctioned off for charity, and you'll board a boring old plane home, oil still staining your fingertips and the smell of burnt rubber, spiced tagine and, yes, success, still up your nose.

ESSENTIAL EXPERIENCES

❋ **Braving the mad roads of Marrakesh, to treat yourself to a night in a *riad* (boutique hotel) and the storytelling, snake-charming craziness of Djemaa el-Fna.**

❋ Breaking down in the middle of nowhere and performing rudimentary repairs with gaffer tape, paper clips and chewing gum.

❋ **Driving in a clapped-out convoy with your fellow rally-goers, stopping now and then to share state-of-car updates and to push each other out of sand dunes.**

❋ Pootling past the skeletons of rusting shipwrecks on the beaches of Mauritania.

❋ **Spending the night in the funky Senegalese island-city of St Louis, a-buzz with jazz clubs and cafes serving fiery fish stew.**

DISTANCE 6000KM | **LOCATION** PLYMOUTH (UK) TO BANJUL (THE GAMBIA), VIA FRANCE, SPAIN, MOROCCO, WESTERN SAHARA, MAURITANIA AND SENEGAL | **IDEAL TIME COMMITMENT** THREE WEEKS | **BEST TIME OF YEAR** DECEMBER TO FEBRUARY **ESSENTIAL TIP** PACK LIGHT (IN CASE YOU NEED TO CADGE A LIFT IN ANOTHER CAR)

MARVELLOUS MAURITANIA

Mauritania is not the easiest place to travel. An increase in kidnappings since 2008 has made driving through the country a far riskier undertaking, and local advice should be sought before attempting it. However, this is one of the most spectacular stretches of the rally. The drive south from Nouâdhibou first passes through the Banc d'Arguin National Park, a haven of birdlife (best seen on a pirogue trip along the waterways). It continues, via uninspiring capital Nouakchott, along one of the world's most dramatic highways, where Saharan sands meet Atlantic spray, and camel caravans meet decaying shipwrecks.

RICH MAN'S RALLY

The original Paris–Dakar Rally – the more highbrow forebear of the Dakar Challenge – was first run in 1979. It's an off-road endurance race, with daily stages of 800km to 900km across punishing terrain. In recent years the rally has changed course, with political troubles in West Africa (plus controversy regarding its damaging effects on the local environment) moving proceedings to South America. The race is split into three classes (motorcycle, car, truck) and is open to both professional and amateur drivers. Vehicles are top of the range, with manufacturers using the event to showcase their wares. Rusting, 25-year-old Skodas need not apply...

THE ADVENTURE UNFOLDS

Under the bonnet, something glows malevolently. The prognosis isn't good. Luckily, you know absolutely nothing of mechanics so decide to simply close the hood and hope the problem goes away... In'shallah.

You and your clapped-out Eastern European clunker have somehow made it from the UK to France, negotiated Paris at rush hour (a white-knuckle ride with a dodgy clutch) and traversed the Spanish sierras, which were a metre-deep in snow. You've mastered the rest of Iberia and puttered off the ferry into Tangier (which is more than can be said for one of your rally-mates who had to be pushed off the boat by a band of Moroccan shopkeepers). You've detoured into magnificent Marrakesh and spent a night beside the seaside at lovely Sidi Ifni. You've crossed an alleged Mauritanian minefield and the soft sands of the Sahara. You've used both of your spare tyres and a lot of gaffer tape; you've wild-camped in the desert under thousands of stars. You even managed to make it across the notorious Senegalese border – albeit with a lighter wallet, having been charged some 'administrative costs' by the avaricious officials.

Now, you're nearly there – it's Banjul or bust! You turn the key. And the tin can groans into life. Your rally-mates cheer: no one among this motley crew – driving old Porsches, ice-cream vans, 2CVs and hearses – wants anyone to fail. Over the past weeks you've been each other's lifeline, sharing laughs, meals and mechanical tips (who knew egg whites could plug a leaky radiator?). There's no race to see who gets there first, there's just the desire to get there at all. Together.

MAKING IT HAPPEN

Dakar Challenge runs the Plymouth–Banjul Rally. There are multiple departures, December to February; participants enter as teams (one vehicle, two people). The vehicle must be left-hand drive (to be more saleable in Gambia); a vehicle costing less than £100 is encouraged. Once accepted, participants pay an entrance fee and start planning, which involves getting visas, jabs and an international driving licence.

AN ALTERNATIVE CHALLENGE

Dakar Challenge also runs a Petra Challenge, a similarly low-budget, high-calamity 'race' that heads east across Europe to Turkey, Syria and Jordan; optional detours and add-ons include Iraqi Kurdistan, Jerusalem and Lebanon. The challenge departs the UK in September/October and takes around 19 days. Highlights include crossing Romania's Transfagarasan Pass and driving through Turkey's fairy-chimney Cappadocia region. Check the current security situation before attempting this route.

301

OPENING SPREAD The ship cemetery of Nouâhadibou on Mauritania's coast. **ABOVE (L)** The hairpin bends of Dades Gorge in Morocco's Atlas Mountains. **ABOVE (R)** Bangers on the way to Banjul strike camp in Mauritania. **LEFT** The Sahara's shifting sands threaten the medieval trading city of Chinguetti.

ARMCHAIR

* *To Dakar and Back: 21 Days Across North Africa by Motorcycle* (Lawrence Hacking & Wil De Clercq) Hacking relives the trials and hardships of the official Paris–Dakar Rally, the most notorious off-road race in the world.

* *West Africa* (Lonely Planet) Practical guide to Morocco, Mauritania, Senegal and beyond, including maps, and restaurant and accommodation listings.

* *Sahara Overland* (Chris Scott) Excellent Trailblazer guide to negotiating this inhospitable region: the bible of desert travel.

* *It'll Be Fine* (John Parry) Firsthand account of one couple's Plymouth–Timbuktu escapade, including encounters with bent border guards, bad traffic and all manner of automotive mayhem.

* *Auto Repair for Dummies* (Deanna Sclar) Handy manual for novice mechanics; includes illustrated how-to instructions for basic problems.

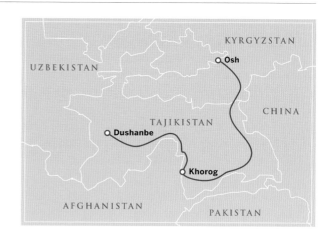

JEEP THE PAMIR HIGHWAY

IN ONE OF ASIA'S LEAST-EXPLORED CORNERS LIES SOME OF THE WORLD'S MOST INCREDIBLE MOUNTAIN SCENERY. THIS JEEP DRIVE TAKES YOU THROUGH THE HEART OF THE ACTION, INTO A LAND OF YURTS AND YAKS KNOWN LOCALLY AS THE ROOF OF THE WORLD.

302

Located in the most remote cul-de-sac of one of the least-known countries in Asia's least-visited region, Tajikistan's Pamir Mountains are deliciously off the beaten track. The immense high-altitude plateau occupies the entire eastern half of the country, but is home to only 3% of its population. Home to the tallest peaks outside the Himalayas, it's one of the highest inhabited places on earth.

The region (also known as Badakhshan) has three environments. The capital, Khorog, lies in the steep and jagged western Pamirs, a knotted chaos of mountain valleys so isolated from each other that each speaks a distinct language. Further south is the Wakhan, a beautiful wide valley shared by Tajikistan and Afghanistan, dotted with forts and villages, and boxed in by the towering 7000m peaks of the Hindu Kush. Finally, to the far east lie the Pamir proper, a series of rolling high-altitude desert valleys and turquoise lakes that spill over into China's Xinjiang Province. Winding through this desolate but incredibly beautiful region is the Pamir Highway, built by Soviet engineers in the 1930s to secure their remotest borders. There is little infrastructure along the road; no hotels, restaurants, shops or gas stations, just the occasional yurt camp or village selling gasoline from roadside buckets.

Upheaval in the post-Soviet 1990s led to unprecedented poverty here. In response, several NGOs started community-based tourism projects, focused around yurt stays and vehicle rental. The result is an easy-to-organise network of reliable, comfortable and cheap homestays in some of the world's most remote surroundings. The region was off-limits for most of the 20th-century, and even now only a handful of people travel from Khorog to Osh each year, following in the footsteps of Marco Polo and Sven Hedin. For modern-day explorers, we rank this as Central Asia's premier road-based adventure.

ESSENTIAL EXPERIENCES

* **Drifting off to sleep under an incredible blanket of stars in a cosy Kyrgyz yurt – perhaps the quintessential Central Asian experience.**

* Picnicking on the shores of Kara-Kul, a huge lake created by a meteorite 10 million years ago, with the 7000m peaks of the high Pamir in the background.

* **Scanning the rolling brown hillsides and ridges for Marco Polo sheep, lammergeiers, ibex and maybe even the odd snow leopard.**

* Absorbing the views of the Hindu Kush from the enigmatic Silk Road forts of Zong or Yamchun in the Wakhan Valley.

* **Milking a grumpy yak at a Kyrgyz herder's camp and then breakfasting on fresh cream in the Pshart Valley.**

DISTANCE 730KM | **ELEVATION** 4665M | **LOCATION** BADAKHSHAN, TAJIKISTAN | **IDEAL TIME COMMITMENT** TWO WEEKS | **BEST TIME OF YEAR** JUNE TO OCTOBER | **ESSENTIAL TIP** BRING SUNSCREEN, SUNGLASSES AND PLENTY OF SPARE BATTERIES, AS ELECTRICITY SUPPLIES ARE FEW AND FAR BETWEEN

YURTS

Toasty warm in winter and cool in summer, spacious, portable and even biodegradable, a yurt offers the perfect accommodation solution for Pamiri nomads and visiting tourists alike. It may look unprepossessing from the outside, but the interior is decorated in a riot of embroidered felts and carpets arranged around a warming yak-dung stove. At the beginning or end of summer, you might be lucky enough to see one being assembled or disassembled. The process takes about two hours, from unwrapping the felt sides and reed walls to prising apart the wooden roof spokes.

PAMIRI HOUSES

Overnight in the Western Pamirs or the Wakhan Valley, and you will most likely stay in a traditional wooden Pamiri house. Such houses are highly traditional structures, whose symbolic numerology dates as far back as Zoroastrianism. The main room is a five-pillared space arranged around a central square depression, whose light comes from a central skylight made from four concentric squares said to represent earth, fire, air and water. Pride of place on the walls is a photo of the Aga Khan, the spiritual leader of the region's Ismaili Muslims and regarded here as a living god.

THE ADVENTURE UNFOLDS

The route kicks off in the mountain-shadowed town of Khorog and detours south to the wide and beautiful Wakhan Valley, once a major Silk Road thoroughfare and still littered with 2000-year-old Kushan forts, Buddhist ruins and Ismaili Muslim shrines decorated with rams' horns. Accommodation is available at homestays in the valley, all offering a flavour of local Wakhi life.

From Langar, the road swings away from the Afghan border and climbs rapidly to join the main Pamir Highway. Viewpoints reveal a landscape of immense salt plains, high-altitude turquoise lakes and yurts set in rolling grassy valleys, broken only by the occasional truck in transit from China's most remote border crossing. The only town is the ex-imperial Russian army outpost, Murgab, an end-of-the-world collection of wooden houses and broken car parts.

The remote valleys around Murgab are dotted with herding yurt camps that take in visitors as part of a local sustainable tourism program. Turn off the paved highway into a pristine mountain valley to a yurt camp, and you can expect to be welcomed with a cup of salty tea, a bowl of fresh yoghurt and a comfy bed. By linking several of these homestays, you can create a host of cutting-edge adventures ranging from camel treks to summit climbs.

The final section of the highway climbs north over the 4665m Ak-Baital Pass to Kara-Kul lake and into the Alay Valley of Kyrgyzstan. Here you can either cross the fabulously remote Irkestham Pass to Kashgar in China, perhaps Asia's most exciting border crossing, or continue over a pass into the Ferghana Valley, the gateway to fabulous Samarkand and Bukhara beyond.

MAKING IT HAPPEN

Foreign visitors need a Tajikistan visa, as well as a Gorno-Badakhshan Autonomous Oblast (GBAO) permit, both of which are easily available from Tajikistan embassies abroad. Several travel companies in Dushanbe and Khorog can arrange vehicle hire, which is the only reliable way to get around the Pamirs. The Murgab Ecotourism Association (META) offers a wide range of yurt stays across the Pamirs and can arrange full tours.

DETOUR

For an adventurous add-on to an already epic road trip, consider the detour southeast from Murgab to Shaimak, right at the junction of Afghanistan, China, Pakistan and the former Soviet Union. For fans of Great Game history, this is the quintessential meeting point of empires. The drive takes you past medieval *kurgans* (burial tombs), a ruined caravanserai and views of 7546m Muztagh Ata peak beckoning from nearby China. And here's the true mark of a great Central Asian adventure – you'll need to secure KGB permission in advance.

OPENING SPREAD Yurt stays can be negotiated in the Pamirs. Kyrgyz, Tajik and Kazakh yurts differ in decor and design. **ABOVE (L)** Family transport, Tajik-style. **ABOVE (R)** Most visitors use a 4WD to drive the highway. **LEFT** Pamirs are skilled on horseback. Take a horse-trekking trips from Bachor.

ARMCHAIR

* ***The Great Game*** (Peter Hopkirk) Details the imperial high jinks between Russian and British spies on the borders of Central Asia, including Francis Younghusband's exploits in the Pamirs.

* ***The Travels*** (Marco Polo) The great Venetian traveller gives a vivid description of the Pamirs, pointing out everything from the lack of birds to the dimming effects of the high altitude on campfires.

* ***The Pamirs and the Source of the Oxus*** (George Curzon) A classic 19th-century travelogue and report to the Royal Geographic Society from the Tory MP and future viceroy of India.

* ***Tajikistan and the High Pamirs*** (Robert Middleton and Huw Thomas) Middleton's chapter on the history of Pamir exploration is a particularly good background read to the region.

DRIVE THE CANNING STOCK ROUTE

THE ULTIMATE DRIVING ADVENTURE, WESTERN AUSTRALIA'S CANNING STOCK ROUTE RUNS FOR 1850KM. THE LONGEST, REMOTEST STOCK ROUTE IN THE WORLD, IT TRAVERSES SOME OF AUSTRALIA'S MOST MAJESTIC (AND DIFFICULT) COUNTRY, AND ITS LEGEND IS AT THE HEART OF AUSTRALIA'S STORY.

306

At the turn of the 20th century, a tick problem meant that East Kimberley cattle couldn't be shipped to Perth for fear of spreading the disease. By opening up a land route from Halls Creek to the south, the stock could be sold directly to the booming gold fields of Kalgoorlie, thereby breaking the monopoly of the West Kimberley cattle barons, and the ticks would die off in the blazing heat of the journey. Keen to keep beef prices down, the government hired Alfred Canning to map a route through the desert that would provide enough water and pasture for large droves of cattle. Canning had already traversed much of Western Australia while surveying the famous Rabbit-Proof Fence.

Canning made his first trip in 1906, with a team of 23 camels, two horses and eight men. They relied on Aboriginal people to help them find water, but their 'guides' were not always voluntary – Canning sometimes used chains and denied his captives water until they led the white men to their precious soaks and waterholes. Two years later, Canning returned to the desert with 30 men, 70 camels, 267 goats and 100 tonnes of food and gear to construct the wells, each one a day's journey from the next. Most of the wells were built on water sources that were both sacred to the Aborigines and essential to their survival.

The first bullocks set out in 1911, but the drovers were killed by desert people at Well 37. A punitive expedition was sent out – nobody was arrested, but the sergeant admitted killing several Aboriginal people. Drovers became afraid to use the track and for the next two decades it was rarely travelled. It reopened in 1931, after repair work – many of the route's wells had been destroyed by Aboriginal people who were unable to draw water from them. After ladders were fitted, the stock route became more peaceful and about 20 mobs of cattle were driven down it over the next 20 years. Since then, the route has not been maintained, making it one of the most unforgiving roads in the world.

ESSENTIAL EXPERIENCES

* **Descending into the eerie Wolfe Creek meteorite crater.**

* Taking a dip before resting under the red cliffs, palm trees and river red gums at Durba Springs.

* **Examining ancient Martu rock art in the Calvert Ranges.**

* Putting your vehicle to the test, climbing dozens of red sand dunes.

* **Washing off the red dust at Desert Queen Baths in Karlamilyi (Rudall River) National Park.**

* Spotting exotic birds at Lake Gregory.

* **Hiding from the cannibal spirits at salty Lake Disappointment.**

* Paying a visit to Aboriginal communities where you can hear stories and buy artwork that tells the Canning tale.

* **Lying on your swag at the end of a day's drive, spotting countless shooting stars in the desert sky.**

DISTANCE 1850KM | **LOCATION** OUTBACK WESTERN AUSTRALIA | **IDEAL TIME COMMITMENT** TWO TO THREE WEEKS | **BEST TIME OF YEAR** APRIL TO SEPTEMBER | **ESSENTIAL TIP** AS THE GIRL GUIDES SAY, BE PREPARED

WALLY DOWLING

Wally Dowling was a legendary drover who rode barefoot along the Canning Stock Route several times in his career. After taking cattle south, Dowling would round up brumbies – wild horses – that he tamed along the way back north before selling them in the East Kimberley. While many white people saw romance in Dowling's way of life, the Aboriginal people, some of whom worked with him, recall him equally for his violence as for his strength and bravery. Dowling drove what was probably the last mob of animals northwards in 1951. He was immortalised in a song by Australian country singer Slim Dusty, 'The End of the Canning Stock Route'.

THE ADVENTURE UNFOLDS

The Canning Stock Route traverses Australia's magnificent Western Desert, passing through the Great Sandy, Little Sandy and Gibson Deserts. En route you'll sail through seas of pale spinifex and plains filled with wildflowers. You'll climb over red sand dunes, gaze across the vast silvery surface of Lake Disappointment and cross the Tropic of Capricorn. You'll visit Aboriginal communities that are at the centre of some of contemporary art's most exciting movements, and share desert oases with wild camels and dingoes.

This is a journey that's about experiencing the outback – as a place and a state of mind. The endless, undulating track – in some places its corrugations can almost shake your teeth out – presents a practical challenge as well as a mental one. This is really remote country. There are no petrol stations or public showers for miles, and you're about as far from civilisation as you can get.

It's a trip that requires meticulous planning and preparation. Once on the road, you're fully committed. There are no quick ways off or shortcuts to easier routes, and all fuel, fresh water and food must be carried with you. Expect to burst a tyre or two. It's extremely unwise to travel the track alone: a team of at least two 4WD vehicles is recommended, and some companies organise guided convoys. Permits are required to cross into some of the Aboriginal lands and national parks, and it's a good idea to let the police know where you're headed.

Learn some history before leaving. Old gravesites, rusted windmills, ancient rock carvings and broken wells tell tales of people who've travelled before you: drovers, pastoralists, and Aboriginal people from 15 different language groups.

MAKING IT HAPPEN

The stock route runs from Halls Creek to Wiluna. Some people start out from Alice Springs, taking the Gunbarrel Highway to Wiluna, then heading north; others begin at Perth. If setting out from Halls Creek, the nearest large cities are Broome on the Western Australian coast, or Darwin, in the Northern Territory. Global Gypsies offers a recommended tag-along tour.

AN ALTERNATIVE CHALLENGE

The section of the Canning Stock Route that runs from Halls Creek to Billiluna is a sealed (though somewhat battle-scarred) road that is also the final 17km leg of the Tanami Track from Alice Springs. The full length of the Tanami Track is some 1000km, and although it makes for a rugged journey, it's shorter and more doable than the Canning Stock Route and offers an adventurous way to get from Alice to the Kimberley. Highlights include the Balgo Aboriginal Community, with its renowned art centre, and the Wolfe Creek meteorite crater.

OPENING SPREAD Between the lines: the Canning Stock Route at Billiluna. **ABOVE (L)** Work by Aboriginal artists can be bought from locally-owned cooperative Papunya Tula. **ABOVE (R)** Shooting stars: Wolfe Creek crater, south of Hall's Creek, is 875m in diameter and less than 300,000 years old.

ARMCHAIR

* **Yiwarra Kuju** (National Museum of Australia) The best source on the Canning Stock Route is the National Museum of Australia's 2010 exhibition catalogue, with a wealth of historical information along with colour photographs and prints of spectacular Aboriginal paintings.

* **Rabbit-Proof Fence** (2002) Set in the 1930s, the film tells the story of three Aboriginal girls who escape from a detention camp to follow the famous fence across Australia home to their mothers.

BLACK HISTORY

According to archaeologists, Australia's Western Desert has been occupied for around 30,000 years, making the Canning Stock Route very recent history. When the Martu people of the Western Desert first saw camel tracks on their land, they called them 'little-fella bums', believing the marks had been left by baby spirits sitting in the sand.

INDEX

GREAT ADVENTURES

INDEX

INDEX

INDEX

INDEX

INDEX

INDEX

RESOURCES

CLIMB

The British Mountaineering Council
The Old Church
177-179 Burton Road, West Didsbury
Manchester, England
+44 (0)161 445 6111
www.thebmc.co.uk
Represents climbers and hill
walkers in England and Wales

École Nationale de Ski et d'Alpinisme
ENSA 35, rue de Bouchet
Chamonix, France
+33 (0)4 50 55 30 30
www.ensa-chamonix.net
France's national mountaineering
and skiing school for guides.

Verband Deutscher Berg und Skifuhrer
Bahnhofstrasse 25, Bad Tolz
+49 (0)8041 793860 6
www.bergfuehrer-verband.de
Ski and mountaineering instruction.

Asociación Española de Guías de Montaña
Carrer San Nicolas, 13, Jaca, Spain
+34 974 355 578
www.aegm.org
Lists schools, local associations and
professional mountain guides.

The Australian School of Mountaineering
166 Katoomba Street, Katoomba
New South Wales, Australia
+61 (0)2 4782 2014
www.asmguides.com
Courses in mountaineering, rock
climbing, bushcraft and navigation.

International Federation of Mountain Guides Association
Moranehuble, Badweidli
Gstaad, Switzerland
www.ivbv.info
Global organisation representing
the world's best mountain guides
and schools.

National Outdoor Leadership School
284 Lincoln Street, Lander
Wyoming, USA
+1 800 710 6657
www.nols.edu
Wilderness education courses.

American Mountain Guides Association
1209 Pearl Street, Boulder
Colorado, USA
+1 303 271 0984
www.amga.com
Accredits mountain guides
in the USA.

Glenmore Lodge
Aviemore, Invernesshire, Scotland
+44 (0)1479 861256
www.glenmorelodge.org.uk
Scotland's national outdoor training
centre with courses in climbing,
mountain biking and paddling.

American Alpine Institute
1515 12th Street, Bellingham
Washington, USA
+1 (360) 671 1570
www.aai.cc
Programs in mountain skills,
high-altitude expeditions, winter
climbing, backpacking, rescue
and first aid.

Nepal National Mountain Guide Association
Gairidhara, Kathmandu, Nepal
+9 77 01 400 4006
www.nnmga.org.np
Accredits mountain guides in Nepal.

New Zealand Alpine Club
Unit 6, 6 Raycroft Street, Waltham
Christchurch, New Zealand
+64 (0)3 377 7595
www.alpineclub.org.nz
Information on where and how to
enjoy New Zealand's mountains.

BIKE

Adventure Cycling Association
150 E. Pine Street, Missoula, USA
+1 800 755 2453
www.adventurecycling.org
Advocacy group providing maps
and advice for long-distance cycling
trips in the US

Cyclist Touring Club
Parklands, Railton Road
Guildford, Surrey, England
+44 (0)1483 238 337
www.ctc.org.uk
British-based advocacy group
for cyclists.

European Cyclists' Federation
Rue Franklin, 28, Brussels, Belgium
+32 (0)2 880 9274
www.ecf.com
Custodian of the EuroVelo project of
trans-Europe cycling routes.

Federation Francaise de Cyclisme
Bat. Jean Monnet, 5, rue de Rome
Rosny Sous Bois, France
+33 (0)1 49 35 69 00
www.ffc.fr
French cycling federation responsible
for racing, touring and routes.

RESOURCES

UK Bike Skills
Hertford, England
+44 (0)7886 342189
www.ukbikeskills.co.uk
Mountain biking courses tend to be
run privately on a small scale. Skills
camps at prime biking locations are
a popular option.

Endless Biking
1401 Hunter Street,
North Vancouver
British Columbia, Canada
+1 604 985 2519
www.endlessbiking.com

FESTIVALS

Banff Mountain Film Festival
October-November, Canada
**www.banffcentre.ca/
mountainfestival**

Kendal Mountain Festival
November, England
www.mountainfest.co.uk

Vail Film Festival
March-April, Colorado
www.vailfilmfestival.com

Edinburgh Mountain
Film Festival
October, Scotland
www.edinburghmountainff.com

WATER

Royal Yachting Association
RYA House, Ensign Way
Hamble, Hampshire, England
+44 (0)23 8060 4100
www.rya.org.uk
Accredits sailing schools that offer
sailing lessons and professional
qualifications for sailors of dinghies
and yachts.

Yachting Australia
Level 1, 22 Atchison Street
St Leonards, Sydney, Australia
+61 (0)2 8424 7400
www.yachting.org.au
Australia's national sailing
organisation offers instruction
and accredits clubs.

American Sailing Association
5301 Beethoven Street, Suite 265
Los Angeles, California, USA
+1 (310) 822 7171
www.asa.com
Certifies sailing schools
and instructors.

British Canoe Union
18 Market Place, Bingham
Nottingham, England
www.bcu.org.uk
Lists approved clubs and centres
in the UK.

National Whitewater Centre
Frongoch, Bala, Wales
+44 (0)1678 521083
www.ukrafting.co.uk
Offers rafting, canoeing and
kayaking courses in Snowdonia
National Park.

Rocky Mountain
Outdoor Center
14825 US Highway 285
Salida, Colorado, USA
+1 800 255 5784
www.rmoc.com
Leading outdoor skills school
in Midwest USA, specialising in
whitewater rafting and kayaking.

Nantahala Outdoor Center
13077 Highway 19 W
Bryson City, North Carolina, USA
+1 888 905 7238
www.noc.com
Specialises in whitewater rafting
and kayaking.

DIVE

PADI
The Professional Association
of Diving Instructors (PADI)
certification is an internationally
recognised standard for scuba
divers. Courses are aimed at
first-timers (Open Water Diver)
and experienced divers (Ice Diver,
Search and Recovery, Master Scuba
Diver) and take place at accredited
schools around the world. Use the
website to find a suitable school.
www.padi.com

FLY

British Hang-gliding and
Paragliding Association
8 Merus Court
Meridien Business Park
Leicester, England
+44 (0)116 289 4316
www.bhpa.co.uk
Accredits clubs and schools
in the UK.

SKI

Ecole du Ski Francaise
www.esf.net
Represents 250 ski schools
around France.

GREAT ADVENTURES

EXPERIENCE THE WORLD AT ITS BREATHTAKING BEST

1ST EDITION

Published October 2012

Publishing Director Piers Pickard

Publisher Ben Handicott

Commissioning Editor Robin Barton

Written by Andrew Bain, Ray Bartlett, Sarah Baxter, Greg Benchwick, Joe Bindloss, Abigail Blasi, Paul Bloomfield, Lucy Burningham, Kerry Christiani, Gregor Clark, Ben Fogle, Jim DuFresne, Sarah Gilbert, Scott Kennedy, Ben Kozel, Bradley Mayhew, Gabi Mocatta, Craig Scutt, Caroline Veldhuis, Steve Waters, Luke Waterson, Rafael Wlodarski

Copyeditors Janet Austin, Patrick Kinsella

Art Direction & Design Mark Adams

Layout Designers Paul Iacono, Jessica Rose

Image Research Rebecca Skinner, Nicholas Colicchia, Mark Adams

Pre-Press Production Ryan Evans

Thanks Larissa Frost, James Phirman, Indra Kilfoyle, Tracey Kislingbury, Jane Hart, Kylie McLaughlin, Chris Girdler, Florian Poppe

PUBLISHED BY

Lonely Planet Publications Pty Ltd ABN 36 005 607 983

90 Maribyrnong St, Footscray, Victoria 3011, Australia

ISBN 978 1 74220 964 7

Introduction © Ben Fogle 2012
Text & maps © Lonely Planet Pty Ltd 2012
Photos © as indicated 2012

Printed in China

10 9 8 7 6 5 4 3 2 1

AUSTRALIA (HEAD OFFICE)
90 Maribyrnong St, Footscray, Victoria, 3011
Phone 03 8379 8000 **Fax** 03 8379 8111

USA
150 Linden St, Oakland, CA 94607
Phone 510 250 6400 **Toll free** 800 275 8555

UNITED KINGDOM
BBC Worldwide, Media Centre, 201 Wood Lane, London, W12 7TQ **Phone** 020 8433 1333

FRONT & BACK COVER IMAGES **Front** (top) Aurora borealis, Wapusk National Park, Manitoba, Canada (Radius Images); (bottom) Hot-air balloon over Bagans temple, Bagan, Myanmar (Felix Hug/Corbis); Tourist snorkelling with whale shark, Ari Atoll, Maldives (Jason Isley - Scubazoo/Science Faction/Corbis) **Back** Tourists riding camels in the desert, Wadi Rum, Jordan (Yadid Levy/Alamy) Tourists in Safari Vehicle, Namibia (Roger de la Harpe/Corbis) FRONT MATTER IMAGES **Pages 2-3** Parc Naturel Régional du Vercors, Isere, France **Page 4** Paria River Canyon, Utah, USA **Page 6** Mt Roraima, Venezuela **Page 7** Þingvellir National Park, Iceland **Page 8** Great Sand Dunes National Park and Preserve, USA BACK MATTER IMAGES **Page 310** Mountain biking in Utah, USA **Page 317** Johnstone Canyon, Banff National Park, Canada